THE BIRDS OF MORAY AND NAIRN

THE BIRDS OF MORAY AND NAIRN

Martin Cook

With illustrations by
Paul Hirst and Robert Proctor
and bird photographs by
John Edelsten

THE MERCAT PRESS
EDINBURGH
1992

First published 1992 by Mercat Press
James Thin, 53 South Bridge, Edinburgh EH1 1YS

British Library Cataloguing in Publication Data
A catalogue record for this book is available from the British Library

ISBN 1873644051

Typeset by Bibloset, Chester
Printed in Great Britain by The Cromwell Press, Melksham

Contents

Text Figures

Illustrations

Plates

Introduction

Few parts of Great Britain can compete with Moray and Nairn for their rich variety of habitats. Within an hour's drive from Elgin lies the choice of the highest mountains, rolling heather moorland, coniferous and broadleaved woodlands, lochs, rivers and coastal scenery of endless variety. The bird fauna is correspondingly rich, 267 wild species (and 10 escapes) have been seen in the Districts of Moray and Nairn and 150 are known to have bred.

Little has been written this century of the general bird life of the Districts but a number of significant contributions were made before 1900. In 1844 George Gordon's *A Fauna of Moray* appeared in the *Zoologist* and this was reprinted, with appendices, as a small book in 1889. In the 1840s/early 1850s Charles St.John spent ten years shooting and carefully observing the local wildlife, a period vividly described in his *Natural History and Sport in Moray* published in 1863. As part of his series of Vertebrate Faunas, John Harvie-Brown, together with T.E. Buckley, produced in 1895 his volume on the Moray Basin, containing much of relevance to the Districts. The detail in many of their species accounts provides interesting comparison with the present day. Although covering only a single parish, Ardclach, the Reverend R. Thomson's *The Natural History of a Highland Parish* (1900) presents a valuable snapshot of the region's wildlife. Since the turn of the century studies have been made, and papers written, on several species or groups including Whooper Swans, seaducks, waders and Dippers.

In most respects the general ornithology of the area has been sadly neglected during the twentieth century until around 1970. At that time systematic collection of records for the Scottish Ornithologists' Club Annual Reports began, and in 1985 an annual Moray and Nairn Bird Report was introduced.

The purpose of this book is to provide an updated picture of the birdlife of Moray and Nairn Districts until the end of 1990. In order to put the modern situation into perspective, historical information is included where this significantly augments, or differs from, the current status of a species. The area covered comprises the post-regionalisation Grampian District of Moray and Highland District of Nairn. This corresponds to the old county of Nairn, Morayshire (omitting a triangle from Lochindorb to Advie to Grantown-on-Spey) and Banffshire (west of a line from Cullen to Marnoch).

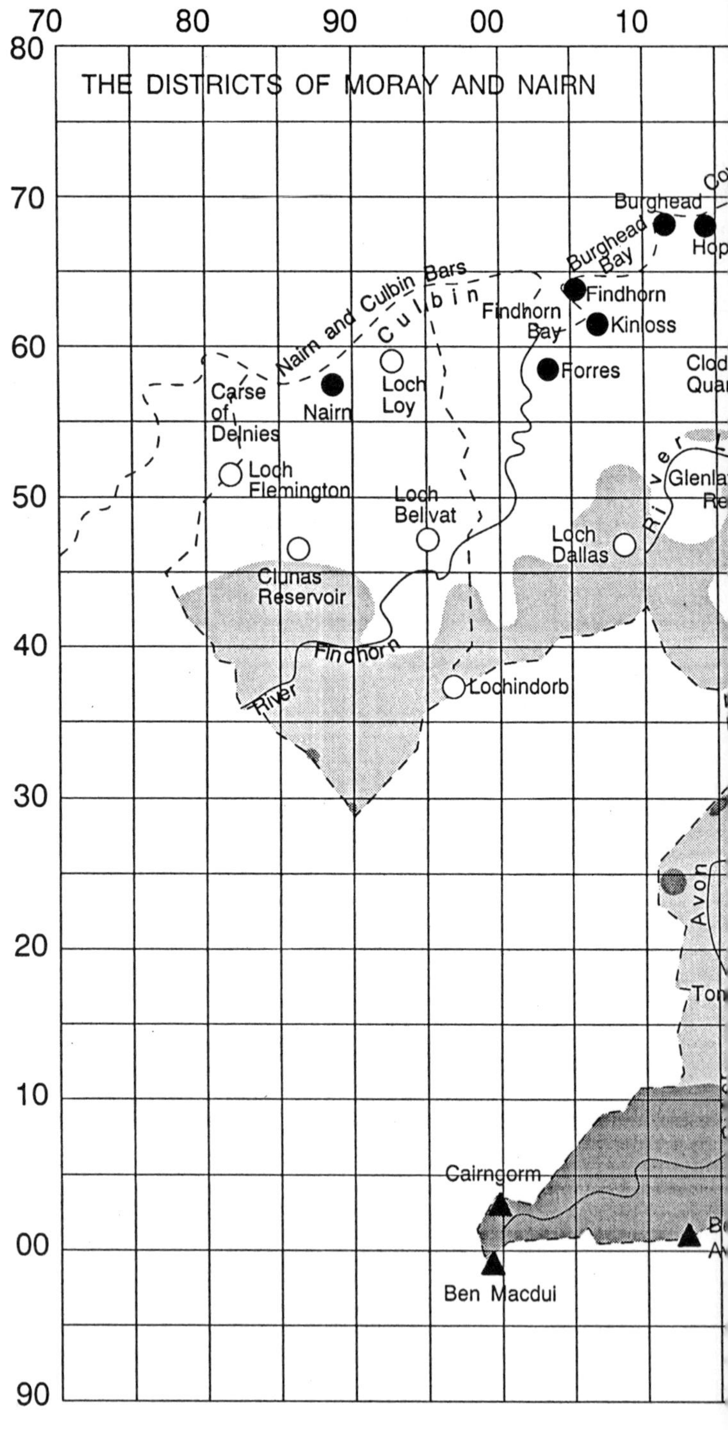
THE DISTRICTS OF MORAY AND NAIRN
70
80
90
00
10
80
70
60
50
40
30
20
10
00
90
Burghead
Burghead Bay
Findhorn
Kinloss
Findhorn Bay
Forres
Nairn and Culbin Bars
Culbin
Nairn
Loch Loy
Carse of Delnies
Loch Flemington
Loch Belvat
Loch Dallas
Clunas Reservoir
River Findhorn
Lochindorb
Avon
Cairngorm
Ben Macdui

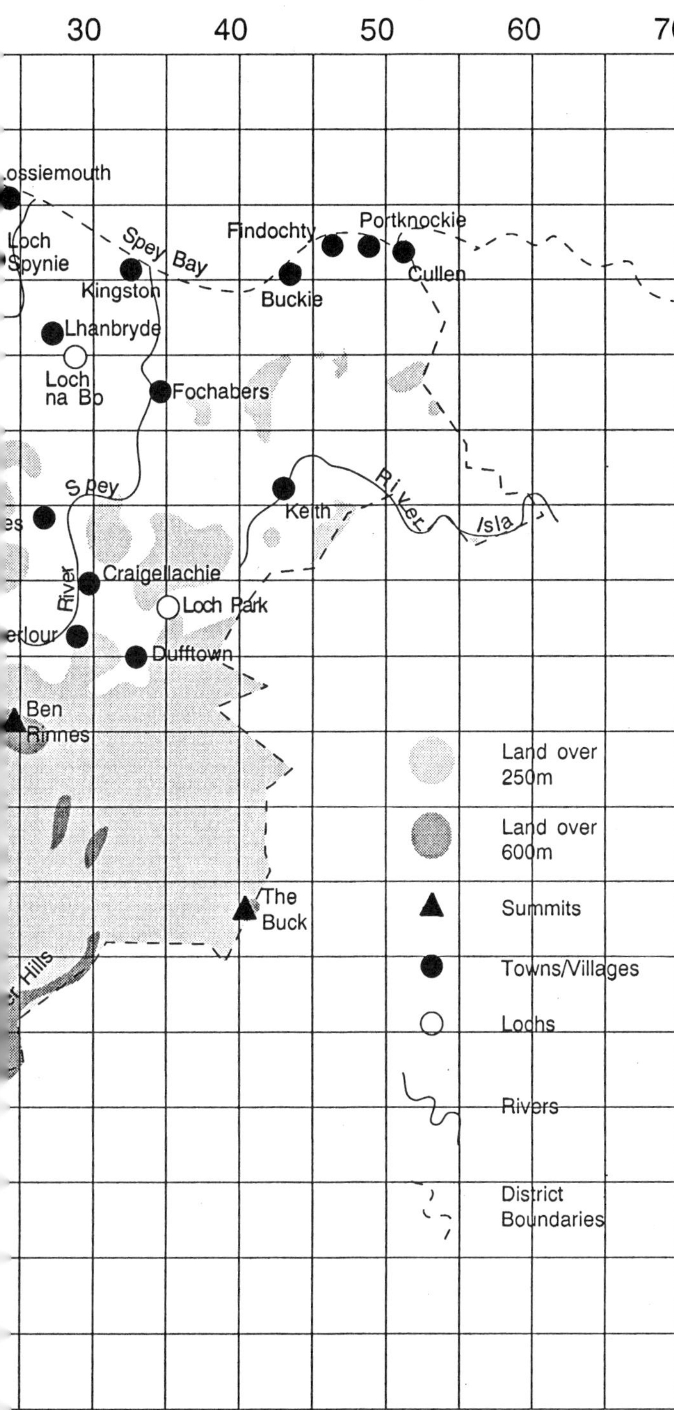
30
40
50
60
70
Lossiemouth
Loch
Spynie
Spey Bay
Findochty
Portknockie
Kingston
Buckie
Cullen
Lhanbryde
Loch
na Bo
Fochabers
Spey
Keith
River
Isla
River
Craigellachie
Loch Park
Dufftown
Ben
Rinnes
The
Buck
Land over
250m
Land over
600m
Summits
Towns/Villages
Lochs
Rivers
District
Boundaries

Acknowledgements

No book of this type is possible without long hours spent in the field by many observers. In recent years the Scottish Ornithologists' Club has provided a focus for the collection and publication of records. At a local level the collation of records has been painstakingly carried out by a succession of SOC recorders, in particular, since 1970, by John Edelsten (1971–77) and Norman Elkins (1977–83), the author taking over in 1984.

I am most grateful to all those individuals who responded to my persistent requests for information and, in particular, to Roy Dennis and Ken Shaw who read the whole manuscript and made valuable suggestions. Bob Swann's comments improved the wader accounts and Roy Dennis and Norman Elkins made available their collections of records.

Thanks for permission to use unpublished data go to the Royal Society for the Protection of Birds, The Nature Conservancy Council and the Wildfowl and Wetlands Trust. Rik Smith kindly allowed me to use his breeding data for Dotterel and Snow Buntings. The involvement of the British Trust for Ornithology and the Nature Conservancy Council in the provision of ringing data is gratefully acknowledged.

The illustrations drawn by Paul Hirst (PTH) and Bob Proctor (RP) have greatly enhanced the appearance of the book. John Edelsten generously permitted me to use his black and white bird photographs.

The publication of this book would not have been possible without financial assistance in the form of grants and sponsorship from a number of sources. In this connection I express sincere thanks to the following: Anderson & England Ltd, furniture retailers, Elgin; Banffshire Educational Trust; Bartlett Taylor Charitable Trust, Witney; W.A. Baxter and Sons Ltd, canners and preservers, Fochabers; Chivas Brothers Ltd, distillers; Herd & Mackenzie Ltd, boat builders and repairers, Buckie; Highland Regional Council; Moray District Council; The Scottish Ornithologists Club; United Distillers; Walkers Shortbread Ltd, Aberlour.

Finally, thanks to my patient family who have endured the writing of this book, especially my wife Jennifer who has often shouldered a disproportionate share of domestic duty.

Habitats for Birds

Mountains

South Moray contains some of the highest montane country in Britain. The arctic-alpine plateau between Cairn Gorm (1,245m) and Ben Macdui (1,309m) presents a harsh ice-bound environment in winter where the Ptarmigan is the only bird likely to be encountered. Even these may move down the mountains in the harshest weather. In summer Ptarmigan, breeding in these windswept boulderfields, are joined by occasional Snow Buntings. Dotterel nest on the drier rounded summits with a few high-level Meadow Pipits and Wheatears.

Moorlands

Below about 1,000m the hostile montane heaths and grasslands give way to gentler conditions where heather dominates and the cackling of Red Grouse is a familiar sound. In summer Meadow Pipits are abundant with a few Twite and, in grassier glens, Wheatears and Skylarks. On rocky outcrops and gullies there may be Ring Ouzels. Golden Plovers are numerous on the higher plateaux of the west Moray moors and the Ladder Hills, joined by a few Dunlin in wetter bogs. Golden Eagles hunt over some slopes and ridges, other scarce moorland predators are Hen Harrier, Peregrine, Merlin and Short-eared Owl. Where gulleys provide shelter for juniper scrub or stunted birches, the bird community may include Wrens, Willow Warblers, Whinchats and the occasional pair of Stonechats. In autumn flocks of Redwings and Fieldfares roam the moors feasting on blaeberries and the fruit of other dwarf shrubs.

Rivers and streams

Two wonderful rivers, the Spey and the Findhorn, lend much to the character of the Districts. Many smaller ones, and innumerable streams, drain the interior into the Moray Firth. Typical breeding species of fast-flowing upland reaches are Dipper, Grey Wagtail and Common Sandpiper, only Dippers remaining through the winter. Goosanders nest high up smaller tributaries bringing broods to the main rivers in summer. Red-breasted Mergansers are scarcer; a few inhabit moorland waters but most are found on the lower reaches of the Findhorn. Shingle islands provide relative safety for nesting Oystercatchers and colonies of gulls and, sometimes, Common Terns. Sandy river banks provide sites for Sand Martin colonies and where the banks are well vegetated they give cover to Reed Buntings, Sedge Warblers and a few Garden Warblers.

Lochs

The number of lochs in Moray and Nairn is relatively small but they differ greatly in character and birds. The only deep valley loch is Loch Avon, holding the occasional Dipper and Common Sandpiper around its shores in summer but invariably birdless in winter. Numerous shallow lochans dot the west Moray moors; these have a much richer breeding community including Mallard, Teal, Little Grebe and Black-headed Gulls. Closer to the coast are the most fertile standing waters, including Lochs Loy, Oire and Spynie. These hold a greater variety of breeding waterfowl with Tufted Duck and occasional Shoveler. They are fringed by emergent vegetation providing cover for nests of Moorhens, Coots and grebes. There may be thickets of willow scrub and reedbeds, as at Loch Spynie, in which Willow, Sedge and Grasshopper Warblers nest and a wide range of passerines feeds in late summer. In winter wildfowl numbers are swollen by influxes of migrants. Wigeon, Teal and Pochard become numerous, Whooper Swans arrive from Iceland

PLATE 1 Cairngorm plateau above Loch Avon. Dotterel, Ptarmigan and Snow Bunting inhabit the wind-swept high tops of southern Moray. *(Martin Cook)*

PLATE 2 River Findhorn at Dulsie Bridge. Downstream from this point the river valley is often steep and thickly wooded. Summer songsters include locally scarce warblers such as Blackcaps, Garden Warblers and Wood Warblers. *(Martin Cook)*

PLATE 3 River Findhorn near Drynachan. The shingles provide feeding areas for Common Sandpipers, Dippers and Grey Wagtails. *(Martin Cook)*

PLATE 4 Loch Spynie, the prime freshwater site for birds in the Districts. Wildfowl, including a large Greylag Goose roost, provide the winter interest while in summer the reedbeds and scrub hold a wide variety of warblers, finches and other songbirds. Local rarities have been found here almost annually. *(Martin Cook)*

PLATE 5 Loch Flemington. Formerly a roost for large numbers of Whooper Swans. Greylag Geese, Wigeon, Mallard and Tufted Ducks are common today, while scarce species in recent years have included Bewick's Swan, Gadwall and Ring-necked Duck. *(Martin Cook)*

and spectacular flocks of Greylag Geese can be watched tumbling in to Loch Spynie to roost each evening. At this season the reedbeds are comparatively quiet, holding little but Reed Buntings and occasionally enlivened by the squealing of a Water Rail.

Coniferous woodland

More than one-quarter of the land surface of Moray is covered by trees, the majority being conifers. Very little of this woodland retains the open character of the natural Scots pine forests, with majestic branching trees and a well-developed under-storey of juniper, rank heather and blaeberry. Instead, most woods are plantations, established this century. The earlier plantings consisted largely of Scots pine with Corsican pine on drier coastal soils. Many plantations of Scots pine have developed sufficient resemblance to native woodlands to permit colonisation by Crested Tits, crossbills, Siskins and Capercaillie, although the latter have now become very scarce. In recent years exotic North American tree species, notably sitka spruce, have predominated in many plantings and in the gloom of these woods with their barren floors the birdlife is of much less interest. When the moorland spruce plantations are young they may provide cover for nesting Short-eared Owls, Black Grouse, Whinchat and Twite but these species are lost as the canopy closes, to be replaced by Coal Tits, Goldcrests and Chaffinches. Mature stands of conifers often contain rookeries and most of the Districts' heronries are in plantations. Crows, both Carrion and hybrid, breed on the woodland edge; their disused nests provide sites for Long-eared Owls and Kestrels. Sparrowhawks are numerous and, when they are tolerated, Buzzards soar over the woods in early spring, most commonly in the west. Roding Woodcocks are a familiar sight and sound of still evenings in early summer.

Broadleaved woodland

The birchwoods of the upland glens come alive with bird song as the days lengthen and leaves unfold in spring. Winter flocks of Redpolls and Siskins break up and Chaffinches move back from farmland, joining Robins, thrushes and many other species which largely desert these woods in winter. Arriving from the south come Willow Warblers, Tree Pipits, Redstarts and Spotted Flycatchers. Bird cherry and rowan are common along gulleys and road sides providing a rich store of berries for autumn and winter. In the lower valleys of the rivers, woodlands are more mixed containing, according to locality, alder, willow, ash, oak, beech and others. Many summer migrants breed in these woods, Willow Warblers are abundant and Chiffchaffs and Blackcaps have been widely reported in recent years. Garden Warblers prefer riverside willows, while remnants of oakwood hold a few Wood Warblers and, very occasionally, Pied Flycatchers. Tawny Owls nest in holes in mature trees,

PLATE 6 Scots pine woodland on the Bin of Cullen. The natural character of this small area of forest attracts Crested Tits, Siskins and crossbills to breed. Only a few Capercaillies remain from a once thriving population. *(Martin Cook)*

PLATE 7 Upland birch woods near Drynachan. Relatively birdless in winter, these woods come alive in spring with the song of Willow Warblers, Chaffinches, Redstarts, Tree Pipits and Cuckoos. *(Martin Cook)*

Great Spotted Woodpeckers are widespread and Green Woodpeckers have recently colonised.

Farmland

The return of singing Skylarks and displaying Lapwings to grassy fields in sunny days of late winter is always a promise of approaching spring. Golden Plovers assemble on the grasslands of the glens before moving onto the moors, Curlew and Redshank may be in rougher, wetter fields. In the Laich of Moray vast acreages of cereal fields attract Oystercatchers but otherwise provide limited cover for breeding birds. Where pockets of Corn Buntings remain, they deliver their jangling song from prominent perches. If farms have rougher corners with gorse and scrub, then a few pairs of Yellowhammers, finches or other small birds can establish territories. Most hedges are too well trimmed to hold many nests. Pheasants and Grey Partridges are common, and in places released Red-legged Partridges and Chukar hybrids have become established. Although usually rare, Quail called throughout the Laich in summer 1989. After the harvest, fields are of more value to birds. Gulls and Rooks seek invertebrates in grass after the silage and hay are cut. The cereal stubbles attract finches and geese to forage in winter. The largest finch flocks are usually in weedy turnip fields where 1,000 or more Chaffinches, Greenfinches, Linnets, Tree Sparrows and others may assemble, sometimes attracting the attention of Sparrowhawks and even Hen Harriers. Elsewhere large Woodpigeon flocks may be a problem to the farmer.

Coast

The Moray and Nairn coastline consists of a rich mosaic of habitat types. Short stretches of cliff run from Hopeman to Covesea and from Findochty to Portknockie but breeding seabirds are restricted to Fulmars, Kittiwakes, the larger gulls and occasional pairs of Shag and Black Guillemot. The best rocky shores are between Burghead and Hopeman, at Lossiemouth and between Portgordon and Findochty. Winter waders are often well accustomed to people and Turnstones, Purple Sandpipers and Oystercatchers can be watched at close quarters. Rock Pipits are numerous especially where seaweed accumulates on the beach. There are three muddy estuaries, the wide expanse of Findhorn Bay and the smaller, but more intimate and easily watched, estuaries of the Lossie and the Spey rivers. Bird numbers are far greater at Findhorn especially during passage seasons and in winter. Redshank, Oystercatchers and Dunlin are the main species but Knot, Bar-tailed Godwits, Lapwings, Ringed Plovers and Curlews all feature strongly and scarcer passage waders occur annually at each site. A variety of wildfowl, gulls and terns feed and roost on the estuaries and fishing Ospreys are a regular thrill in summer. Offshore Burghead Bay and Spey Bay are well-known for their flocks of wintering sea

PLATE 8 Agricultural land below the Bin of Cullen. The mosaic of fields and woodland holds a varied songbird community with winter feeding among the stubbles and turnips. The ruined barn may provide a breeding site for Swallows, Pied Wagtails or even Barn Owls. *(Martin Cook)*

PLATE 9 Heather moors and rough grassland above Glen Fiddich. Encroaching forestry renders this type of habitat unsuitable for breeding waders and moorland birds of prey. *(Martin Cook)*

ducks. In the 1970s the water was frequently covered with bobbing rafts of Common and Velvet Scoters but in recent years numbers have been greatly reduced. The flock of Long-tailed Ducks roosting in Burghead Bay is still of international importance, thousands of birds entering the bay each evening. For a few weeks in autumn Red-throated Divers appear offshore to moult in hundreds. When the wind blows them close to the coast Fulmars, shearwaters, Gannets and skuas are buffeted past headlands such as Lossiemouth – the watcher in the shelter of a car will be briefly rewarded with a glimpse of species seldom occurring in the Districts under any other conditions.

PLATE 10 Rocky shore at Buckie. In winter Oystercatchers, Knot, Purple Sandpipers, Redshanks and Turnstones can be watched at close quarters. *(Martin Cook)*

Watching Birds in Moray and Nairn

Loch Flemington

A small freshwater loch set among farmland and surrounded by patches of gorse and broom scrub.

Access: drive west from Nairn on the A96 and after 5 miles turn left on the B9090. After 0.4 mile turn left and the loch is on the right, easily viewed from the road.

Summer: Mute Swans and Little Grebes breed with a few pairs of Mallard, Tufted Ducks and Coots. Reed Buntings, Yellowhammers, Whitethroats and Sedge Warblers are in the surrounding scrub.

Autumn/winter: Greylag Geese often roost on the loch and, until 1988, there were large numbers of Whooper Swans. Other regular wildfowl include Mallard, Wigeon, Tufted Ducks and Goldeneye. Little Grebes gather in autumn. Local fields often hold good flocks of finches and buntings.

Carse of Delnies

A large flat area of grassland and saltmarsh inundated by the sea to a varying extent. A long shingle spit, covered in grass and low scrub, leads out to Whiteness Head.

Access: 1 mile west of Nairn leave the A96 onto the B9092. Turn first right to Hilton of Delnies and continue past the farm to a locked gate. From here progress can be made only on foot, along the track to the west.

Spring: main interest is provided by 2,000–3,000 Pink-footed Geese which graze the area in March/April. Redshank, Lapwings and Ringed Plovers defend territories and many Skylarks are in song. Migrant Wheatears and White Wagtails pass through.

Summer: Great Black-backed Gulls nest on Whiteness Head, over the Nairn boundary, and the gorse on the spit sometimes holds a pair of Stonechats. In August Wheatears become numerous. Offshore Manx Shearwaters may be seen and there is a moulting flock of Red-breasted Mergansers.

Autumn: good numbers of seabirds, including skuas and shearwaters, pass along the shore when forced close in by the weather. The Merganser flock increases and Long-tailed Ducks appear. Passage waders such as Greenshank feed along the creeks in the saltings while much larger flocks of Knot, Redshank, Oystercatchers and Bar-tailed Godwits are usually just west of the District boundary. Meadow Pipits and Pied Wagtails are numerous in the grasslands.

Winter: herds of Whooper Swans may visit the grassy fields. Offshore are divers, mostly Red-throated, Mergansers and other sea ducks. Wandering groups of Snow Buntings are often encountered.

Culbin Forest and Bars

Formerly a wide expanse of sand dunes and shingle ridges, the area has been transformed by the extensive plantations created since the 1920s. Scots and Corsican pine are the main tree species. The Nairn Bar is of shingle, well vegetated with scrub and some stunted trees. Culbin Bar is sandy, covered only with marram and other low-growing grasses and herbs. Between the Bars and the Forest is extensive coastal marsh with mud and sand flats exposed at low tide.

Access: the Forest is a Forestry Commission plantation to which access on foot is unrestricted. There is a carpark at Wellhill (NH 997614). Travel west from Forres on the A96. After 1.2 miles cross the River Findhorn bridge and turn right almost immediately over the railway. Take the second turn on the right and follow signposts to Kintessack. Continue through the village and soon turn left. This road ends at the carpark after 0.8 mile. Much of the coastal marsh and the Bars is an RSPB reserve but public access is uncontrolled. The area can be reached on foot by various routes through the forest (about 3 miles from Wellhill). A closer approach can be made from the west. Entering Nairn from the east follow the A96 under the railway bridge and turn first right along Lochloy Road. After 1 mile a track leads off left down to the shore. Take great care in this area as the channel between Nairn Bar and the shore floods rapidly on a rising tide. Alternatively follow Lochloy Road for 2.6 miles before a forest path on the left gives access to the shore.

Birds in the Forest

All year: a few Capercaillie remain, although they are much scarcer than formerly, and Woodcock can be flushed in damper parts of the Forest. Commoner passerines associated with conifers are present in good numbers and Scottish Crossbills, Crested Tits and Siskins all breed, joined in summer by occasional pairs of Redstart and Tree Pipit.

Birds at the Bars

Spring: flocks of seaducks depart and wader numbers fall. Ringed Plovers nest. Breeding species of Nairn Bar scrub include Linnet, Reed Bunting and, probably, Stock Dove. Meadow Pipits and Skylarks are numerous and Wheatears nest in some years.

Summer: Eider and Shelduck have broods. Stock Doves are regular on the saltmarsh and among the scrub. Small numbers of Bar-tailed Godwits and Knot oversummer and wader passage starts in July. Occasional summer plumaged divers of all three commoner species are seen offshore. Sandwich Terns with their young move up to the area to feed from the east coast of Britain.

Autumn: Red-throated Divers are common offshore and seaduck numbers build up. Large flocks of Bar-tailed Godwits, Knot, Oystercatchers and Redshank feed on the mud.

Winter: wader numbers are high and flocks of Long-tailed Ducks, Common and Velvet Scoters are regular offshore. Wigeon feed on the mudflats and a small flock of Sanderlings inhabits the shore. Snow Buntings forage along the Bars.

Findhorn Bay

Situated at the mouth of the River Findhorn, the bay empties almost completely at low tide to leave wide expanses of mud and sand, with shingle west of Findhorn village. The eastern and southern shores are fringed by saltmarsh and Culbin Forest closely approaches to the west.

Access: from Kinloss take the B9011 north to Findhorn, and the eastern shore of the bay is accessible at numerous points. To reach the southern shore, turn right at the eastern roundabout on the Forres by-pass and after 0.3 mile take the first minor road on the left, signposted Netherton. After 0.7 mile, turn left at a T-junction. After the humpback bridge over a burn, turn right and continue past Netherton Farm. At the corner by the next house a rough track leads off to the shore on the right. Access to the western side of the bay is possible through Culbin Forest.

Spring: thousands of Greylag Geese roost and feed in the area in March/April. Substantial numbers of migrant Knot, Redshank and Ringed Plovers pass through in April/May. Shelduck become widespread and a few Pintail occur annually.

Summer: wader passage is in full swing in August. As well as good numbers of the common species, scarcer migrants such as Spotted Redshank, Ruff and Little Stint frequently stop over. Common, Arctic and Sandwich Terns feed and rest in the bay, as do Ospreys.

Autumn: waders continue to appear including, in some years, good numbers of Grey Plovers, Black-tailed Godwits and Curlew Sandpipers. Several Ospreys may be fishing together. Pink-footed Geese pass through in late September, to be followed by the first Greylags and Whooper Swans in October.

Winter: Dunlin, Redshank and Oystercatchers dominate the wader scene. Golden Plovers, Bar-tailed Godwits and Knot can be expected and a few Greenshank overwinter in most years. Wigeon are usually present in hundreds. Meadow Pipits are numerous in the saltings where the occasional Hen Harrier, Merlin or Short-eared Owl hunts.

PLATE 11 Findhorn Bay. At low tide the wide expanse of mud provides rich feeding for wildfowl and waders. In late summer and autumn more than 20 species of wader might be present on a good day. Baird's and Pectoral Sandpipers and Wilson's Phalarope are among recent rarities. *(Martin Cook)*

PLATE 12 River Spey estuary at Kingston. A small area of mud and creeks, at its best for birds in summer and autumn. It attracts a good variety of waders, and fishing Ospreys quarter the shallows. *(Martin Cook)*

PLATE 13 Covesea cliffs, which support a few hundred breeding pairs of seabirds. Main species are Kittiwake, Fulmar and Herring Gull. The clifftop gorse is good for Stonechats. *(Martin Cook)*

PLATE 14 Bow Fiddle Rock, Portknockie. A few Kittiwakes and other gulls nest here and the Rock holds a large Shag roost in winter. *(Martin Cook)*

Burghead Bay

A wide, shallow bay between Findhorn and Burghead. There is a long sandy beach fringed by dunes and a conifer plantation.

Access: at the western end enter Findhorn village on the B9011 from Kinloss and turn right where 'Dune Area' is signposted. Drive through the dunes to the car park and view the bay from the adjoining beach. For access to the centre of the bay, travel east for 2.7 miles along the B9089 from Kinloss and turn left to the Forestry Commission car park at the shore. The eastern end of the bay is reached by taking the B9089 to the tip of Burghead promontory which reveals a fine panorama.

Autumn/winter: Red-throated Divers appear in good numbers in October; a few Black-throated and Great Northern Divers may also be found as may Slavonian Grebes. Fewer divers are present in mid winter when seaducks are most numerous. Spectacular numbers of Long-tailed Ducks flight into the bay to roost each evening. Scoter numbers fluctuate annually but hundreds can usually be seen and a Surf Scoter is found in most winters. Guillemots and Razorbills are common, especially in autumn, and a few Goldeneyes and Red-breasted Mergansers are regular.

Covesea cliffs

Three kilometres of sandstone cliffs containing numerous caves and a stack. Extensive areas of gorse cover the clifftops.

Access: travel west from Lossiemouth on the B9040. After 2.9 miles from the edge of the town take a track on the right, just before a plantation. Proceed to the top of the hill and descend the slope to the coastguard lookout tower. Walk west (for Kittiwakes) or east along the clifftop, or along the shore at low tide. Take great care both along the clifftop and along the shore from which access back to the footpath is not always easy on a rising tide.

Spring/summer: Covesea cliffs hold the largest seabird colonies in the Districts. There are several groups of Kittiwakes' nests with numerous Fulmars and Herring Gulls. Occasional pairs of Great and Lesser Black-backed Gulls also breed. Cormorants rest on cliff ledges but have not nested recently. In most years there are a few Stonechats breeding in the gorse on the clifftop.

Lossiemouth

The River Lossie flows out at the East Beach through an estuary in which sand and mud are exposed at low tide. Sparsely vegetated dunes separate the estuary from the sea. Between the West Beach and the harbour the shore is rocky. The headland just west of the harbour provides a good vantage point for seawatching.

Access: West Beach: enter Lossiemouth on the A941 from Elgin. On the outskirts of the town bear left up the hill and follow signposts for 'West Beach'. *East Beach*: turn right off the A941, opposite the playing fields, along Church Street. On reaching the shore continue to the right and park in front of the caravan park.

Summer: on the Lossie estuary return wader passage begins in July and August when Dunlin, Ringed Plovers and Sanderling appear. Scarcer waders include Whimbrel and the occasional Spotted Redshank. At low tide large flocks of Kittiwakes, Great Black-backed Gulls and terns rest on the mud flats.

Autumn: further waves of passage waders pass through, Little Stints, Grey Plovers and Ruff are usual in small numbers and Curlew Sandpipers are seen in some years. Brent Geese may stop briefly in the estuary. In suitable weather, usually north-easterly gales with rain, seabird passage can be exciting off the headland with the three commoner skuas, Manx and Sooty Shearwaters, Gannets and Fulmars all likely to pass close inshore.

Winter: fewer waders are on the estuary but the rocky shores to the west hold good numbers of Turnstones, Purple Sandpipers, Redshank and Oystercatchers. Goldeneye, Mallard and Eider feed offshore and other seaducks fly past the headland. A flock of Snow Buntings is usually on the East Beach dunes, while careful inspection of the mudflat gull flocks sometimes reveals Glaucous or Iceland Gulls.

Loch Spynie

Now only 1 km long and less than half that in width, the present loch is only a remnant of the 13 km^2 Loch Spynie which was largely drained by 1870. Nevertheless a rich variety of habitats remains. Much of the open water is surrounded by reedbeds and there is extensive reed and marsh to the west of the loch. Willow scrub has developed at the northern and southern ends while the south-eastern side is sheltered by a mature pine plantation.

Access: the loch and surrounding area is an SSSI on privately owned land and is not open to the public. Permission to visit is usually given to organised groups e.g. local branches of bodies such as RSPB, YOC, Scottish Wildlife Trust, Moray Field Club, etc.

Spring: Greylag Geese remain common in the area until April, When numbers of Pink-footed Geese are also high as passage birds stop over. Fewer ducks remain after April although a build-up of Shovelers is noted at this time. Breeding activity in the heronry is in full swing and in May the reedbeds and scrub come alive with bird song. A high proportion comes from migrant species such as Willow and Sedge Warblers. Large flocks of newly-arrived hirundines, and later Swifts, hawk for insects over the loch.

Summer: broods of Mallard, Tufted Ducks and Coots are on the water, and Shoveler and Great Crested Grebe have nested in recent years. Innumerable small passerines forage in the willows and reeds, including tits, Willow and Sedge Warblers, Whitethroats, Wrens and Reed Buntings. In smaller numbers are Chiffchaffs, Blackcaps and Garden, and occasionally Grasshopper, Warblers. In recent years unexpected August visitors have included Marsh Warbler and Nightingale.

Autumn: spectacular roosts are a feature of this season. Thousands of Swallows gather each evening in the reeds in September and by mid October the evening flights of Greylag Geese never fail to thrill. Swarms of Starlings perform synchronised aerobatics before plunging into the reeds as the light fades. Numbers of Coots and ducks build up, especially Mallard, Teal, Wigeon, Tufted Ducks and Pochard with fewer Goldeneyes, Goosanders and Shovelers.

Winter: few passerines remain in the reedbeds, although Water Rails are often heard and Hen Harriers sometimes visit. Greylag Geese are rarely silent, although the roost size steadily declines. Other regular wildfowl include Mute and Whooper Swans and, sometimes, huge numbers of Wigeon.

Kingston and Spey Bay

Kingston village overlooks the small muddy estuary of the Spey. Offshore, Spey Bay extends between Lossiemouth and Buckie, bordered by sandy beaches in the west but largely shingle to the east.

Access: Kingston is reached at the end of the B9015 which runs north from Mosstodloch. Drive through Kingston until the road turns sharply to the left. On the right at this point is a carpark and picnic area, giving views and access over the muddy estuary and creeks. Alternatively, continue west through Kingston until another carpark is reached. This lies beside the shingle beach from which Spey Bay can be scanned. All of this area is a Scottish Wildlife Trust reserve but access on foot is unrestricted.

Spring: Common Terns arrive and move up river and a few pairs of Shelduck breed above high tide mark. Only small numbers of waders remain on the estuary; Redshank, Ringed Plovers and Lapwings all breed in the area. Seaducks may still be numerous in the bay until mid May.

Summer: Common Terns commute overhead from the river to the sea to feed and a few pairs of Arctic Terns may nest on the shingle with one or two pairs of Common Gulls. Wader passage resumes in July and, although numbers are usually not large, scarcer species such as Whimbrel, Little Stint and Ruff are regular visitors. Just off the river mouth are moulting flocks of Eiders and Goosanders.

Autumn: wader passage continues in September and Teal and Wigeon are frequent on the estuary. Hundreds of Red-throated Divers moult in the bay in October but only occasional Black-throated and Great Northern are seen. Common and Velvet Scoters arrive and Guillemots may be numerous.

Winter: in some years the bay holds huge flocks of Common and Velvet Scoters, although there have been fewer recently. Long-tailed Ducks and

Eiders are also common with small numbers of divers and Red-breasted Mergansers. The Lein area holds Snipe, pipits and sometimes Snow Buntings.

Buckie shore

The foreshore is mostly rocky with shingle between Portgordon and Buckpool and a sandy beach at Strathlene.

Access: straightforward at numerous points from the A990, between Buckie harbour and Portgordon, and the A942 between the harbour and Strathlene.

Autumn/winter: from September onwards the usual rocky-shore wader species can be watched at close quarters at several spots along the coast. Most numerous are Turnstones, Oystercatchers and Redshank. Purple Sandpipers can be relied on around Portessie, while Curlews, Golden Plovers, Dunlin and Ringed Plovers are usually to be found between Portgordon and Buckpool, occasionally with Knot. Gulls are abundant and worth checking for Glaucous, especially around Buckie harbour. Rock Pipits flit among the beach boulders. Off Strathlene are regular Eider and Mallard flocks and, at low tide, Craigenroan Reef provides a resting place for Cormorants.

Early and late dates for Migrant Species

Given below are the first and last dates on which migrant species are known to have occurred in the Districts.

Summer visitors

	Earliest	*Latest*
Osprey	27 March 1982/91	26 Sept 1982
Corncrake	29 April 1858	29 Sept 1982
Whimbrel	11 March 1978	16 Oct 1973
Common Sandpiper	14 April 1991	16 Oct 1969
Sandwich Tern	18 March 1990	31 Oct 1968(i)
Common Tern	14 April 1979	16 Nov 1985(ii)
Arctic Tern	8 April 1985	3 Oct 1976
Little Tern	5 May 1984	7 Oct 1979
Cuckoo	25 April 1985/87	3 Sept 1978
Swift	5 May 1988	6 Nov 1985
Sand Martin	14 March 1880	12 Nov 1892
Swallow	23 March 1968	22 Nov 1981/87
House Martin	12 April 1988	15 Nov 1984
Tree Pipit	9 April 1988	
Redstart	23 April 1902	13 Oct 1988
Whinchat	25 April 1987	16 Oct 1981
Wheatear	24 March 1989	10 Nov 1976
Ring Ouzel	22 March 1844	6 Nov 1982
Grasshopper Warbler	28 April 1961	13 Aug 1985
Sedge Warbler	22 April 1984	25 Sept 1988
Whitethroat	19 April 1850	25 Sept 1988
Garden Warbler	11 May 1981	22 Oct 1968
Blackcap	24 April 1982	o
Wood Warbler	8 May 1894	
Chiffchaff	1 April 1988	o
Willow Warbler	9 April 1984	24 Oct 1982
Spotted Flycatcher	5 May 1987	3 Oct 1990

Notes: o last date confused by wintering birds
(i) there are also two midwinter records
(ii) there is also one midwinter record

Winter visitors

	Earliest	*Latest*
Whooper Swan	18 Sept 1983	*
Pink-footed Goose	15 Sept 1986	12 May 1986
Greylag Goose	17 Sept 1978	*
Waxwing	7 Oct 1970	18 May 1971
Fieldfare	21 Aug 1983	29 May 1988
Redwing	27 Sept 1980	*
Brambling	28 Sept 1985	3 May 1970
Snow Bunting (coast)	13 Sept 1969	5 May 1972

Note: * last date confused by summering birds

Species Accounts

Accounts are given of all species which have occurred in Moray and Nairn at any time. Escapes are placed in square brackets, while round brackets are used for those few species whose records are of debatable authenticity. The order follows that proposed by Voous in his *List of recent holarctic bird species* (1977).

Each account starts with a summary of the recent status of the species in which the terms used have the following meaning:

Breeding species

Occasional - has bred but none in most years
Rare - 1–10 pairs in most years
Scarce - 11–50 pairs in most years
Numerous - 51–500 pairs in most years
Common - over 500 pairs in most years
Introduced - originally released or escaped but now breeding in the wild

Non-breeding visitors

Accidental - less than five records
Rare - 5–20 records
Scarce - not rare but less than 50 most years
Common - more than 50 most years
Escape - formerly captive individuals now surviving in the wild

Where references are given in the text, bold numbers in square brackets relate to the main reference list. Other abbreviations are as follows:

ASNH - *Annals of Scottish Natural History*
BB - *British Birds*
MNBR - *Moray and Nairn Bird Report*
NCC - Nature Conservancy Council
RSPB - Royal Society for the Protection of Birds
SB - *Scottish Birds*
SBR - *Scottish Bird Report*
SN - *Scottish Naturalist*
SOC - Scottish Ornithologists' Club

Map references of places mentioned in the text can be found in Appendix 1.

For certain species the pattern of occurrence is shown by means of histograms of monthly or half-monthly totals. Unless otherwise stated, individuals are included for every month, or half month, of their stay. The distribution of selected species is illustrated by a map based on a 5 km-square grid. These maps have been compiled from records received during the decade 1981–1990 only. The symbols on the maps have the following meaning:

● Proved to breed at least once. Categories of evidence accepted were:

1. nest containing eggs or young;
2. used nest (same season) or egg shells;
3. recently fledged young or downy chicks;
4. adult sitting on, or leaving, inaccessible nest;
5. adult carrying food for young or faecal sacs;
6. distraction display.

• Present in the breeding season in suitable nesting habitat but no proof of breeding obtained. Singing birds have been included here. Probable migrants are excluded.

❄ Recorded only outwith the breeding season

The species accounts have drawn on all available information up to the end of December 1991.

Red-throated Diver

Gavia stellata

Rare breeder. Common autumn and winter visitor offshore.

Breeding was first confirmed in the Districts in 1986 when one pair raised a chick. A pair nested at the same lochan in 1987 (unsuccessful), 1988 (two young), 1989 (one young), 1990 (unsuccessful), and 1991 (unsuccessful). A second pair bred at another lochan in 1989. Elsewhere one at Loch Builg on 5 May 1975 is the only inland record.

In October large moulting flocks gather offshore in shallow bays. The highest counts for each favoured locality are shown below:

Nairn/Culbin Bars	993	(1982)
Burghead Bay	373	(1985)
Spey Bay	621	(1987)

The largest total count for the whole coastline was 1,414 in October 1982. By mid-November, numbers are much lower and midwinter counts seldom exceed 50 at any site. Very few are seen on the sea from May to July but small numbers are again present from August onwards. Most birds are within 2 km of the shore with only a few frequenting rocky shorelines.[1]

The origin of our autumn and winter flocks has been indicated by three birds found dead between Burghead and Nairn. Two had been ringed as adults, at Hvalrosodden (Greenland) in July 1969 and on Yell (Shetland) in July 1979, while the third was marked as a chick on Hoy (Orkney) in August 1979.

Black-throated Diver

Gavia arctica

Scarce autumn and winter visitor offshore. Has bred.

A pair nested at Lochindorb from 1845 until about 1851 [2] but there were no further inland records until one was seen on the same loch from 13–24 July 1988. Two were there for two days in early April 1989 and another was on Loch Builg on 1 July 1990.

Prior to 1895, several were caught in salmon nets in Burghead Bay [4] and this bay, together with the Findhorn–Culbin coast, remains the chief haunt today where birds regularly appear in autumn. Numbers rarely exceed ten at any time, although 18 were counted on 23 September 1985 and on 19 October 1987. Fifty divers in Burghead Bay in November 1985 were believed to be Black-throated.[5] A few can be seen in this area throughout the winter and also in Spey Bay where, exceptionally, there were 19 on 31 August 1980 and 29 on 12 November 1983. Spring counts are usually small, although there were 18 in Burghead Bay on 22 March 1989, and only occasional birds are seen offshore in summer.

Great Northern Diver

Gavia immer

Scarce visitor offshore, rare in summer.

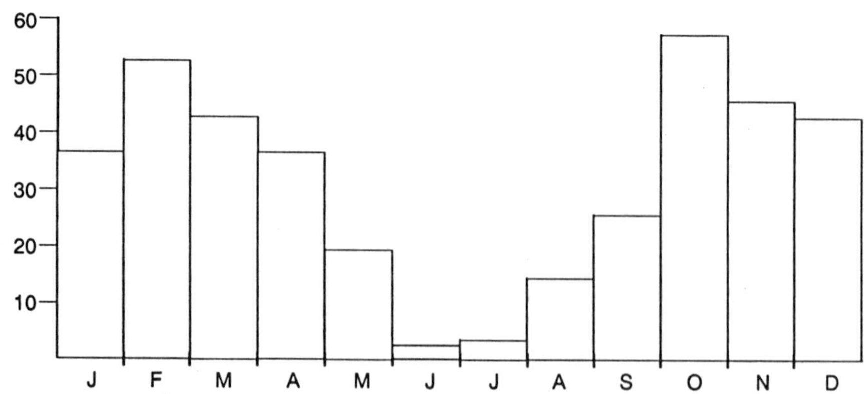

Figure 1 Great Northern Diver monthly totals 1970–91

Reported as 'not uncommon' in winter last century,[**3**,**6**] they remain regular in small numbers, usually in Burghead Bay and Spey Bay. It is unusual to see more than five at one time. The monthly distribution of records is shown in the histogram, revealing peaks in autumn and spring. Highest counts were 12 in Burghead Bay on 19 April 1984, 13 in Spey Bay on 15 May 1984 and 12 there on 14 March 1991.

There have been three inland records, one on Loch na Bo on 20 January 1908, one dead at the roadside at Alves following storms on 26 February 1927 and one flightless, moulting bird found dead at Loch Spynie on 21 February 1988.

White-billed Diver

Gavia adamsii

Accidental.

There are few accepted records for Moray and Nairn. Two of these relate to birds found dead on the shore, in Spey Bay on 2 January 1955 and at Findhorn on 1 February 1970. In 1972 one frequented Buckie harbour from 5 March until 20 May.[**99**] Another was seen at the mouth of Findhorn Bay on 14 December 1975 (BB **71**: 487).

Little Grebe

Tachybaptus ruficollis

Scarce breeder, scarce in winter.

In 1863 Little Grebes were described as 'not uncommon' [**3**] and the same remains true today. Since 1984, breeding has taken place on at least 29 different lochs and pools up to 350m altitude on the moors at Loch Noir and Loch of the Cowlatt. Most waters hold only one or two pairs but more have bred on Loch Flemington (max. five pairs in 1986 and 1987), Loch Belivat (four pairs in 1989) and Loch of Blairs (three pairs in 1985).

Largest autumn numbers regularly occur on Loch Flemington where there were 39 on 31 August 1989 and 35 on 16 August 1991. Few remain there by late November and a general exodus from the Districts takes place in

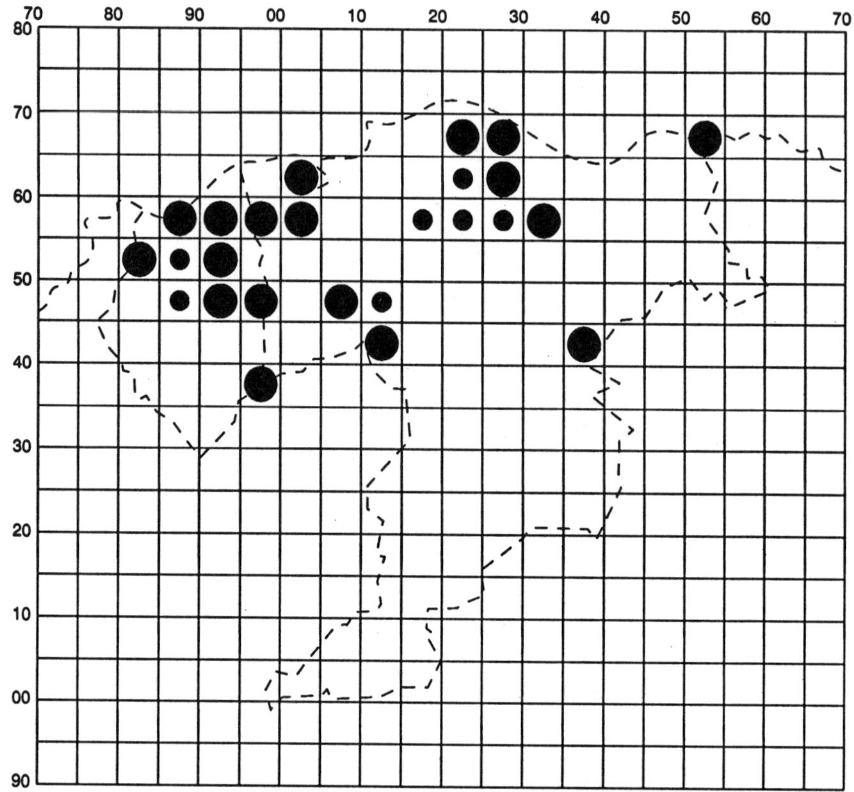

Figure 2 Little Grebe summer distribution 1981–90 (March–August)

late autumn. Up to five may winter around Findhorn Bay but there are very few other coastal records. The breeding lochs are usually reoccupied in late February and March.

Great Crested Grebe

Podiceps cristatus

Rare breeder and scarce migrant.

As a breeding species the Great Crested Grebe has been lost and regained at least three times during this century. In 1912 a pair summered on Loch Spynie but there was no evidence of nesting. In 1913, however, a pair returned and one young was hatched (SN 1914: 46). One pair continued to breed there until 1929.[2] There were no further records until one pair bred again from 1954–6. In 1984 a pair again nested on Loch Spynie and reared three young. They continued to breed there successfully until 1987. In 1988 and 1989 only a single adult was present during summer, briefly joined by a second in late July and August 1988, perhaps the same bird as that seen on Loch Flemington on 30 June 1988. In 1990 there were up to four adults, and one pair raised a chick. In 1991 one pair nested unsuccessfully.

Only small numbers are seen offshore, most commonly, in autumn. The monthly distribution of birds is shown below:

Jan	Feb	Mar	Apr	May	Jun	Jul	Aug	Sep	Oct	Nov	Dec
2	3	2	1	0	0	3	1	4	14	6	2

All records are of one to two birds except seven at Nairn Bar on 29 October 1989, part of a small influx mirrored elsewhere in the Moray Firth.

Red-necked Grebe

Podiceps grisegena

Scarce migrant.

There were four records in Moray between 1876–9 [7] but no others were reported until 1970, when one was found dead at Findhorn. Since then 34 have been seen mostly in Spey and Burghead Bays, and one found dead. The monthly distribution of birds and annual pattern of occurrence are shown below:

Jan	Feb	Mar	Apr	May	Jun	Jul	Aug	Sep	Oct	Nov	Dec
4	5	2	1	0	0	0	0	2	6	8	6

All records have been of singles except for four at Burghead Bay on 9 November 1982, and two off Nairn Bar on 11 December 1991. There have been only two on fresh water: one on Loch na Bo from 9–17 November and one on Loch Flemington on 13 November, both in 1991.

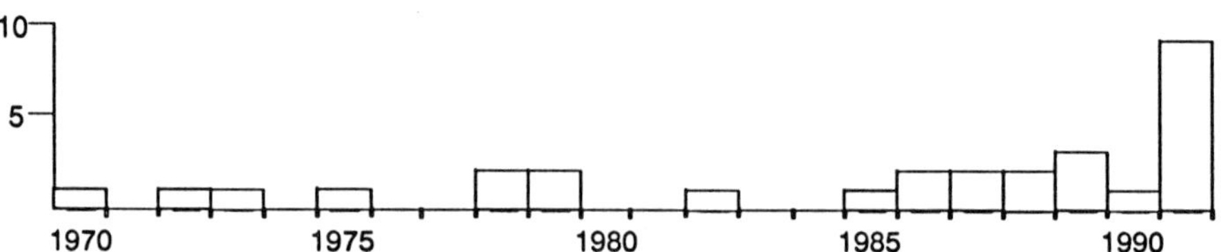

Figure 3 Red-necked Grebe annual totals 1970–91

Slavonian Grebe

Podiceps auritus

Rare breeder. Scarce offshore in winter.

St.John, writing in 1863, described the species as a rare visitor and noted its occurrence at Loch Spynie (in winter), Loch Loy and on the Spey.[3] In 1895 Harvie-Brown and Buckley stated that 'young birds are common on the coast in winter' but they gave only three coastal records, and three inland ones, from 1876–90.[4]

Slavonian Grebes first bred in the Districts in the 1950s and the stronghold has traditionally been on one loch. During the 1970s the population at this site dwindled but since 1980 a number of other waters have been colonised and six lochs have held birds in summer, although never all in the same year. The number of sites occupied and total number of breeding pairs in Moray and Nairn since 1971 are given below:

	1971	1972	1973	1974	1975	1976	1977	1978	1979	1980	1981
Sites	1	1	1	1	1	1	2	1	1	2	2
Pairs	7	6	5–6	5–6	4	4–6	4–5	4	5–6	4–6	6

	1982	1983	1984	1985	1986	1987	1988	1989	1990	1991
Sites	2	2	3	4	3	4	4	5	4	4
Pairs	5	5	6	4	7	7–8	8–9	10–11	11	13

The colonisation of new sites is a welcome development as breeding success at the original well-known and much disturbed loch has been very low in recent years. The increase in pairs is also encouraging although only seven young were raised in 1990, and 10 in 1991.

In winter they are regular in Burghead Bay and off the Nairn and Culbin Bars. Most records are of one to three birds but there may be ten or more in Burghead Bay, with a maximum of 21 on 14 January 1991. Few are seen elsewhere. Breeding lochs are usually reoccupied from mid March; the earliest was on 29 February 1976.

Black-necked Grebe

Podiceps nigricollis

Rare visitor.

There have been six records:

1 River Lossie (nr. Aldroughty)	1833 [**53**]
1 Morayshire	22 Jan 1861 [**4**]
1 Loch Spynie	June 1919 (SN 1923:174)
1 Loch Loy	Jan 1948 (R.Richter)
1 off Culbin	19 Jan 1975 (SB **9**:180)
1 Nairn Harbour	11–12 Dec 1978 [**9**]

(Black-browed Albatross

Diomedea melanophris)

An albatross, probably of this species, was seen and photographed from a ship 14 km north of Cullen on 5 September 1990. This record has yet to be accepted by the British Birds Rarities Committee.

Fulmar

Fulmarus glacialis

Numerous breeder, common offshore.

The first recorded occurrences of the Fulmar were around Culbin Sands where there were 'several' in 1881 and singles were found dead in 1885 and 1886. [**4,7**] The establishment of the first breeding colony, between Hopeman and Covesea, proceeded as follows [**10,11**]:

1919	Birds prospecting
1922	20 sites occupied, breeding not proved
1923	5–6 pairs laid eggs
1929	43 occupied sites
1934	86 occupied sites
1945	98 occupied sites

In 1987 there were 186 apparently occupied sites in this area, with a further 104 between Findochty and Portknockie. Prospecting birds were first reported around Cullen in 1945 and again in 1959. A few pairs have bred close to the town since at least the late 1960s, sometimes on the old viaduct. The most remarkable colony in the Districts is 13 km inland in Ternemny quarry near Knock Hill. There were no Fulmars there in the mid 1970s but they were well established by 1984 when there were nine adults and three nests. In 1985 two nests were seen, in one of which a chick was reared (A.Anderson, S.T.Buckland). One adult was incubating beneath a gorse bush on 17 June 1990.

Colonies are largely deserted in September and are reoccupied by the early New Year. In late autumn Fulmars are usually scarce, but they are otherwise common at sea. Largest numbers are seen during adverse weather in autumn, e.g. 3,000 flew west past Lossiemouth in one hour on 3 September 1984. A small dark Fulmar was found dead at Nairn on 16 December 1978.

Six ringed Fulmars have been found in Moray and Nairn between May and September. They had been marked on Fair Isle, Orkney (two) and in Ross and Cromarty (three).

Sooty Shearwater

Puffinus griseus

Scarce migrant in late summer and autumn.

The first report was not until 1976 when one flew east past Lossiemouth on 29 August. Since then birds have been seen on 19 occasions between August and October, the largest count being 26 off Lossiemouth on 24 September 1988. Most are seen passing close inshore during north/north-easterly gales.

Manx Shearwater

Puffinus puffinus

Scarce offshore in summer and autumn.

Manx Shearwaters are seen offshore in small numbers in most years, usually on passage in August and September. The strongest passage noted was in

1984 when best counts were 30 past Burghead on 26 August and 90 past Lossiemouth in one hour on 3 September. In 1988 a regular flock of birds was found off Delnies in late summer; the highest count was 135 on 16 July. This flock, apparently feeding in the area, was again present in 1989 when Shearwaters were seen on each of seven visits in July and August, usually 35–65 but up to 180 on 19 August. Only occasional birds were there in 1990, however, and none in 1991. Few are seen off the Districts' coasts after September, the latest in autumn being singles off Findhorn on 16 and 17 November 1985. In midwinter, one passed Lossiemouth on 20 January 1991.

There have been two inland occurrences: the remains of an individual were found in a Peregrine eyrie near Dufftown in April 1988 and another was picked up alive, and apparently healthy, at Clochan on 8 September 1990. This bird, having been ringed and released at Portgordon, was found oiled near Sao Paulo, Brazil on 9 December 1990. Another, ringed on Rhum in August 1973, was found dead at Lossiemouth two weeks later.

Storm Petrel

Hydrobates pelagicus

Summer and autumn visitor offshore.

In 1844 Gordon described Storm Petrels as frequent in the Moray Firth and stated that they were sometimes driven ashore during storms.[**6**] Harvie-Brown and Buckley also called them frequent and described the curious event of a bird found frozen to a telegraph wire in Burghead railway station during the winter of 1879.[**4**]

This century there have been only four sightings of live birds:

1 past Buckie	4 Oct 1981
1 off Lossiemouth	7 Aug 1986
1 off Lossiemouth	21 Aug 1988
1 Speymouth	13 Sept 1988

In addition one was found dead in a Burghead street after gales on 11 November 1986. It is very probable that on summer nights there are many more birds in the vicinity of our coasts than the small number of daytime records would suggest.

Leach's Petrel

Oceanodroma leucorhoa

Scarce visitor.

There is an old report of one found dead at Cluny Hill on 29 November 1897 (ASNH **7**:53) and Forres Museum records show that one was killed against a tree in the town's St Leonard's Road on the same date after a severe north-easterly gale. The big Scottish 'wreck' of Leach's Petrels in autumn 1952 was represented locally by one bird found dead at Nairn and received by the Royal Scottish Museum on 4 November.[**12**] It is likely that this largely nocturnal species is more regular offshore than these records indicate.

Gannet

Sula bassana

Common offshore in summer and autumn, fewer in winter.

Hundreds of Gannets are sometimes attracted to feed on shoals of small fish in shallow coastal waters, e.g. 300 off Culbin Bar on 18 October 1989. Counts of up to 50 are, however, much more usual. In autumn during adverse weather and onshore gales large movements of Gannets can sometimes be seen; the best passage yet noted was 465 past Lossiemouth in one hour on 7 October 1990. Those which remain in the Firth during winter are mostly adults although *c.*1,000 Gannets off Burghead on 17 November 1972 included numerous juveniles, as did a flock of 300 off Nairn on 24 December that year.

Storm-driven birds have been found well inland on four occasions: at Rothes in 1820, Pluscarden in 1865, Glen Fiddich on 3 October 1962 and Archiestown on 4 April 1966. One was on Spynie canal on 20 February 1987.

Ten ringed Gannets have been found dead in the Districts. They had been ringed as chicks in the gannetries on the Bass Rock (seven) and Hermaness, Shetland (three). An adult released at Findhorn in April 1977 was caught in the Bay of Biscay in January 1978.

Cormorant

Phalacrocorax carbo

Scarce resident and common winter visitor. Has bred.

Breeding has taken place only once when a single pair nested at Covesea in 1962 (SB **5**:374). Two other reports of breeding, in 1969 (SB **6**:70, [**57**]) and in 1987 [**110**], are now considered unacceptable following a review of the original data held by the Seabird Monitoring Programme. Up to 20 non-breeders are regular on the Covesea cliffs in summer and were first noticed there in the middle of last century [**3**].

In autumn and winter numbers increase and flocks of 50 or more are regular at favoured sites such as Findhorn (highest count 105 on 18 February 1967), the mouth of the Spey (max. 120 on 23 October 1988) and around Buckie harbour (max. 121 on 20 November 1989). The main night-time roosts are on the cliffs at Covesea (max. 150 on 30 December 1989) and at Portknockie (max. 130 on 15 October 1975).

A few are regularly seen inland in winter, usually up the Spey as far as Aberlour and up the Findhorn to Sluie. Twelve were on Loch Spynie on 12 April 1981. There have been occasional summer records on various inland lochs.

Over 60 ringed Cormorants have been recovered in Moray and Nairn. All had been marked as chicks, three in north-east England and most of the rest in Caithness, Orkney or Shetland.

Shag

Phalacrocorax aristotelis

Rare breeder and common visitor, chiefly in winter.

Breeding was not confirmed in the Districts until 1986 when two pairs nested at Portknockie. There was one pair there in 1987, none in 1988, and one pair raised three young in 1989 and in 1990. In 1991 there was an increase to five pairs. Non-breeders are regular in this area in summer; the highest count was 140 on 15 June 1991.

In autumn there is a big increase along the rocky coastline eastwards from Buckie, although relatively few are seen elsewhere. There is a large roost around the Bow Fiddle Rock at Portknockie, where 2,084 were counted on 15 January 1991, and a much smaller one on the cliffs at Covesea (e.g.

PLATE 15 Cormorant in wing-drying posture *(John Edelsten)*

50 on 30 December 1989).

The daytime whereabouts of the Portknockie birds is uncertain, particularly as flocks joining the roost arrive predominantly over the sea from a north-westerly direction. Colour ringing in June 1989 in the Caithness breeding colonies, around Helmsdale and Berriedale, has yielded at least 12 winter reports from Portknockie.

There have been 42 other recoveries of Shags, mostly ringed as nestlings in various Scottish colonies although seven came from north-east England. An adult ringed on the Isle of May in 1990 was seen at Portknockie in February 1991.

Bittern

Botaurus stellaris

Rare visitor.

There were eight documented occurrences during the nineteenth and early twentieth centuries, all involving single birds:

Brodie	1839 [**13**]
Loch na Bo	before 1863 [**3**]
Loch Spynie	before 1863 [**3**]
Loch Spynie	Feb 1879 [**7**]
Loch Flemington	20 June 1884 [**4**]
Elgin	1888 [**4**]
Coulmony House	19 Nov 1891 [**4**]
near Cawdor	10 Jan 1900 (ASNH **9**:122)

In addition there are imprecise references to others near Dufftown,[**4**] Grange [**14**] and at Loch Spynie.[**53**]

In more recent years there have been only two, at Loch Park in February–March 1964 (R.Hewson) and at Loch Spynie on 24 January 1985 (SBR 1985).

American Bittern

Botaurus lentiginosus

Accidental.

A male was shot at Loch na Bo, around December, in 1888. [**4,104**]

Little Egret

Egretta garzetta

Accidental.

One stayed in Findhorn Bay from 21–26 June 1983 (BB **77**:511).

Grey Heron

Ardea cinerea

Numerous breeder and winter immigrant.

At least six heronries have been occupied during the 1980s; the known history of each is as follows:

Ordiga (Fochabers)	Occupied 1872, 35–40 pairs in 1913, 13 in 1974 and 9 in 1981. Deserted in 1986 after trees were felled.
Culbin	*c.*7 pairs in 1946, 14 in 1975 and still occupied in mid 1980s.
Loch Spynie	First noted Pitgaveny area in 1911 (9 nests). Nested Caysbriggs where 13 pairs in 1954 and 12 in 1974. Trees felled in 1975 when moved to Loch Spynie where 8–9 nests in 1986–8, 11 in 1989 and 12 in 1990. In 1981 one pair nested in the reedbeds.
Parkmore (Dufftown)	*c.*9 pairs in 1966, 5 in 1985. Deserted in 1989 after felling in the area.
Hillockhead (Keith)	8 pairs in 1976, 3 in 1980. Wood then felled.
Kinermony (Aberlour)	8–10 pairs in 1986–9, 11 pairs in 1990.

In an area as heavily forested as Moray and Nairn small heronries must be easily overlooked and there must be more Herons breeding in the Districts than the 30–35 pairs contained in the three surviving colonies noted above.

The best documented heronry of last century was sited on cliffs on the banks of the Findhorn below Sluie. St.John reported 'plenty' of birds there in 1850 but the extinction of the colony in 1863 due, he claimed, to predation of the eggs by Jackdaws.[**3**] Other heronries, now extinct or not recently counted, were at Ballindalloch (20 pairs in 1939, 22 in 1954 and 32 in 1974), Loch Loy (13 pairs in 1927, 11 in 1974), Miltonduff (three nests in 1973), Loch Park (one pair in 1954, formerly large) and Ordiquish (two nests in 1976). Watt listed other heronries at Altyre, Darnaway, Drumin and Kirkmichael but no counts are available.[**15**]

In favoured feeding areas considerable numbers of birds may gather, the highest counts at each site being 30 in Findhorn Bay on 22 August 1973, 19 beside Spynie canal on 22 February 1986 and 12 at Speymouth on 31 August 1991.

Evidence of immigration in winter is provided by the recovery of three Norwegian birds, ringed as chicks and found dead at Portgordon (September

1964), Findhorn Bay (October 1971) and Keith (March 1985). Six individuals have moved into the Districts in winter from Scottish heronries (Highland (two), Tayside (three) and Fife) and one came from Cumbria.

(Purple Heron

Ardea purpurea)

Gordon gave a record of one killed at Loch na Bo in 1888.[7] Curiously he made no mention of the American Bittern there the same year. There appears to be no other supporting evidence for the Purple Heron occurrence and some suspicion must therefore exist of confusion between the two species. The record is not now considered acceptable.

Black Stork

Ciconia nigra

Accidental.

One was seen at Dulsie Bridge on 17 July 1977 (BB **73**:496), from where it moved upriver to Tomatin, Inverness-shire.

White Stork

Ciconia ciconia

Rare visitor.

There have been eight occurrences, probably relating to six individuals:

Auldearn	17 April 1964 (BB **58**:357)
Tomintoul	31 May 1971 (BB **65**:327)
Mulben, Keith	4–5 June 1972 (BB **66**:336)
Auldearn	27 April 1975 (BB **69**:329)

Birnie, Elgin	7–10 May 1975 (BB **69**:329)
Dufftown	18 April 1977 (BB **71**:491)
Geddes, Nairn	22–23 April 1979 (BB **73**:496)
Fochabers	20–22 June 1979 (BB **73**:496)

It is likely that the two records in 1975 refer to the same bird, as do the two sightings in 1979.

Glossy Ibis

Plegadis falcinellus

Accidental.

There are three records of single birds from the early twentieth century:

1 shot on a small loch near Forres on 2 October 1902 (ASNH **12**:186)
1 shot Lein Burn, Speymouth in September 1907 (ASNH **17**:50)
1 obtained near Nairn some years prior to 1913 [2]

In April of 1936 or 1937, three birds spent two days near Hatton Farm, Kinloss. Two of these were later found at Loch Spynie where they stayed into June (R.Richter).

Spoonbill

Platalea leucorodia

Accidental.

Spoonbills have been seen on three occasions:

1 Culbin Bar	19 Oct 1964 (SB **3**:310)
1 Findhorn Bay	2 July 1977 (SB **10**:120)
1 Loch Spynie	11 July 1984 (SBR 1984)

[Chilean Flamingo

Phoenicopterus chilensis]

Escape.

Flamingoes of this species have spent a fortnight in Moray on two occasions:

Lossiemouth	16–17 Oct and Speymouth 17–30 Oct 1976 (SB **10**:82)
Fochabers	14–30 April 1979 (SBR 1979)

Mute Swan

Cygnus olor

Scarce resident breeder and short-distance migrant. Common in winter.

As early as 1526, Mute Swans were reported to be breeding plentifully on Loch Spynie [**16**] but there is little other local information of substance until the middle of this century.

Today they nest almost exclusively on freshwater lochs with occasional pairs occupying slower-flowing stretches of rivers such as the Isla and the Lossie. National censuses were carried out in Scotland in 1955–6,[**17**] in 1978,[**18**] in 1983 [**19**] and in 1990. The results for the first three surveys, using the old county boundaries of Banff, Moray and Nairn, were as follows:

		1955	1978	1983
Banff:	Breeding pairs	5	5	3
	Non-breeding birds	7	2	6
	Total birds	17	12	12
Moray:	Breeding pairs	23	13	10
	Non-breeding birds	16	88	2
	Total birds	62	114	22
Nairn:	Breeding pairs	3	4	0
	Non-breeding birds	0	2	2
	Total birds	6	10	2

The 1983 census was incomplete, at least for non-breeders. In 1990 there were 15 breeding pairs in Moray and Nairn Districts and 61 non-breeders. During the 1970s a moulting flock was present in summer at the mouth of the Spey, 40 birds being counted in 1976 and 30 in 1979. By 1981 the flock had dwindled to 18 and by the mid 1980s had disappeared. In 1990 and 1991, however, a flock of *c.* 20 birds was once again present. A summer flock of 30–40 (61 in 1991) is now regular in Findhorn Bay.

In winter the largest numbers, usually 30–50, are on Loch Spynie. Over 100 were regular there in the 1960s and 1970s, the best count being 148 on 22 December 1973. Unless the loch freezes, numbers usually increase from October to a midwinter peak and decline in March. The Lossie estuary holds a winter flock of variable size (max. 74 on both 12 January 1975 and 16 March 1990) and there are sometimes 30–40 on Loch Flemington (max. 63 on 16 November 1969). Up to 50 wintered around Loch Loy in the 1970s (max.

88 on 18 January 1976). When severe weather freezes inland lochs, swans are sometimes seen in Findhorn Bay but flocks seldom exceed 20. Mute Swans are occasionally seen swimming on the open sea, e.g. two off Buckie on 28 December 1981.

Lead poisoning of swans in Moray is a less serious problem than in some other parts of the country. In 1984 blood samples from birds on Loch Oire, Spynie Canal and Cooper Park, Elgin showed only low levels of contamination but three other swans from Sanquhar Loch, Forres carried blood lead counts of 78, 108 and 112 parts per million which they had accumulated from taking in discarded lead angling weights (*Northern Scot*, 17 November 1984). Poisoning may also be caused by ingesting lead gunshot: the gizzard of a swan found dead near Elgin in 1982 contained 944 pellets.[**20**]

Many Mute Swans have been ringed in Moray and Nairn and about 30 have been recovered outside the Districts, all within 100 km except one adult which moved from Findhorn to Aberdeen in early 1990. Several have been found in a summer flock at Inverness. Three birds marked in the moulting flock at Loch of Strathbeg in July 1983 were found at Delnies, Forres and Findhorn in subsequent years and a cygnet from Loch Ness was reported in winter at Lossiemouth.

Bewick's Swan

Cygnus columbianus

Rare visitor in winter.

St.John claimed that Bewick's Swans 'usually come in smaller companies than the Whooper . . . usually four or five' and never more than eight together. His only detailed records concern two at Loch Spynie on 13 March 1853 and two killed elsewhere in Moray on 23 February 1854.[**3**] Another was shot at Forres on 29 October 1889.[**4**] Assuming that there was no confusion with Whoopers in St.John's reports, the situation since then has been very different. Bewick's Swans have only been seen on three occasions this century: three were near Culbin Bar on 15 November 1963, three others fed among Whoopers in flooded fields at Milton Brodie from 22–28 November 1984 and two were on Loch Flemington on 3 December 1987.

Whooper Swan

Cygnus cygnus

Common migrant and winter visitor.

Evidently Whooper Swans have always been numerous autumn and winter visitors to Moray and Nairn in the last 150 years. St.John usually saw them in flocks of less than 20, although 200–300 were in Findhorn Bay in October 1844. He thought that they were more numerous on autumn passage than in midwinter.[**3**]

The first Whoopers occasionally arrive in late September (earliest were two on Loch Spynie on 18 September 1983) but more usually in early October. Numbers peak in late October and November and fewer remain through midwinter. Recently the only regular winter flock has grazed fields in the extreme east of Nairn District, also commonly feeding in the vicinity of Inverness airport. Until the winter of 1988/9 they roosted at night on Loch Flemington, sometimes in impressive numbers; the highest count was 184 on 15 November 1981. They were still using the loch in autumn 1988 (166 on 9 November) but thereafter numbers declined and in winters 1989/90 and 1990/91 very few Whoopers were seen there. Since autumn 1988 a small roost has existed intermittently on Loch Loy or Cran Loch (max. 33 on 22 December 1988 and 28 November 1991). A return passage through the Districts is evident in March, and few are left by late April. Single birds, mostly disabled, remained all summer in 1968, 1970, 1972, 1973, 1977, 1983 and 1989. Most were at Kingston or in Findhorn Bay; in summer 1979 there was a bird at each site and in 1991 two were in Findhorn Bay in June and July.

Loch Park, near Dufftown, was a well-known Whooper Swan site by 1880. They were studied there by Hewson between 1955–68.[**21,22**] He found a regular pattern in autumn, the herd forming in early October, reaching a peak about a month later and most birds leaving by late November. The average brood size varied annually between 2.27 and 4.00, and first-winter birds formed from 15.2% up to 34.1% of the flock. The maximum counts for each season are shown below:

1955	1956	1957	1958	1959	1960	1961	1962	1963	1964	1965	1966	1967	1968
135	160	205	200	170	117	130	130	40	50	60	50	30	10

Very few Whoopers visit the loch now.

Two swans ringed at Caerlaverock on the Solway Firth were found dead near Loch Flemington in subsequent winters. One seen at the loch on 15 February 1989 had been ringed in Iceland in August 1985.

[Black-necked Swan

Cygnus melanocoryphus]

Escape.

One was in Findhorn Bay on 4 March 1986 and at Loch Flemington from 2 December 1987–18 March 1988.

Bean Goose

Anser fabalis

Rare winter visitor, formerly common.

This was once the commonest grey goose on the southern side of the Moray Firth. According to St.John, in 1863, they were chiefly autumn and spring migrants, passing through in immense flocks in October and returning in mid March when they fed on newly sown crops and roosted in Findhorn Bay. Few remained in winter.[**3**] Macgillivray also reported 'multitudes' roosting in Findhorn Bay at night.[**23**] A great decline took place around 1870–90 after which Bean Geese were only rare visitors.[**2**] In the last 20 years there have been only nine records, mostly of one to two birds:

1 Lossiemouth	9 Jan 1977
10 Buckie	7 Jan 1979
1 Lossiemouth	25 March 1985
1 Findhorn Bay	March 1985, perhaps the same as the Lossiemouth bird
2 Findhorn Bay	4 Oct 1987
2 Coxton	13 March 1989
23 Findhorn Bay	3 May 1989, stopped to roost in the evening
1 near Nairn	26 May 1989, possibly an escape
3 Milton Brodie	27 Dec 1990

Pink-footed Goose

Anser brachyrhynchus

Common migrant, scarce in winter.

In 1863 Pink-footed Geese were regular visitors but far less numerous than Bean Geese.[**3**] In the latter part of last century numbers began to increase and by the late 1880s large flocks were moving through Moray on passage. Between 1910–30 further increase took place and by the late 1920s they were described as appearing 'by the acre' in autumn, and remaining in mild winters. By 1939 there were fewer but still a very large spring passage.[**25**]

Today the species is a common migrant in autumn and spring but they are generally scarce in winter. In most years the first birds arrive in the second half of September, the earliest on 14 September 1991, and, except in western Nairn, only stragglers are seen after October. Few flocks stop to feed, most passing straight through. In winter months a few birds often accompany the Greylags but larger numbers are unusual in Moray. In the 1970s and 1980s only 11 flocks of more than 10 birds were reported in the December–February period, all after 1983. Recently in western Nairn many more have overwintered; 500–1,000 in 1989/90 and 1990/1. The main return passage takes place in late March and April with more flocks stopping over than in autumn especially west of Nairn, where a build up of 2,000–3,000 birds takes place in the Drumdivan/Delnies area (max. count 3,730 at Tomhommie on 24 March 1989). Similar numbers may be roosting in Findhorn Bay at this time, and feeding around Miltonhill/Coltfield (where 6,000 were counted on 19 April 1991). A thousand or more regularly make a brief stop around Loch Spynie but 3,000 on 22 April 1988 was a lot more than usual. Most have left the Districts by the end of April, latest were 50 at Kinloss on 12 May 1986. Single disabled birds spent the summer in Findhorn Bay in 1977, at Kingston in 1987 (where an apparently healthy individual was seen on 30 June 1988) and at Loch Flemington in 1989.

Fifteen birds ringed on the Icelandic breeding grounds in summers 1951–3 were reported, mostly shot, in Moray and Nairn in later winters. Other local recoveries have resulted from birds ringed in southern and central Scotland (seven), Lancashire and Lincolnshire.

White-fronted Goose

Anser albifrons

Scarce winter visitor.

St.John noted only a few groups of six to twelve birds arriving in October and departing in April.[**3**] In the 1930s, also, small numbers sometimes wintered in Moray, [**25**] perhaps of the European race *A.a.albifrons* which was common in winter on Tayside at that time.[**24**] This race has, however, been identified only once in the last 30 years, a single bird near Lhanbryde on 13 December 1967.

Today very small numbers of White-fronts are seen in most winters. These are all of the Greenland race *A.a.flavirostris*. They mainly frequent the Drainie area, often associating with Greylags and roosting with them on Loch Spynie. Usually fewer than 10 are involved; highest counts have been 24 on 24 February 1985 and 17 on 18 January 1990. A flock of 32 flew over Cairn Gorm on 4 October 1964.

One ringed at Egedesminde, Greenland in July 1946 was shot at Speymouth in November 1947.

Greylag Goose

Anser anser

Common winter visitor.

Last century the Greylag was described as a rare visitor [**3,4**] and by 1939 it was still only an irregular autumn visitor in small flocks, although the nearby Beauly Firth saw a big increase after 1920.[**25**]

Today the species is abundant in the Districts in autumn and winter. A few are sometimes seen in late September (the earliest were 79 at Loch Spynie on 17 September 1978) but the main arrivals take place in October. The largest numbers are then present during late October and November, with a decline thereafter as fewer stubble fields remain unploughed for geese to graze. The main roost is at Loch Spynie and the best feeding grounds usually lie in the Laich of Moray between the loch and Findhorn Bay. Some flocks commute considerably further; in December 1987 nearly 1,000 fed daily in the vicinity of Newmill and Aultmore, up to 25 km east of Loch Spynie. This habit has persisted in subsequent early winters; in early November 1990 *c.*2,500 passed over Clochan each morning and returned west in the evening. Regular counts

at the Loch Spynie roost began in 1960. The maxima for each winter are shown in the histogram below. Between 1985–8 the increase was dramatic: on 22 October 1988 a record 13,070 were counted entering the roost. In 1989, however, there were considerably fewer. Some Greylags from the west of the Districts, around Nairn, head north in the evening, probably to roost on Loch Eye, while a very variable number roosts in Findhorn Bay, up to 3,300 in winter 1989/90. Elsewhere a few hundred geese may roost on Loch Flemington and, since autumn 1989, on a dam near Deskford, where there were *c.*1,500 in November 1990. In October–November 1991 nearly 2,000

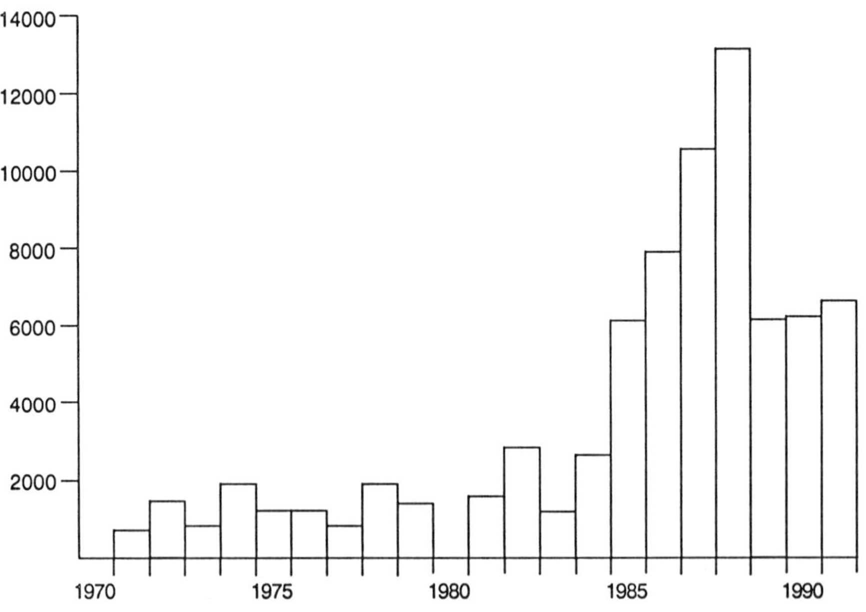

Figure 4 Greylag Goose: Loch Spynie roost maximum autumn counts 1970–91

roosted on Loch Belivat. In addition to stubble fields, wintering geese graze on grass, and sometimes young cereals and turnips. In November–December 1986 the water level at Loch Spynie dropped and geese were able to feed from the bottom sediments. As a result, large quantities of lead shot were ingested and at least 285 Greylags were found dead [**109**].

In spring, numbers increase again as flocks move north. Up to 5,000 frequent the area of Findhorn Bay in March and April, often roosting in the bay. Most have left by May. A few birds, either injured or escapes, or perhaps from the Scottish breeding population, are sometimes seen in summer; seven were at Kingston on 10 June 1987 and six at Loch Spynie on 7 June 1991. Breeding has not been recorded in Moray or Nairn.

Greylags ringed on their Icelandic breeding grounds were shot at Spynie in December 1979 and Findhorn Bay in November 1985. Five other birds recovered in the Districts had been ringed in earlier winters in Tayside (four) and Kirkcudbright, one of them 11 years previously.

[Bar-headed Goose

Anser indicus]

Escape.

An adult was seen at Kingston on 28 August 1977 (SB **10**:125) and two were on Loch Spynie and the Lossie estuary on 6 June 1991.

Snow Goose

Anser caerulescens

Rare visitor or escape.

On 27 August 1933, a flock of 16 Snow Geese was seen at Lochindorb. They were described as 'old birds as they were pure white except for the black wing tips'. One, an adult female, was shot as they passed within 30 yards of the observer (BB **27**:236). The date, number and apparent tameness suggests that these were unlikely to have been wild birds. A possible origin was the flock of about 15 Snow Geese reported by the Duchess of Bedford to have left Woburn in late August. It is curious however, that these were apparently young birds (BB **27**:21). Another flock spent two weeks near Elgin in autumn 1935.[**25**]

More recently, Snow Geese have visited Moray on seven occasions:

- 2 Loch Spynie 15 Jan 1967 (SB **4**:511)
- 1 Loch Spynie 3 June and Findhorn Bay 14 June–16 Sept 1979 (SBR 1979)
- 1 Loch Spynie area 6 Nov-10 Dec and Findhorn Bay 19 Dec 1985 (SBR 1985)
- 2 Lossiemouth 5 May, Kellas 21 May and Kinloss 22 May 1987
- 2 Miltonhill–Roseisle area 20 Feb–6 March 1988, 1 until 9 March
- 2 Coltfield area 24 Feb 1990, 1 there 28 Feb–7 March
- 1 around Loch Spynie 6–20 Oct 1990, in Findhorn Bay 25 Oct and at Miltonduff 9 Dec

It is impossible to be certain whether any of these birds are genuine vagrants. However, the October 1990 bird consorted closely with a newly-arrived flock of Greylags and gave every impression of at least having migrated with them from Iceland.

[Ross's Goose

Anser rossii]

Accidental or escape.

An adult remained with Greylags near Lossiemouth from 23 March–16 April 1991. The same bird was probably in Findhorn Bay on 15–19 March (*Birding World* 4:137–140).

Canada Goose

Branta canadensis

Scarce migrant in summer, rare in winter.

The first record was of 18 seen at Findhorn on 2 May 1887, two of which were shot. The rest of the flock apparently spent the summer in the area, being progressively shot, and the remaining five were last seen on 1 October.[**4**]

Since the early 1960s Canada Geese from the Yorkshire breeding population have established a regular summer migration to moult in the Beauly Firth. This doubtless explains the increased frequency of records in the Districts in the 1970s and 1980s, indeed four birds ringed on the Beauly Firth have later been shot around Findhorn Bay. Since 1971, when ten flew west over Buckie on 28 April, flocks of 12–50 have been seen briefly in the Districts between 25 May–21 July on eight occasions in five different years. Other stragglers have been seen in summer and also in January (1975, 1977, 1982 (three), 1984 and 1991), September (1973, 1982 (two) and 1985) and October (1982 and 1991 (staying throughout the winter)). In 1988 birds moulted in Moray for the first time, when six remained in Findhorn Bay from 17 July–2 September. In 1990 11 (ten after 18 August) were seen briefly at Garmouth and then moulted at Loch Spynie from 20 June–25 August, latterly moving to the Lossie estuary on occasions.

A small, pale bird showing the characters of one of the North American races *B.c.parvipes* or *B.c.hutchinsii* was feeding among Greylags near Lossiemouth on 16 April 1988 (MNBR 1988). This record is still under consideration by the British Birds Rarities Committee.

Barnacle Goose

Branta leucopsis

Scarce migrant and winter visitor.

Described in 1939 as an irregular winter visitor in small numbers, [**25**] the Barnacle has apparently never been common in Moray and Nairn. Although the increased number of records in the 1980s may partly reflect the increase in observers, it would appear that the species is now far more numerous, at least on passage. Quite large flocks of migrants occasionally pass through in late September or October *en route* from Svalbard to their wintering grounds on the Solway Firth, e.g. 112 over Culbin on 25 September 1982 and 85 off Burghead on 5 October 1979. Most records, however, relate to the very small number of birds which infrequently overwinter, often in company with Greylags. In winter 1985–6 up to six birds were regularly present in the Lossiemouth–Loch Spynie area between 13 December–15 February. A few migrants pass through in spring and there are three summer records, of singles at Nairn (injured) on 11 July 1963, at Loch Spynie on 10 June 1979 and at Kingston from 24–27 June 1982 and from 6–10 June 1991. Some or all of these birds were likely to have escaped from captivity.

A Barnacle found dead at Tomnavoulin in November 1976 had been ringed on the breeding grounds in Svalbard 14 years earlier. Another, marked at Caerlaverock on the Solway Firth in October 1978, was dead at Lossiemouth in October 1986.

Brent Goose

Branta bernicla

Scarce migrant.

During the nineteenth century Brent Geese were far more abundant in Moray than at present, although their numbers were prone to huge fluctuations. The winters of greatest influx were 1866/7, 1880/1, 1890/1 and also in 1909/10 when over 2,000 were shot.**[25,26]** St.John described 'great numbers' arriving in late September and early October and departing in late April,**[3]** while Harvie-Brown and Buckley wrote that Brent Geese 'literally swarm during some winters' and in Findhorn Bay in 1890/1 they were 'almost covering the surface of the water'.**[4]** In 1939 there were still several thousand in the Moray Firth as a whole but a considerable decline had taken place, apparently due to overshooting.**[25]**

Since the Second World War Brents have become scarce, although they still occur almost annually, usually in very small numbers. The largest recent flocks have been 47 at Findhorn Bay, 19 September 1971; 150 at Loch Spynie, 3 November 1974; 54 at Lossiemouth, 17 September 1978; and 37 at Nairn Bar, 18 January 1987. Earliest autumn dates were one at Lossiemouth on 17 July 1984 and four there on 26 August 1988. The best recent year was 1988, with an autumn influx of ten flocks totalling 112 birds at four localities.

The great majority are of the pale-bellied race *B.b.hrota* but small groups of the dark-bellied race *B.b.bernicla* have been identified on 12 occasions; the largest flock was 11 at Culbin Bar on 17–18 November 1988.

Ruddy Shelduck

Tadorna ferruginea

Accidental and probable escape.

Six arrived at the mouth of the Findhorn in early July 1892 and one, a female, was shot on 6 July (ASNH **1**:269–70). A second bird was also shot on 19 October.[**4**] As the arrival of this flock coincided with a huge influx by the species into northern Europe, it seems certain that these birds were wild vagrants.

Two adults, almost certainly escapes, were seen at a variety of places from Auldearn to Portgordon between 4 April–21 May 1987 (MNBR 1987) and again in the Mosstodloch/Lhanbryde area in September–October 1988 (MNBR 1988). In 1989 one was in Findhorn Bay on 27–28 April and a female stayed on Loch Spynie from 8 July–13 August (MNBR 1989).

Shelduck

Tadorna tadorna

Numerous summer visitor and breeder. Scarce in autumn.

Shelduck are mostly encountered on the muddy estuaries of the Findhorn, Lossie and Spey rivers, and inside the Nairn and Culbin Bars. Birds start to arrive on the estuaries in December or January but numbers are usually small until February and peak between March and May. Spring maxima on the estuaries in the last 15 years have ranged as follows:

Findhorn Bay/Bars	118–250 (max. only 140 in 1988–91)
Lossie estuary	10–31
Speymouth	14–30

Ducklings are seen from early June until early August with breeding success varying widely from year to year. The highest duckling count made in Findhorn Bay was 189 on 5 July 1969, but recent numbers have been much smaller. Most birds leave the estuaries in late summer to move to their moulting grounds at the Helgoland Bight. There have been three movements of ringed birds between Findhorn/Culbin and the Bight. Very few Shelduck are in Moray from September until the return commences in late December.

Birds occur sporadically on many inland waters but regularly only on Loch Spynie and its canal; the highest count was nine on 18 September 1977.

Ducklings ringed at Newburgh (Grampian) and in the Lothians have been found in the Delnies area in later summers.

Wigeon

Anas penelope

Common winter visitor and scarce breeder.

Breeding was first proved satisfactorily for the Districts in the late 1950s but colonisation probably took place many years earlier. Summering birds were first reported at Loch Spynie in the early 1880s, when a nest was reputedly found, and on lochans at the head of the Blackwater near Glenlivet in 1891.[4] Since 1970, when four broods were found in western Moray, breeding has been regular on moorland lochans there and has also occured in Nairn District. Pairs were present on nine lochs in 1988 and it is unlikely that the population greatly exceeds 10–15 pairs in any year.

Wintering Wigeon arrive in September and October. Numbers vary considerably from site to site and from year to year. The average annual maximum and peak count for the main coastal and freshwater sites in recent years is shown below:

	Loch Spynie		Findhorn Bay	
	Av. max.	*Peak*	*Av. max.*	*Peak*
1960/1–1969/70	378	1,150	1,490	3,558
1970/1–1979/80	628	3,000	629	1,200
1980/1–1989/90	733	1,700	1,486	6,256

Substantial flocks of Wigeon also appear periodically on the coast at Speymouth and Lossiemouth (up to 100, occasionally more) and inside the Nairn and Culbin Bars (usually 300–800, max. 1,290). They are also sometimes seen on the open sea, e.g. 1,550 at Burghead Bay on 15 February 1984 and 800 at Spey Bay on 29 January 1979. Other than Loch Spynie, favoured inland lochs (with highest recent counts) are Loch Flemington (940), Loch Loy/Cran Loch (520) and Loch na Bo (395).

In the Moray Basin as a whole, peak Wigeon numbers are usually present in October although the Moray and Nairn peak is often later. Most have left by late March and there is no evidence of a spring passage.

The origin of our wintering birds is indicated by six chicks ringed in Iceland and found in Moray and Nairn in October-February. A full-grown Wigeon, ringed in Holland in July 1954, was shot at Dyke in January 1956. Two others, marked in October in Suffolk and Essex, were shot at Delnies (February) and Findhorn Bay (November) in subsequent years.

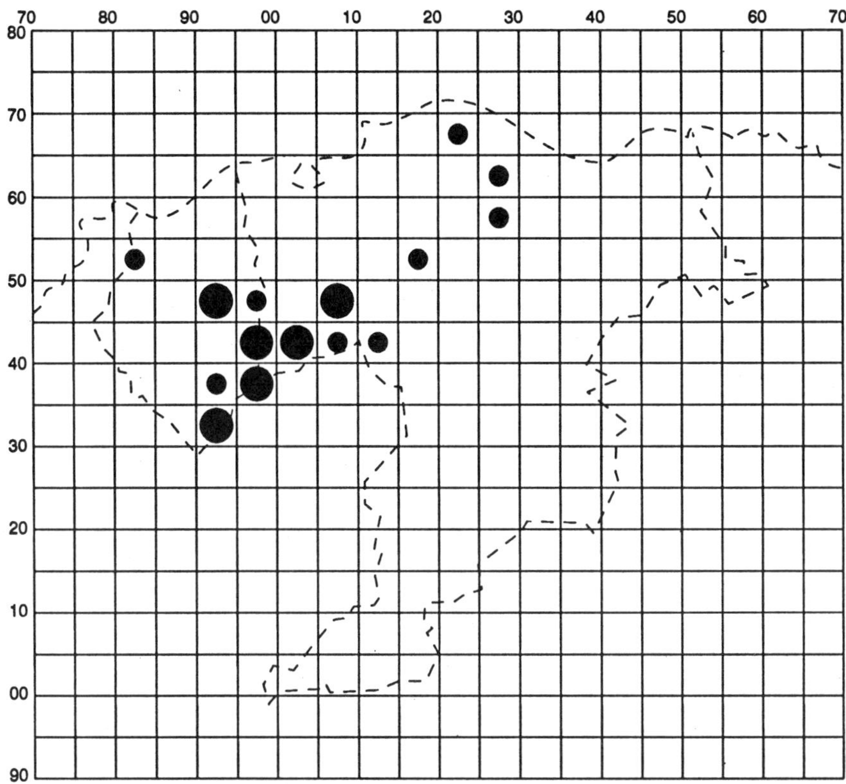

Figure 5 Wigeon summer distribution 1981–90 (May–July)

American Wigeon

Anas americana

Accidental.

A male, first seen at Loch Loy on 10 November 1986, subsequently frequented the area around the Nairn Bar until 11 January 1987 (BB **81**:546).

Gadwall

Anas strepera

Scarce visitor.

The only old records were of two killed in Morayshire in March 1859 [**4**] and others shot at Loch Spynie about 26 August 1892 and on 4 February 1898 (ASNH **7**:117).

Since 1960, Gadwall have occurred in 18 years. Most have been at Loch Spynie with occasional records at Fochabers (1971 and 1972), Gilston (1976), Lossiemouth (1981 and 1991), Loch Flemington (1987, 1988 and 1991), Sanquhar Loch (1991), Findhorn Bay (1991) and Loch Loy (1991). The monthly distribution of birds is shown below:

Jan	Feb	Mar	Apr	May	Jun	Jul	Aug	Sep	Oct	Nov	Dec
4	12	2	6	3	4	0	1	11	14	16	12

Most records refer to one or two birds. At Loch Spynie there were five on 16 September 1973, seven on 17 February 1980 and four on 12 October 1980. At Loch Flemington there were five on 23 October 1991 and six from 13–27 November 1991.

Baikal Teal

Anas formosa

Accidental.

A female was shot at Loch Spynie on 5 February 1958. The skin is preserved at the Harrison Zoological Museum in Sevenoaks, Kent (BB **74**:460).

Teal

Anas crecca

Scarce breeder and common winter visitor.

As a breeding species, the Teal is widely but thinly distributed over most parts of the Districts. They nest by the larger lowland lochs, in forest pools and at

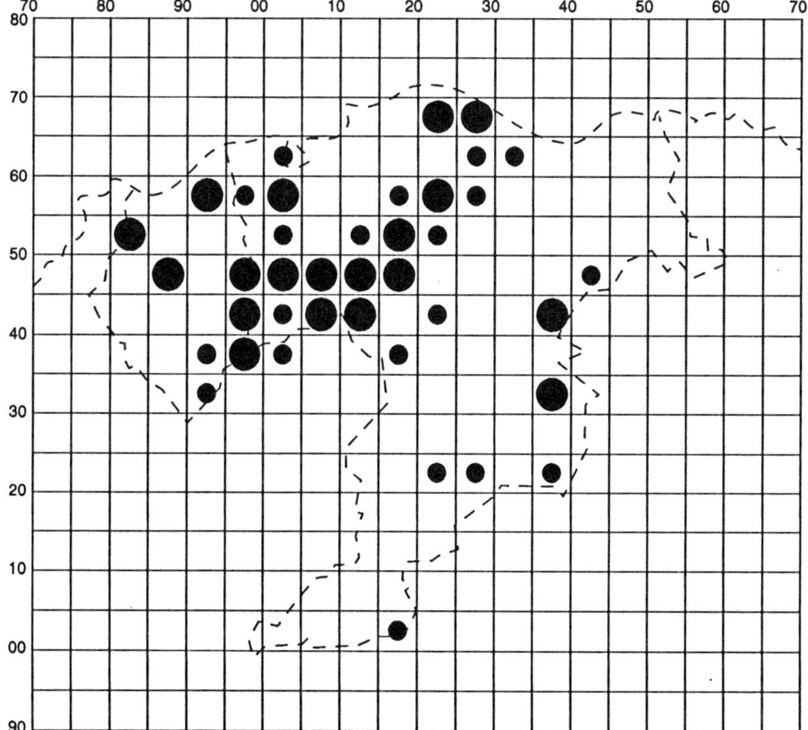

Figure 6 Teal summer distribution 1981–90 (April–July)

moorland lochans and marshes, as high as 500m near Loch Builg.

In autumn numbers are greatly swollen by the arrival of immigrants from northern Europe and even Iceland, from where a bird, ringed in August 1949, was shot at Kellas in November 1953. Winter numbers at the main sites in recent years are shown below:

	Av. Sept–March max.	*Peak*
Cloddach Quarry (1984/5–90/1)	244	380 on 21 Sept 1986
Loch Spynie(1960/1–90/1)	136	500 on 15 Dec 1985
Cran Loch/Loch Loy (1960/1–90/1)	95	320 on 15 Oct 1967
Findhorn Bay (1971/2–90/1)	65	217 on 17 Feb 1991

Loch Flemington has also held up to 200 on a few occasions around 1970 but numbers here are usually much lower. There were 80 on Loch Belivat on 31 October 1989.

There have been five recoveries of British-ringed Teal in the Districts: they came from Northern Ireland, Essex (two), Stranraer and Inverness.

Mallard

Anas platyrhynchos

Numerous resident breeder and common winter visitor.

Mallard have apparently always been common in Moray and Nairn, **[4,6]** although adverse affects on the population of increased land drainage and cultivation were already being noticed by the turn of the century.**[27]** They remain our most numerous breeding ducks, occurring widely in summer on rivers and lochs, although only thinly on upland waters to about 400m.

In autumn and winter, numbers are greatly increased by the arrival of foreign immigrants. A juvenile ringed in Finland in July 1962 was found dead at Rothiemay in February 1963 and an adult caught at Loch Spynie in March 1939 was shot in Denmark in October 1940. Large flocks build up on lowland lochs, many birds moving to the sea when these waters freeze over. Winter numbers at the main freshwater sites in recent years are shown below:

	Av. Sept–March max.	*Peak*
Loch Spynie(1960/1–90/1)	467	1,360 on 18 Oct 1981
Cloddach Quarry (1984/5–90/1)	281	417 on 16 Jan 1988
Cran Loch/Loch Loy (1960/1–90/1)	218	410 on 18 Nov 1973

Other lochs which may hold 50–200 birds are Lochs Oire, na Bo, Boath, Belivat and Blairs, and Clunas and Glenlatterach reservoirs. Up to 400 were formerly recorded on Loch Park,[**21**] but many fewer are seen there now.

Large Mallard flocks also occur on the sea in winter. Regular concentrations in recent years have been as follows:

	Regular	*Peak*
Burghead Bay	250	1,209 in winter 1982/3 [**31**]
Strathlene	250	358 on 9 Feb 1988
Findhorn Bay area	100	400 on 25 Feb 1978
Covesea/Lossiemouth	100	2,485 in winter 1981/2 [**31**]

British ringing has produced six winter recoveries from outwith the Districts, five of them from the vicinity of East Anglia. Evidence of emigration was provided by the duckling marked at Garmouth in June 1974 and shot in Denmark in August 1975.

A duck showing the characters of a hybrid Mallard × Black Duck *Anas rubripes* was seen at Loch Loy on 16–23 November 1986. Another bird seen on the Lossie estuary on 19 February and in November–December 1991 was probably a hybrid Mallard × Wigeon.

Pintail

Anas acuta

Scarce winter visitor and migrant. Has bred.

In the mid nineteenth century St.John saw Pintails in summer at Loch Spynie but found no nest and classed them otherwise as occasional winter visitors.[**3**] Breeding was proved at Loch Spynie before 1914 (SN **111–112**:37–42) and this was presumably the 'one locality in Morayshire where the species nests with fair regularity' described by Berry in 1939.[**25**] The origin of this claim is uncertain. Breeding was not proved again in the Districts until a female with ducklings was seen on a Dava lochan on 18 June 1970 (SB **6**:357). There is no subsequent record of nesting.

In the 1950s small numbers regularly wintered around Cran Loch, Loch Loy and the nearby shore; occasionally up to 50 were present. This flock disappeared in the 1960s and between 1970–91 only 28 birds were seen in Moray and Nairn in the November–February winter period. Most records today are from Findhorn Bay in early spring, presumably of migrants returning north. In most years up to five are seen but there were ten in April 1984 and 1985 and 15 on 17 April 1979. Autumn sightings in the bay are unusual but there were eight on 29 October 1989.

Garganey

Anas querquedula

Accidental in spring.

Only four records exist:

1 'obtained' Cullen	spring 1841 [**97**]
1 pair Loch Oire	6 April 1971 (SB **7**:119)
1♂ Gilston	13 May 1978 (SBR 1978)
1♂ Loch Spynie	17 May 1991 (MNBR 1991)

Shoveler

Anas clypeata

Rare breeder and scarce migrant.

Shovelers were first proved to breed at Loch Spynie in 1851 when a nest was found on 19 May.[**3**] Further nests were found in 1852 and 1853 when at least three pairs were present in the latter year.[**32**] In 1885 four or five pairs were there [**4**] and two broods were seen in 1897.[**32**] Elsewhere two pairs bred at Loch of Cotts in 1878.[**7**] Breeding was again proved on a pool near Loch Spynie in the 1950s and on 13 May 1989 a female was watched on the loch with two tiny ducklings. Small numbers are now regular there in spring, usually up to six birds but nine males and five females were present on 11 April 1988. Males regularly display and it seems probable that breeding occurs more often than the proved records suggest. During the 1960s and early 1970s Shovelers were seen in spring in a marsh at Kinloss airfield, usually only one pair but five pairs were there on 6 April 1966. Any breeding attempts were curtailed by the efforts of the RAF to discourage a large colony of Black-headed Gulls.

There is a small but regular autumn passage through Loch Spynie in October–November where the peak count was 13 in 1988 and 1989, and 15 in 1990. Very few overwinter. There have been occasional records in Findhorn Bay, usually in spring, but otherwise Shovelers are now rarely seen away from the Spynie area.

[Red-crested Pochard

Netta rufina]

Accidental or escape.

There have been five records of seven birds, all since 1982. Most, if not all, were probably escapes:

1 ♂	Cloddach Quarry	10–21 March 1982 (SBR 1982)
2 (♂ + ♀)	Loch of Blairs	11 Nov 1984
(the male remaining until at least 13 Dec (SBR 1984))		
1 ♀	Loch Spynie	29 Oct 1985 (SBR 1985)
2 (♂ + ♀)	Loch of Blairs	3 Feb 1989
1 ♀	Loch Spynie	13 Aug–2 Nov 1989

Pochard

Aythya ferina

Common winter visitor and occasional breeder.

Last century the Pochard was described as not uncommon in winter and breeding may have taken place at Loch Loy in 1848.[3] By 1885 they were breeding on Loch Spynie and Loch na Bo. They continued to breed at Loch Spynie 'in small numbers' in 1891 and 1892 and 10–12 pairs were nesting there by 1920. By 1895 they had also bred on Loch Flemington.[4,25] Although Berry reported a gradual expansion of breeding by 1939, [25] this seldom happens now and the most recent breeding took place at Loch Spynie in 1977 (two broods) and in 1978 (three broods) and on a pool in Lossie Forest in 1979 (one brood).

In winter significant numbers are present only on Loch Spynie where the build-up usually begins in September. Peak numbers and the pattern of attendance at this loch have changed since the mid 1970s, as shown below:

	Seasons with peak count occurring in		*Av. Sept–March max.*	*Range*
	Sept–Dec	*Jan–March*		
1960/1–1974/5	2	14	52	7–141
1975/6–1989/90	13	2	118	32–380

The highest count, of 380, was on 12 November 1978 and recent numbers have been very much lower. Elsewhere in winter a few Pochard are regular at Loch Oire, Loch na Bo, Cloddach and Loch Flemington. In autumn at Loch na Bo Pochard were unusually numerous in 1990 (max. 49) and 1991 (max. 45). A party of 12 were on Lochindorb on 4 September 1975.

The origin of our wintering birds is indicated by the duckling ringed in Latvia in June 1981 and shot at Loch Spynie in November of the same year.

(Ring-necked Duck

Aythya collaris)

A female briefly visited Loch Flemington on 12 January 1990. This record has yet to be submitted to the British Birds Rarities Committee.

(Ferruginous Duck

Aythya nyroca)

Harvie-Brown and Buckley, quoting from a Mr Small's 'List of Birds sent for Preservation', reported one received from Morayshire on 10 February 1857. The bird was bought from a poulterer's ship in Edinburgh, having been shot on the Moray Firth by a punt-shooter.[4] Unfortunately this record cannot be corroborated.

Tufted Duck

Aythya fuligula

Scarce breeder and common winter visitor.

The exact timing of the colonisation of Moray and Nairn by Tufted Ducks is uncertain. They were rare winter visitors last century, first reported in 1845 in Dyke and Moy parish [**13**] and subsequently at Loch Spynie in 1860, 1878 and 1880 during severe weather.[**7**] By 1895, however, they were described as 'not rare' in winter and breeding may have taken place in 1891 at Loch of the Clans, where several young birds 'only recently able to fly' were killed.[**4**] By 1936 they were breeding regularly at Loch Spynie and at Loch Oire.[**2**]

Today they breed widely on lochs and pools throughout the lower part of the Districts, and on moorland lochans up to around 300m. In 1988 11 lochs were occupied and in 1991 a minimum of 20 pairs bred on seven waters.

The main wintering lochs in recent years have been Lochs Spynie, Flemington and Oire/na Bo:

	Av. Sept–March max.	*Range*
Loch Spynie(1960/1–90/1)	88	35–194
Loch Flemington (1960/1–90/1)	34	2–71
Loch Oire/Loch na Bo (1984/5–90/1)	53	29–80

In most years highest numbers are not present until December or January. The highest count was 194 at Loch Spynie on 18 January 1981. Other waters sometimes holding 10–30 birds are Cloddach Quarry, Loch Belivat, Loch of the Clans, Cooper Park (Elgin), Loch Loy and Cran Loch. In the past, sizeable numbers have occurred at Loch Park (max. 49 on 17 October 1966) but only a few winter there now.

Tufted Ducks are uncommon on the sea, but they sometimes frequent the lagoon at Kingston from where they flight onto the sea in Spey Bay. Seventy-two were counted there on 21 January 1979 and 52 on 9 October 1987.

Scaup

Aythya marila

Scarce winter visitor.

The occurrence of Scaup offshore in winter is erratic but there is no evidence of substantial numbers before the 1970s. Peak winter counts since that time are shown in the histogram below. There has never been more than one site holding a significant flock (over 20 birds) in one winter. Highest flock counts were 400 off Findhorn in December 1972, 300 there in November 1973 and 600+ in Spey Bay in January 1979.[**9**] In 1913 it was claimed that 'considerable parties of Scaup' visited Loch Spynie every winter [**102**] but by 1939 only 'odd Scaup' were seen there.[**25**] However, in winter 1982/3 a flock remained on the loch for two months. On 6 March there were 12, increasing to 32 on 13–19 March (12♂♂, 20♀♀) and declining to 15 on 17 April. On 1 May there were still 17. In the 1940s up to 24 wintered on Loch Loy and Cran Loch. The only inland winter record since 1983 was one female on Cran Loch on 14 February 1989.

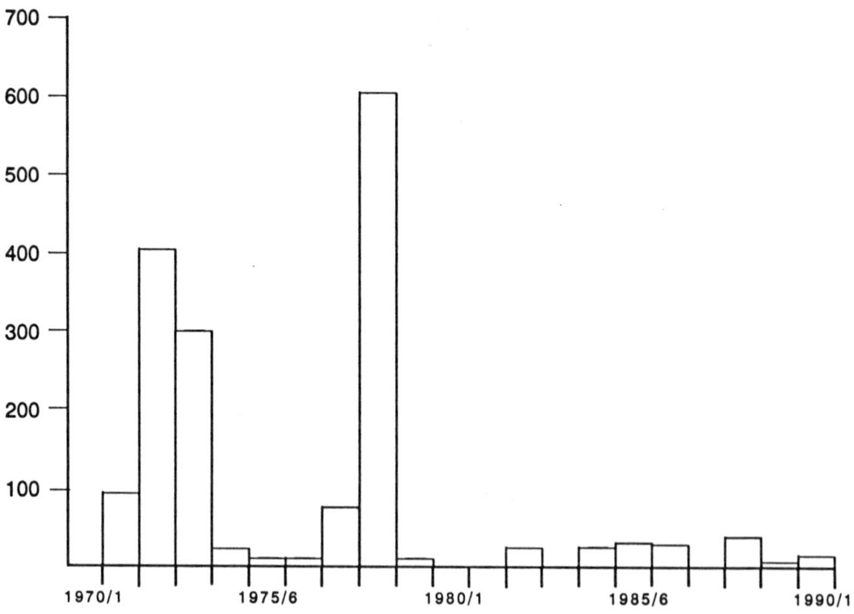

Figure 7 Scaup maximum winter count 1970/1–90/91

Breeding has never been suspected, but there are five inland records in summer: 1 ♂ Loch Spynie in May 1880[**7**], 1 ♂ Loch Oire 12 June 1961 (SB **2**:106), 1 ♂ Loch Builg on 14 May 1972 (SB **7**:337), 1 ♂ 2 ♀ ♀ Loch Spynie 19 June 1991 and 1 ♂ there 13 July 1991 (MNBR 1991).

There is one local ringing recovery of a male marked at Newburgh (Grampian) in January 1963 and found dead at Nairn the following June.

A duck seen on Loch Spynie on 29 March 1984 was considered to be a hybrid Scaup × Tufted Duck.

Eider

Somateria mollissima

Scarce breeder, common offshore.

Last century the Eider was only a rare visitor to the coast [**3**,**7**] although apparently more frequent by 1895.[**4**] A female and young were reported at Culbin in 1913[**102**] but there is no other suggestion of breeding until two broods were seen behind Culbin Bar on 7 August 1961.[**33**] Since that time breeding has become well established between Delnies and Findhorn Bay and has also been proved at Covesea, Speymouth and Buckie. The number of pairs, however, remains very small, probably not more than 10–15.

Large Eider flocks off the Moray coast were not recorded before the mid 1960s and are apparently a quite recent development.[**34**] In 1965 a moulting flock was noted off Hopeman–Covesea and by 1971 178 were there in August. In January 1972, 280 were counted in Burghead Bay.[**34**] Since then, a pattern of regular flocks in certain favoured sites has become established. During June–August summer flocks of, almost exclusively, moulting eclipse males build up in the following areas:

	Av. June–Aug peak (1984–91)	*Range*
Culbin/Burghead Bay	242	250–274
Hopeman/Covesea	199	60–269
Spey Bay	551	145–1,070
Strathlene (Buckie)	394 (1988–91)	327–536

These flocks appear to be increasing, especially in Spey Bay where 1,070 were counted on 3 July 1991. By September the moulting flocks can fly again and most of the Spey Bay birds leave the bay. From October until March winter flocks are in the following areas:

	Av. Oct–March peak (1981/2–1990/1)	*Range*
Culbin/Burghead Bay	596	300–900
Burghead/Lossiemouth	315	94–500
Spey Bay	117	43–514
Portgordon/Strathlene	119	82–153

At most sites peak numbers are present in October–December and decline thereafter, perhaps moving to the eastern Grampian coast.[**5**] Adult males predominate, usually forming 55–70% of the winter flocks.[**31**] There are no inland records of Eiders.

The origin of at least some of our wintering Eiders is indicated by three recoveries in the Districts of birds ringed at Newburgh (Grampian). Of two ducklings marked at Culbin in August 1966, one was found near Fraserburgh in December 1968 and the other at Aberdeen in July 1984, 18 years later.

King Eider

Somateria spectabilis

Accidental.

There have been seven records, all since 1976:

1♂ Covesea Skerries	14–15 Feb 1976 (BB **70**:418)
1♂ Covesea Skerries	17–24 March 1979 (BB **73**:501)
1 imm ♂ Burghead Bay	13 Feb–7 March 1982[**31**]
1 imm ♂ Burghead	3 Feb 1986 (BB **80**:529)

1 ♂ Burghead	28 April 1991 (MNBR 1991)
1 ♂ Burghead	25 May 1991 (BB **85**:519)
1 ♂ Kingston	12 June 1991 (BB **85**:519)

The 1991 records may all relate to the same bird.

Long-tailed Duck

Clangula hyemalis

Common winter visitor offshore.

Long-tailed Ducks have apparently always been common offshore in winter.[**3,4**] They remain so today although numbers fluctuate considerably from year to year. Very few are seen between June and August, first arrivals usually taking place in September with large flocks present by late October. The monthly pattern during winter at different sites varies as birds redistribute themselves within the Moray Firth, but numbers fall after February and, although still plentiful in April, few remain by late May. Since winter 1977/8, surveys of Long-tailed Ducks, in common with other sea ducks, have been undertaken by the RSPB[**9,31,34,36,37,38**] as part of a monitoring programme for Britoil. Maximum counts in each winter at each main feeding site since 1971/2 have been as follows:

	Spey Bay	*Burghead/ Burghead Bay*	*Off Nairn and Culbin Bars*
1971/2	350 (Apr)	2,350 (Jan)	nc
1972/3	300 (Apr)	3,000 (Dec)	nc
1973/4	1,500 (Apr)	7,000 (Jan)	nc
1974/5	nc	3,115 (Dec)	nc
1975/6	1,300 (Jan)	5,000 (Dec)	nc
1976/7	750 (Nov)	nc	nc
1977/8	2,155 (Dec)	3,000 (Feb)	2,000 (Nov)
1978/9	2,607 (Dec)	6,500 (Feb)	520 (Nov)
1979/80	nc	3,500 (Oct)	nc
1980/1	nc	nc	nc
1981/2	491 (Jan)	3,000 (Nov)	902 (Dec)
1982/3	2,000 (Dec)	2,188 (Jan)	922 (Nov)
1983/4	1,000 (Dec)	1,143 (Feb)	1,927 (Feb)
1984/5	761 (Feb)	3,230 (Oct)	4,700*
1985/6	750 (Apr)	545 (Dec)	3,500*
1986/7	279 (Apr)	2,008 (Oct)	465 (Feb)
1987/8	509 (Dec)	1,330 (Nov)	235 (Feb)

1988/9	386 (Dec)	3,710 (Nov)	970 (Nov)
1989/90	325 (Dec)	3,455 (Oct)	457 (Nov)
1990/1	847 (Mar)	2,174 (Dec)	1,712 (Nov)

* flocks off the Bars in mid Firth and not countable from land

It would, of course, be invalid to add the site totals to obtain a Moray and Nairn total for any one year as the counts were not made simultaneously and interchange of birds from one site to another is known to occur.

Accurate assessment of numbers is made difficult as the flocks are often well offshore. Another method of counting is to watch the birds flying to roost. The major roost for the south Moray Firth coast is in Burghead Bay, 3–4 km from the shore. Peak counts of birds entering this roost in recent years have been as follows:

1977/8	5,000 (Dec)	3,000 arriving from west, 2,000 from east
1978/9	6,500 (Jan)	almost all from west
1981/2	15,637 (Feb)	⅓ from north-east, most others from north-west, very few from east
1982/3	7,370 (Feb)	
1983/4	10,000 (Feb)	
1984/5	4,673 (Feb)	almost all from west
1985/6	3,538 (March)	
1986/7	3,740 (Nov)	
1988/9	7,000 (Nov)	
1989/90	2,034 (Nov)	
1990/1	3,056 (Nov)	

In 1978/9 a second, smaller, roost was detected in Spey Bay. In that winter it held 1,500 birds and 700 were using it in 1984/5.

Long-tailed Ducks have visited inland fresh waters on 14 occasions, at Loch Spynie (October 1981, October–November 1982, November 1986, March–April 1987, October 1988, November 1988, January 1989, October–November 1990 (two), October–November 1991), Loch Flemington (October 1964 (three), November 1985, November–December 1988 (up to four)), Loch na Bo (November 1985 (two)) and Loch Loy (November 1991).

Common Scoter

Melanitta nigra

Common winter visitor.

Although numbers were described as 'considerable' in the middle of last century,[**3**] there is nothing to suggest that scoters were particularly abundant. In the mid 1960s no large flocks were known but in the 1970s and early 1980s huge numbers were regularly present in winter. Since then a considerable decline has taken place. The main wintering areas, usually within 1 km of the shore, are in Spey Bay, Burghead Bay and off the Nairn and Culbin Bars. Since the winter of 1977/8 regular surveys of seaducks have been organised by the RSPB.[**9,31,34,36,37,38**] Before that time counting was less systematic, especially in Spey Bay, and caution must be exercised when making comparisons. Average maximum winter counts at the three main sites are shown below for Common Scoters and for all scoters, including Velvets and those not specifically identified:

Common Scoters only

Winters	*off Bars*	*Burghead Bay*	*Spey Bay*
1971/2–1975/6	*	6,716	1,250
1976/7–1980/1	*	1,714	6,500
1981/2–1985/6	584	1,413	1,918
1986/7–1990/1	422	850	253

All scoters

Winters	*off Bars*	*Burghead Bay*	*Spey Bay*
1971/2–1975/6	*	7,711	1,553
1976/7–1980/1	*	2,194	10,500
1981/2–1985/6	1,889	2,414	3,561
1986/7–1990/1	541	1,299	334

* Counts available for less than three winters in the period

Even allowing for inconsistencies in counting effort, it is evident that Common Scoter numbers were at their highest in the 1970s and have declined steadily since then. The greatest usage of Spey Bay was in the late 1970s and early 1980s when Burghead Bay numbers were well past their peak. Highest single Common Scoter counts in each bay were 14,000 at Burghead Bay on 13 January 1974 and 7,000 at Spey Bay on 13 April 1978. Little interchange is thought to take place between Spey Bay and the flocks further west.[**34**] No dusk flighting has been observed, the ducks apparently remaining to roost in their feeding areas.

The flocks build up during September and October but the pattern thereafter is inconsistent, with fluctuating numbers through the winter and most birds leaving by mid May. In some years an increase is apparent in late March and April as passage birds move through the Firth. Since the mid 1970s, at least, a moulting flock has been present in summer in Burghead Bay. This held 930 birds on 29 July 1986.

There are only two inland records of Common Scoter, one male at Loch Spynie on 19 May 1973 and a pair there, occasionally displaying, from 9 April–6 May 1989.

A male of the American and east Siberian race *M.n.americana* (Black Scoter) was seen off Findhorn on 29 December 1979 (BB **75**:495). Another male was off Culbin Bar from 22 January–8 February 1989 and the same bird, presumably, was back there on 11 December 1989 (BB **83**:455).

Surf Scoter

Melanitta perspicillata

Rare visitor.

This distinctive North American scoter was not recorded in Moray until 1964 but during the years of great scoter abundance in the 1970s and early 1980s they occured regularly with up to eight present in 1979. All records are listed below, extending for some winters the dates published in *British Birds*:

Winter 1964/5	Findhorn	1♂ 14 Oct (BB **58**:358)
Winter 1975/6	Burghead	1♂ 26 Oct (BB **69**:331)
	Spey Bay	1♂ 14 March (BB **70**:417)
Winter 1977/8	Spey Bay	1♂ 6 Jan–23 April (BB **72**:516)
Summer 1978	Spey Bay	2♂♂ May–early June, 1♂ from 15 July–10 Aug when 2♂♂ seen. 2♀♀ 2 June, 1♀ until 20 July (BB **72**:516)
Winter 1978/9	Spey Bay	3♂♂ 23 Sept, increasing to 4♂♂ on 21 Nov and a peak of 7♂♂ on 3 Jan. 1♀ 3–21 Jan. Down to 2♂♂ on 23 Feb and last 1 14 April (BB **72**:516, BB **74**:464)
	Burghead	1♂ 4 Feb and 14 April (BB **73**:501)
Winter 1979/80	Spey Bay	1♂ 3 April (BB **74**:464)
Winter 1980/1	Spey Bay	1♂ 22 April–5 May (BB **75**:495)
Winter 1981/2	Spey Bay	2♂♂ 11 Dec, rising to 5♂♂ on 2 Jan. 3♂♂ on 7 Jan, 1 until 14 Feb. 2♀♀ on 11 Dec[**31**]
	Burghead Bay	1♂ 12 Nov, 2♂♂ 1 Dec (BB **77**:516)
Winter 1982/3	Spey Bay	2♂♂ 17 Oct–12 Nov, 3♂♂ 24 Nov, 4♂♂ 2 Dec–16 Feb, 2 until 24 Feb,[**31**] 1 until 3 April when 2 (poss. 3)♂♂

		(BB **77**:516)
	Burghead Bay	1♂ 15 Oct and 4 Nov (BB **77**:516)
Winter 1983/4	Spey Bay	2♂♂ 17Oct–atleast31Dec. 1imm.♂ 17 April (BB **77**:516)
	Burghead	1♂ 10–20 Dec (BB **77**:516)
Winter 1984/5	Spey Bay	2♂♂, 1♀ 12 Dec, 1♂, 1♀ until 5 Feb (BB **78**:539)
Winter 1985/6	Burghead	1♂ 5–23 Feb
	Spey Bay	1♂ 25 Feb, probably the same bird (BB **80**:530)
Winter 1986/7	Burghead Bay	1♂ 15 Oct–1 Nov
	Spey Bay	1♂ 13 Dec, probably the same bird (BB **80**:530)
Winter 1987/8	off Culbin Bar	1♂ 26–29 Nov
	Burghead Bay	1♂ 20–25 Feb (BB **82**:518)
Winter 1988/9	Burghead Bay	1♂ 28 Sept (BB **82**:518) and 26 Feb–11 March (BB **83**:455)
Summer 1989	Spey Bay	1♂ 7 July–9 Sept
Winter 1989/90	Burghead Bay	1♂ 17 Oct–12 Dec and 26 March, 2♂♂ on 18 Oct
	off Culbin Bar	3♂♂, 1♀ 11 Dec (BB **83**:455)
	off Hopeman	1♂ 7 Jan
Winter 1990/1	Burghead Bay	1♂ 26 Oct and 13 Dec, 2♂♂ 16 Dec–14 Jan, 1♂ on 14 Feb
	off Culbin Bar	1♂ 6–8 Nov, 14–16 Dec and 20 March (BB **84**:464)

The great majority of records are of adult males. It seems likely that, in view of the greater difficulty of identification, at least some females are overlooked. Records for the winters of 1981/2 and 1982/3 were apparently not submitted to the British Birds Rarities Committee. However they appear in RSPB reports and are therefore included here.

Velvet Scoter

Melanitta fusca

Common winter visitor.

St.John, in 1863, described Velvet Scoters as 'common in small companies', [**3**] a statement which apparently remained true until the late 1960s when they started to become very much more abundant. Average maximum winter counts at the three main sites are shown below:

Winters	*off Bars*	*Burghead Bay*	*Spey Bay*
1971/2–1975/6	*	1,244	303
1976/7–1980/1	*	*	3,000
1981/2–1985/6	53	573	674
1986/7–1990/1	126	201	49

* counts available for less than three winters in the period

As with Common Scoters, the largest numbers in Spey Bay were present some years later than in Burghead Bay. Peak counts at each site were 5,000+ at Spey Bay on 13 April 1978 and 2,500 at Burghead Bay on 27 October 1975. Over the last few years they have once again become very much scarcer, especially in Spey Bay. Males are usually far more numerous than females; in 1977/8 77% of Velvet Scoters in Spey Bay were adult males, doubtless well over 80% males if immatures are included.

Goldeneye

Bucephala clangula

Rare breeder and common winter visitor.

Pairs were seen inland in summer in 1978 and 1979 but breeding did not take place until 1986 when a female with four ducklings was found on a moorland lochan in Moray. They bred again at the same site in 1987 and 1990 and possibly in 1988 and 1989. One pair probably bred at a different loch in 1991. With the recent provision of nest boxes it is to be hoped that the population will increase.

Immigrants start to arrive in October, mostly wintering at sea with a few on inland waters. The most important coastal site was formerly off Burghead maltings where the effluent discharge attracted a large flock of birds. There were regularly 200–300 with peak counts of 494 on 19 January 1975 and 420 in January 1978, representing about one-third of the whole Moray Firth Goldeneye population.**[34]** In October 1978 the outflow was redirected to over 1 km offshore and numbers declined rapidly to, usually, less than 50, only about 5% of the Moray Firth population.**[31]** Other coastal sites where birds have congregated have been at Findhorn and Speymouth. Off Findhorn 150–200 were regular between 1973–82 with an exceptional 400 on 4 April 1982. Less than 50 have usually been seen there in recent winters, although there were 76 on 15 March 1987. At the mouth of the Spey 100–200 were seen annually in late winter between 1969–76, peak count was 220 on 17 March 1973. Recently many fewer have been seen, 30–50 at most. Elsewhere only small numbers of Goldeneye are seen along the coast, especially off rocky shores such as Lossiemouth (up to 45) and between Portgordon and Buckie (up to 30).

Most larger inland lochs hold a few Goldeneye in winter when unfrozen, notably Loch Spynie where up to 10 are usual with more in spring e.g. 30–32 in March–April 1988 and 1989, and 41 on 29 March 1990.

Smew

Mergus albellus

Rare winter visitor.

There have been 18 records since the early nineteenth century, involving a total of 22 birds. The monthly pattern of birds' known arrival dates is shown below:

Jan	Feb	Mar	Apr	May	Jun	Jul	Aug	Sep	Oct	Nov	Dec
5	3	3	1	0	0	0	0	0	6	2	1

Fifteen of the records involved single birds, there were pairs on Loch Flemington in January 1961 and Loch na Bo/Loch Oire in March 1968, and three were at Cloddach on 29 October 1989. Of birds where the sex was noted, 13 were redheads and five were adult males. Loch Spynie (six) and Loch Flemington (four) account for ten of the records; furthest inland was one shot on Lochindorb on 7 February 1912 (SN 1912:116). The only bird on the coast was one at Speymouth on 20–23 February 1982.

Red-breasted Merganser

Mergus serrator

Scarce local breeder and common visitor.

In 1895 Harvie-Brown and Buckley wrote that the Merganser 'literally swarms all along the banks of the Findhorn, nesting in thick gorse coverts close to the river-side'. Only a few years previously the species was described as 'scarcely known, and then only as a comparatively rare winter visitant'.[**4**] There was evidently a very great increase around 1885–90.[**25**] By 1896 there were several pairs on the Spey at Ballindalloch and on the Avon. They were found commonly in Morayshire in May–June 1936[2] and also nesting widely on the lower reaches of the large rivers in the early 1960s.

Today they nest commonly only on the lower Findhorn, where at least eight broods were seen between the Bay and Cothall in summer 1987. On the Spey a survey of breeding sawbills in 1987 revealed only one pair of Mergansers between the sea and Millton, these were near Fochabers. None was found on the River Avon between the Spey and Coire Grealach, or on the River Lossie. Elsewhere only scattered pairs breed, as far inland as Loch Builg and Lochindorb.

In June and July males leave the females and broods and gather with non-breeders on the sea to moult, mostly in the Riff Bank area between Nairn and Whiteness Head. About 200 were there on 22 June 1921 and on 1 July 1967. More recently there were 152 on 4 July 1987. In the same area large numbers also build up in autumn and winter before declining by February. Peak recent counts were 1,800 in October 1984 and January 1986. Burghead Bay and Spey Bay regularly hold a few Mergansers in autumn and winter. Numbers seldom exceed 30 at either site, although 61 were in Burghead Bay on 22 March 1989 and 95 were at Findhorn on 15 November 1989.

Evidence of emigration from the area is provided by the bird ringed as a chick on the Muckle Burn, Forres in July 1976 and found in Hordaland, Norway in December 1980.

Goosander

Mergus merganser

Widespread but scarce breeder and common winter immigrant.

Breeding was not proved until 1895, in Nairn District,[2] but may have taken place before then as earlier inland summer records exist, e.g. at Cawdor in May 1864 and a pair on the Spey at Aberlour on 28 April 1885.[4] During the present century, they have become widespread despite persecution for their perceived threat to fish stocks and by 1977 the combined population of the old counties of Banff, Moray and Nairn was estimated at 50–100 pairs.[**40**]

In summer 1987 a survey of sawbills indicated that Goosanders were widely but thinly dispersed on the Spey, Fiddich and Findhorn but the Avon, Livet and Lossie held few or none (MNBR 1987). They breed on smaller headwaters and tributaries than Mergansers, although females conduct the broods to larger rivers to feed.

In mid and late summer a moulting flock forms at the mouth of the Spey. This regularly holds 50–100 birds; peak count was 148 on 30 August 1987. In recent years, in early autumn, large numbers have roosted on Glenlatterach reservoir; at least 180 were there on 25 September 1986. In winter upland breeding areas are largely deserted, but Goosanders remain on larger lowland lochs, especially Loch Spynie where a midwinter maximum of 30–50 is usual; best count was 66 in February 1984.

Winter immigration to the Districts has been demonstrated by two ducklings ringed in Northumberland in July 1972 and found in Moray and Nairn in September and November of the same year. Some of these incomers evidently remain here; another Northumberland chick was shot in Glenlivet in late May, two years later.

Ruddy Duck

Oxyura jamaicensis

Accidental.

There are five records, all since 1980:

2 ♀♀ Nairn 25 Sept 1982 (SBR 1982)
1 ♂ Loch Spynie 6 May 1984 (SBR 1984)
1 ♀ Loch Flemington 25 June 1986 (SBR 1986)
1 ♂ Loch na Bo 6–7 Sept 1987 (MNBR 1987)
1 ♂ Loch Flemington 9–23 Oct 1991 (MNBR 1991)

Honey Buzzard

Pernis apivorus

Rare summer visitor.

St.John included a report of a bird feeding on a wasp's nest near the Findhorn.[**3**] A further nine occurrences followed between 1867 and 1896, including five in 1882. This, together with the claim by Thomson that they were 'irregular stragglers' to Ardclach parish,[**27**] suggests that breeding may have taken place at that time.

More recently single Honey Buzzards have been seen in 1975, 1983 and 1985.

Black Kite

Milvus migrans

Accidental.

One was seen in the Cabrach on 14 July 1974. Despite initial rejection this record was accepted by British Birds Rarities Committee following a reconsideration (BB **73**:502).

Red Kite

Milvus milvus

Formerly numerous breeder, now being re-introduced.

Red Kites were 'numerous' in 1775 [**28**] and remained so in the first half of last century. At Ballindalloch in the 1840s four or five were often seen together in autumn and winter. St.John, writing in 1850, described them as formerly common but by the middle of the century persecution was taking its toll and in 1842 they had disappeared from Forres. Having once been described as the commonest hawk around Spynie, none was seen after 1848. In the 1850s they were generally very rare and the only subsequent report was of two seen by Harvie-Brown soaring over woods at Wester Elchies near Craigellachie for several days in spring 1885.[**4**] There have been no certain records of vagrants this century.

In 1989 the RSPB and NCC began a programme of re-introduction of Red Kites to the Highlands using young birds imported from Sweden. Several of these have spent periods of time in Moray and Nairn:

1 Roseisle–Elgin	27 Aug 1989–15 March 1990+
1 Glenferness	for *c.* 2 weeks in early Sept 1989+
1 Altyre	16–26 March 1990+
2 Glenferness	29 March–17 April 1990 (1 until 21 April)
2 Glenferness	3 Oct 1990
1 Glenferness	23 Oct–30 Nov 1990+
1 near Cawdor	29 Nov 1990
1 Glenferness	7 dates from 23 May–5 Dec 1991, 2 on 10 Dec 1991
1 Logie	6 Oct, 30 Oct and 10 Dec 1991

2 Drynachan	7 Nov 1991
1 Achnatone	26 March 1991
3 Dava	26 March 1991
1 Brodie	17 June and 10 Oct 1991
1 Forres	4 Dec 1991

+ = all different (wing-tagged) birds

White-tailed Eagle

Haliaeetus albicilla

Accidental.

There were two records in the nineteenth century. Gordon, writing in 1844, described the finding of one 'a few years ago . . . in a disabled state on the sandy beach near Innes House'.[6] In his 1889 book he mentions another on Innes Links in 1878.[7] The coincidence of locality is remarkable.

Marsh Harrier

Circus aeruginosus

Rare visitor.

The first record was not until 1969 when a pair frequented Spynie marshes from May until July. There was no evidence of breeding. Since then there have been 18 reports, all involving single birds except two at Kinloss on 1 May 1986 and two at Loch Spynie on 6 June 1991. Only three have been identified as males, 15 of the others being females or immatures.

The monthly distribution of birds, since 1969, is as follows:

Jan	Feb	Mar	Apr	May	Jun	Jul	Aug	Sep	Oct	Nov	Dec
0	0	0	2	9	3	1	3	1	0	1	1

Most sightings have been at Loch Spynie (eight) or in the Findhorn Bay area (four).

Hen Harrier

Circus cyaneus

Rare resident breeder and scarce winter visitor.

Gordon, in 1844, described the Hen Harrier as the most abundant and destructive of larger hawks.[6] St.John, while also reporting them as formerly common throughout the county, remarked on their destruction of young grouse, a habit which brought them into conflict with game keepers.[3] During the second half of the last century they were persecuted to extinction and the last possible breeding attempt was by two pairs reported as nesting near the source of the Conglass Water close to Tomintoul in 1884.[4] Thomson, writing of Ardclach in 1900, observed that 'for many years not a single specimen has been known within the bounds'.[27] Reduced keepering during the last war permitted a recolonisation and breeding again took place on the Moray moors in 1944 and 1945.[96] Other pairs were found in 1949 and 1950. In the 1960s and 1970s the population may have risen to 20–30 pairs, although they largely failed to colonise young plantations which they occupy elsewhere in Scotland. Illegal persecution has continued on certain grouse moors and this, combined with ploughing of their open heather moorland habitat for forestry, has prevented further increase — indeed a recent decline is evident and the present population is unlikely to exceed ten pairs.

In winter birds move onto lower ground and are joined by immigrants; there have been three local recoveries in winter of chicks ringed in Orkney and one from near Inverness. They can be seen quartering marshland and will sometimes become attendant on large finch flocks for food. During January–March 1982, two ringtails roosted among reeds near Loch Spynie. The most distant recovery of a locally ringed chick was at Inchture (Tayside) in April of the following year. A wing-tagged bird at Aberlour from 10 Sept–3 Oct 1991 had been marked as a nestling in Tayside.

Goshawk

Accipiter gentilis

Rare resident breeder.

In the mid nineteenth century they apparently bred regularly in Darnaway Forest.[3] During the last 20 years breeding has again taken place in the Districts and on five occasions single birds have been seen in winter, at

Fochabers on 16 January 1977, Loch Spynie on 25 February 1979 and Hopeman in late November 1983. The other two records relate to ringed birds recovered in Moray in winter in 1976 and 1977. Both had been marked in summer 50–60 km outside the Districts.

Sparrowhawk

Accipiter nisus

Numerous resident breeder.

Sparrowhawks were described as 'common' or 'abundant' by all writers last century, although Thomson noted their persecution by gamekeepers around Ardclach [**27**] and this was doubtless common practice elsewhere. Despite having destroyed all the nests in their woods, Innes House keepers killed

PLATE 16 Sparrowhawk, male at nest *(John Edelsten)*

33 birds in August 1907 or 1908 (ASNH **20**:117). Despite this level of destruction, Sparrowhawks survived in good numbers and now nest in conifer plantations and broadleaf woods throughout the Districts. In a heavily wooded study area of *c.* 150 km^2 near Forres, 25–30 pairs usually nested in the 1980s (B.Etheridge). On 22 July 1990 one flew over Feith Buidhe, Cairngorm plateau at 1,100m.

Sixty-three Sparrowhawks ringed in Moray and Nairn have been recovered, 42 of them within the Districts. Thirty-six birds moved between 10–100 km and four, marked as chicks, travelled over 100 km, to Tayside (two), Fife and, most remarkably, to South Uist. Evidence of winter immigration of northern Continental birds is provided by the female ringed on Fair Isle on 9 October 1955 and found dead at Cawdor on 29 December the same year.

[Red-tailed Hawk

Buteo jamaicensis]

Presumed escape.

A bird of this species was seen in the Cabrach in spring 1989. It was relocated in spring 1990 near Dufftown, where it remained until at least late June.

Buzzard

Buteo buteo

Scarce resident breeder, chiefly in the west.

The fortunes of the Buzzard in Moray and Nairn have reflected the intensity of keepering. They were apparently widespread in the Districts at the beginning of last century but by 1863 they were 'much less common than formerly'.[3] The persecution continued until Harvie-Brown and Buckley, in 1895, called them one of the rarer birds of prey in Moray.[4] In 1900 they were very rare in the Ardclach area of the Findhorn valley where they were once common.[27]

By the 1950s the situation was starting to improve and Moore gave a breeding population for 1954 of around 11 pairs in 408 square miles in Morayshire.[29] Today, were they are tolerated, breeding densities can be high e.g. up to 22 pairs/100 km^2 south of Forres (B.Etheridge). To the east of Elgin numbers are much lower, seldom reaching five pairs/100 km^2. Increased afforestation, providing nest sites where previously none existed, has contributed to the growth in numbers as has a general decline in persecution. In certain areas, however, shooting and trapping goes on and poisoned bait continues to be used. On one estate, where Buzzards were absent, keepering ceased in 1981 and by 1983 there were four pairs breeding. Although nesting pairs occupy small clumps of woodland well up the glens, the individual over Cairn Lochan at 1,150m on 3 May 1990 was unusually high.

Thirteen Buzzards ringed as nestlings in Moray and Nairn have been recovered. Four left the Districts; the furthest travelled 66 km to Alford. A chick marked at Cannich, south-west of Inverness, in June 1990 was found dead at Burgie nine months later, a distance of 83 km.

Rough-legged Buzzard

Buteo lagopus

Rare winter visitor.

There have been 11 records in all, the earliest of singles at Cawdor in 1832, 1839 and 1840.[4] There is a curious report of one of a pair trapped at Knockando on 4 May 1921 (SN **127–128**:121). Recently there have been seven sightings:

1 Kinloss	7–21 Nov 1982
1 Dufftown	9 Jan 1983 (SBR 1983)
1 Milton Brodie	24 Nov 1984 (SBR 1984)
1 The Buck	7 April 1988 (SBR 1988)
1 Cabrach	6 Nov 1988 (SBR 1988)
1 Cabrach	16 Oct 1989 (MNBR 1989)
1 Knock of Braemoray	20 March–1 April 1990

(Spotted Eagle

Aquila clanga)

An eagle, probably of this species, was seen at Darnaway on 28 June 1976. The record was rejected by British Birds Rarities Committee but is to be resubmitted by the observers (R.H.Dennis).

Golden Eagle

Aquila chrysaetos

Rare resident breeder.

There have probably never been more than two or three breeding pairs since the middle of the last century. In 1844 the remains of a disused nest were visible on Ben Rinnes [**4**] and there was an eyrie on Ben Avon in 1845.[**13**] In 1891 a pair first nested in a birch tree in Glen Fiddich and persisted, unsuccessfully, for at least three years.[**4**] Breeding currently continues in three localities, all with long histories of occupancy. It is not uncommon for wandering juveniles to be seen in the uplands well away from occupied home ranges.

One chick, ringed in Moray, was found dead near Ballater a year later and another, ringed elsewhere, moved 29 km into the Districts.

Osprey

Pandion haliaetus

Scarce summer visitor and breeder.

Although St.John wrote, in 1863, of Ospreys as 'frequently seen on the lower Findhorn, Loch Spynie and other places' he made no mention of breeding.[**3**] Knox, in 1872, said that they were occasionally seen around the lower Spey, Blackwater and Glen Fiddich areas.[**100**] Harvie-Brown and Buckley also gave no breeding records but included reports of single birds shot in the Cabrach in August 1889 and at Mayen near Rothiemay in 1890.[**4**] About 1906 a bird was seen in spring at Loch na Bo (ASNH **20**:117) and there were others at Fochabers in June 1936, Findhorn in June 1950 and Nairn Bar in July 1954. In the 1960s records increased and the first pair built a nest in 1966 and raised two young in 1967.

Birds arrive in the last days of March or in early April, the earliest was on 27 March in 1982 and in 1991, and most have left by mid September, latest on 26 September 1988. In autumn shallow estuaries are favoured fishing areas and several birds often congregate in the best sites; the highest count was 10 in Findhorn Bay on 20 August 1986. In 1987 an Osprey was seen high over the Cairngorms on 31 May and others were seen there on 6 and 19 July 1988.

Locally ringed Ospreys in, or travelling to and from, their West African wintering ground have been recovered in Belgium (September), France (September), Morocco (April and February) and Gambia (January). Birds have also been found in subsequent summers in Iceland (May) and the Faeroes (June).

Kestrel

Falco tinnunculus

Widespread but scarce resident breeder and migrant.

Described as common by all writers last century, they remain widespread today. Kestrels breed in quarries, on inland and coastal cliffs, on ruined buildings and in woodland in holes and the disused nests of other birds. While most pairs nest at low levels, they have been found up to 500m near Tomintoul. The breeding population varies, even from one year to the next, presumably in relation to the supply of their small mammal food.

In late summer the juveniles disperse away from the breeding areas and may appear anywhere from the coast to the high tops of the Cairngorms, e.g. two at 1,200m on Ben Macdui on 26 August 1984. Ringing recoveries of nestlings show that this dispersal may take some Kestrels as far as the Continent; two chicks ringed near Dallas in June 1985 reached France (December) and West Germany (November) in the same year. Other locally ringed nestlings have been reported from Cumbria, Yorkshire (two), Warwickshire, Northamptonshire and Cornwall. Return movement was shown by the adult ringed in Shropshire in April and found later at Ardclach. Evidence of movement through Moray from more northerly regions is provided by the 11 birds seen to fly in from the sea at Findhorn on 23–24 August 1970 (SB **6**:365). A chick ringed in Orkney in 1961 was killed at Ballindalloch in January 1963.

Merlin

Falco columbarius

Scarce resident breeder and migrant.

The historical status of Merlins is hard to ascertain, writers last century variously describing them as 'not infrequent', 'not particularly abundant' and 'scarce'. In recent years breeding numbers have declined in several areas as the species' open heather moorland habitat has been surrendered to forestry plantations. Extensive fieldwork between 1986–91 has revealed about 22 active sites in Moray and Nairn, of which about three-quarters were occupied in any one year (B.Etheridge, J.J.C.Hardey). Most nests are in long heather on sloping ground, although there are records of breeding in trees in the old nests of other species.

After the breeding season birds occasionally visit the highest ground (e.g. one on Cairngorm/Ben Macdui plateau on 2 August 1987) but in autumn and winter they feed in low-lying and coastal areas, and upland breeding sites are deserted. Dispersal of first-winter Merlins is evidenced by movements of five local nestlings to Peterhead, Aberdeen, Tayside, Lancashire and Cambridgeshire. A chick ringed in Kincardineshire in July was found near Elgin 16 months later and another, from Tayside, was dead near Dallas the following summer.

Hobby

Falco subbuteo

Rare visitor.

There are only five records:

1 killed Rothiemay	July 1863 [**4**]
1 killed Innes (Urquhart)	late June 1910 (ASNH **20**:117)
1 nr. Dufftown	19 Oct 1938 (SN **235**:29)
1 Garmouth	16 June 1980 (SBR 1980)
1 Darnaway	24 May 1989

[Lanner

Falco biarmicus]

Escape.

A Lanner wearing jesses was seen at Lossiemouth on 17 October 1976. This bird did not originate from nearby RAF Lossiemouth (SB **10**:90).

Gyrfalcon

Falco rusticolus

Accidental.

St.John mentioned birds seen at Loch Spynie and near Elgin a year later but gave no dates.[**3**] Harvie-Brown and Buckley included an extra record of one 'taken' near Elgin in 1865 [**4**] — the undated report from Lossie Green given by Gordon probably refers to the 1865 Elgin bird, which had previously been wounded by a keeper in Duffus.[**7**] The only recent record is of one at Williamston near Duffus on 24 November 1977 (BB **71**:497).

Peregrine

Falco peregrinus

Scarce resident breeder, some dispersal in autumn and winter.

Although detailed information is lacking, it appears that Peregrines were quite common in the Districts last century despite collecting and persecution on grouse moors. St.John relates how at one site, in 1851, he shot a pair on 22 April and a new pair had occupied the territory by 19 July.[**3**] During the national decline in the 1960s, caused by pesticides, the eastern Highlands (of which Moray and Nairn form part) were relatively unaffected except in coastal areas.[**30**] The population today remains high (*c.* 20 pairs) although persecution and thefts of eggs and young continue. Most breeding takes place in the uplands but one costal site has been sporadically occupied for at least 100 years.

In winter, while one or both adults may stay in the vicinity of the breeding territory, juveniles disperse and are regularly seen hunting in coastal areas such as Findhorn Bay.

Scottish ringed birds found in Moray and Nairn have all come from Highland Region, the furthest travelled 179 km from Cape Wrath to Tomintoul. Local nestlings have been found in Poolewe and Blairgowrie.

Red Grouse

Lagopus lagopus

Common resident breeder.

Red Grouse breed on heather moorland throughout the Districts from at least 800m down to 250m only 4 km from the sea on the Bin of Cullen. They occur at widely varying densities, populations remaining highest on those drier south-eastern moors where a burning rotation is practised to ensure a plentiful supply of young heather shoots. In winter heavy snow causes the grouse to gather into packs in better feeding areas. In 1988 *c.*1,100 were counted in two or three groups over *c.*5 km^2 of moorland at Bowmans, Cabrach.

Grouse were very abundant last century [**6,27**] but over the last 80 years they have declined greatly in many areas. Although the population remains high on some moors in south and east Moray, numbers are much reduced over the greater part of the Districts. This has been caused by a variety of factors such as less efficient moor management, tick-borne disease and widespread afforestation, although the latter has often taken place only after declining grouse stocks rendered the moors uneconomic. Disease was already a serious problem by 1917 when grouse were temporarily almost exterminated in the Tomintoul area (SN **82**:241).

Considerable mobility was shown by two birds ringed at Pitchroy near Ballindalloch in December 1911 and shot at Lhanbryde in August 1912 and Pluscarden in October 1914.

In 1907 an unsuccessful attempt was made to introduce the Continental Willow Grouse *L.l.lagopus* near Craigellachie (ASNH **16**:117).

Ptarmigan

Lagopus mutus

Numerous resident breeder.

Apparently Ptarmigan were once more widespread, and on lower hills, than is the case today. Harvie-Brown and Buckley, in 1895, reported breeding in the Glenfiddich, Glenlivet and Cabrach areas on 'quiet ridges' and some 'lower hills'.[4] Watson gave former occurrence in summer on Cook's Cairn (Glen Fiddich) and the Ladder Hills.[**105**]

They are now almost confined to the mountainous uplands around Cairn Gorm and upper Glen Avon usually above about 900m, although a few breed on Creag Mhor down to 850m or lower. Remarkably a few birds have persistently inhabited the isolated summit of Ben Rinnes at around 800m. First reported there in the 1790s [**14**] they were also noted as present in 1844, when up to 14 were seen,[6] in 1863,[3] 1895,[4] the 1920s, 1953 and 1955, when a few were also seen in the Ladder Hills in February.[**105**] More recently there were two coveys on 26 July 1970 and a few birds in most years since; the highest count was 14 on 29 December 1987. Breeding was confirmed in 1989, when a pair with four chicks was feeding around the rocks of the summit cairn on 2–11 July, and took place again in 1990. Three pairs were found on 10 March 1991. They have certainly been absent from Ben Rinnes in some years so recolonisation of this outlying hill appears to have taken place on several occasions. In about 1983 two Ptarmigan spent many months around the summit of Ben Aigan at only 450m altitude.

In winter birds may gather into large flocks e.g. 74 on Ben Avon, 12 November 1983 and 85 at Coire Raibeirt, 13 December 1988. When very deep snow makes feeding difficult a move towards lower altitudes may take place.

Black Grouse

Tetrao tetrix

Numerous resident breeder.

Black Grouse were described as abundant in suitable woods in 1863 [3] but a serious decline started around 1900 and they became scarce nesters in Moray and Nairn. This decline was documented by Rintoul and Baxter in 1927. Large decreases between 1900–25 were reported from Altyre, Findrassie,

Fochabers, Cabrach, Arndilly, Glenlivet and Cullen. By contrast they were still numerous in 1918 around Dufftown and Tomintoul.[42]

By the 1960s/70s there had been some recovery in numbers due, at least in part, to increases in afforestation. Glen Avon estate held two leks each with *c.*25 cocks. More recently, however, Black Grouse have become scarcer again and less than 10 cocks remain on Glen Avon. Elsewhere other leks have dwindled or vanished and birds are now only thinly spread through the Districts. Most are seen in or close to young open plantations (where numbers fall as the canopy closes) and around the moorland/woodland edge. They are found down to 200m only 4 km from the sea near Cullen. The largest numbers currently appear to be in the Glenlivet and Cabrach areas where at least four leks exist. These usually hold only six to ten cocks each although, exceptionally, 19 were at one site in early March 1990.

Capercaillie

Tetrao urogallus

Scarce resident breeder.

Shaw wrote, in 1775, that the 'chief Fowl in the Woods . . . the Caperkylie is become rare'.[28] Within a very few years the bird was extinct. The subsequent process of reintroduction has been described by Pennie [43] and can be summarised as follows:

1852 Introduced Loch na Bo, failed
1878 Introduced again Loch na Bo, failed
1882 Unsuccessful attempt to rear birds from eggs Glenferness [27]
1883 Young reared from eggs Clunas woods
1884 Nest and three coveys young at Darnaway – probably originated from the Clunas stock
1886 Reared from eggs Aultmore
1887 One nest Aultmore, none in subsequent years
1888 Reared from eggs Gordon Castle, Fochabers but all dead within 18 months
1892 Nine nests Darnaway (but none found in 1894)
1897 2♂♂ and several ♀♀ released Gordon Castle and became established
1898/9 Several 'arrived' Arndilly
1906 At least 12 nests Arndilly, *c.*30 birds Gordon Castle were probably survivors from the 1897 stock

From these and perhaps other introductions the Capercaillie slowly spread through the Districts, being reported at Carron (1903), Binn Hill, Garmouth (1906), Pluscarden (1906), Cullen (1916) and Culbin Forest (before 1922). The Darnaway stock seems to have survived (12 killed there in 1912) and by 1922 they were becoming 'plentiful' there. The first bird was shot in Roseisle in 1945 and they were present, although not yet proved to breed, in Lossie Forest in 1948. In 1949 breeding was reported in Speymouth Forest, Teindland, Pitgaveny and Monaughty with good stocks in Newtyle, Altyre, Darnaway, Cawdor and Culbin Forests.

In recent years the process of expansion has been reversed and the Capercaillie is once more an uncommon bird in Moray and Nairn. Since 1968 their presence in the 33 10 km-squares in the Districts has declined as shown below:

PLATE 17 Capercaillie, cock threatening an intruder *(John Edelsten)*

	10 km-squares surveyed	*10 km-squares occupied*
Summers 1968–72 [**65**]	33	23
Winters 1981/2–1983/4 [**68**]	33	14
Summers 1988–90	33	8

By the late 1980s Darnaway, and perhaps Monaughty, were the only forests where reasonable numbers persisted. Birds were seen at 12 localities in Darnaway Forest during summer 1987. A programme of release of captive-reared Capercaillies was started in Altyre in 1988 and birds from this stock have also been liberated at Cawdor.

Capercaillies inhabit mature woods and plantations of Scots Pine, but will forage on adjoining farmland in autumn and winter. Small leks containing one or more males are formed in early spring, often on forest tracks or clearings, and it is important that such sites are not disturbed.

An interesting movement was made by a female, ringed at Abernethy in April 1991, which was traced to Carn Meilich, Strathavon in September 1991. It remained there and bred in 1992.

Red-legged Partridge

Alectoris rufa

Introduced scarce breeder.

The earliest record concerns one which was shot at Rafford in 1870.[**4,53**] In the early 1890s four pairs were released at Pitgaveny and in the next two years birds were shot at Findhorn (two) and Covesea, and a covey was seen near Roseisle.[**4**]

No further introductions, for sporting purposes, are known until *c.*1970, when Seafield Estates began large-scale releases at Cullen. Since then birds have been turned out on many estates including Pitgaveny, Cairnfield, Tulchan, Kellas, Orton, Glen Rinnes and Altyre. Some releases have been of pure Red-legged Partridges while others were of Red-legged × Chukar *A. Chukar* hybrids. Individuals may travel several miles and records have come from 26 localities since 1970, mostly in the arable lowlands but as far up-country as Inverharroch (Cabrach) and Tomdow. Feral breeding has occasionally been proved (e.g. at Clochan in 1988) but the extent to which self-supporting populations have become established is unclear.

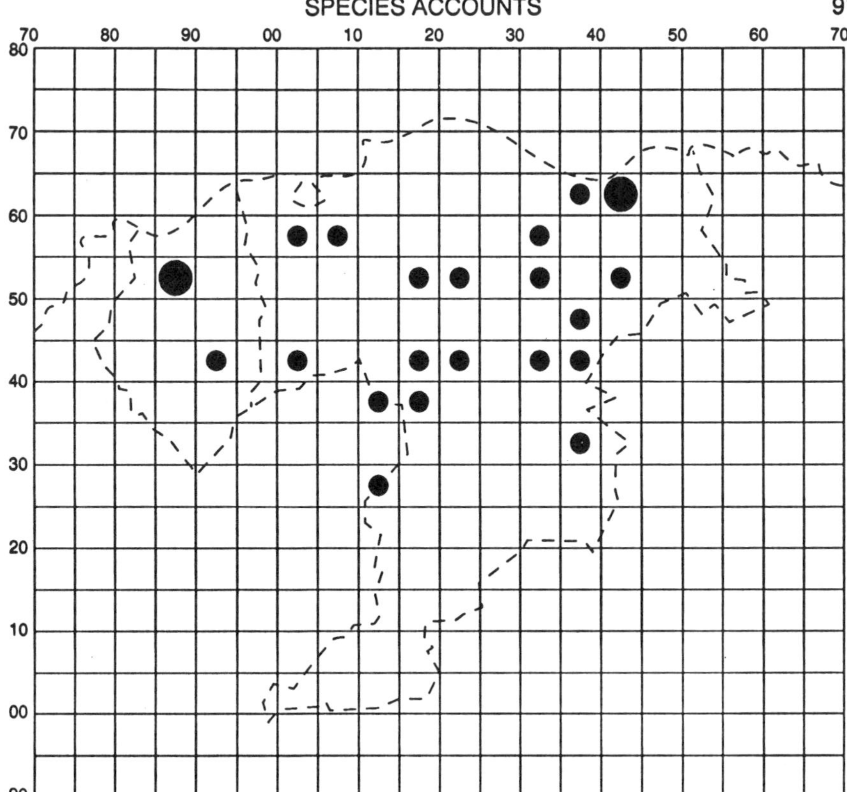

Figure 8 Red-legged Partridge summer distribution 1981–90 (May–July)

Grey Partridge

Perdix perdix

Numerous resident breeder.

The Grey Partridge is widespread throughout the cultivated lowlands and ranges up some grassy glens to 400m. A few also inhabit the coastal sand dunes and scrub at Findhorn and Culbin; five were on Nairn Bar on 28 November 1971. They are probably less numerous now than in the last century but the effects of recent changes in agricultural practice, such as increased chemical spraying and autumn ploughing, are uncertain. Chick survival is greatly affected by cold, wet weather but coveys of 15–20 are still frequent in a good season; the largest recently recorded was 38 at Milton Brodie on 24 November 1984. Three coveys in close proximity at Roseisle on 1 January 1990 held 54 birds.

Quail

Coturnix coturnix

Rare summer visitor and breeder, occasionally numerous.

Around 1844 Quail were found annually in the Elgin area and other 'sheltered parts of the province' of Moray.[6] They bred at Dyke and Moy in 1842 [2] and were regularly shot around Duffus and seen or heard near Forres every spring.[3] In 1893 they seem to have been unusually numerous; they nested near Portgordon and near Nairn, and several were seen or shot in autumn at Forres, Kinloss, Alves and Elgin.[4]

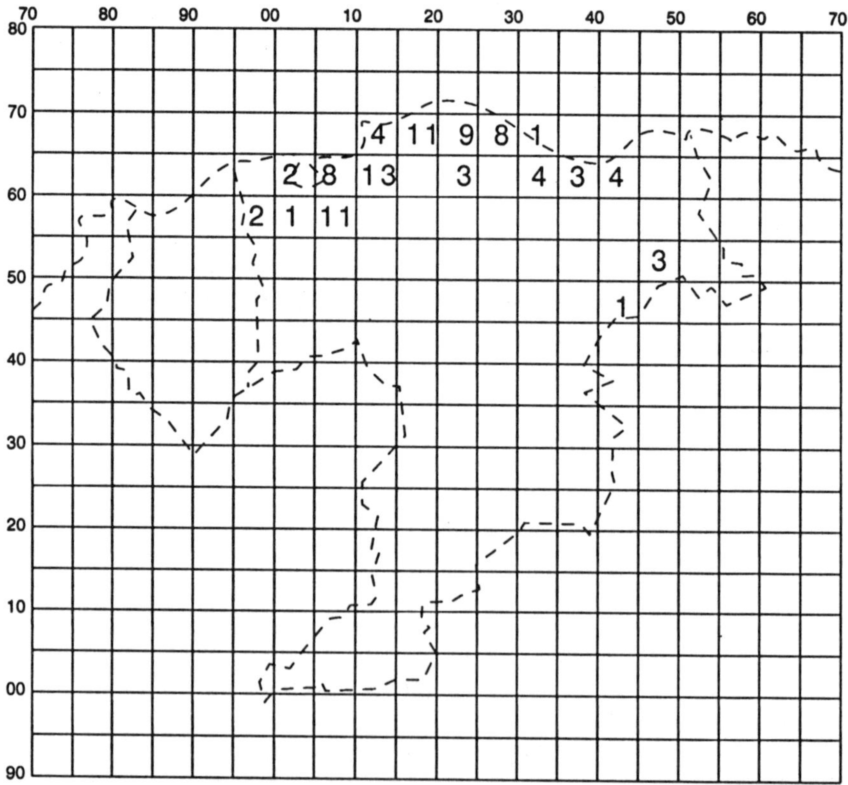

Figure 9 Distribution by 5km squares of calling Quail in summer 1989

This century, prior to 1989, the few Quail records have mostly come from the Duffus area. One called there every summer between 1933–7 and again in 1982–3 and 1986. Other records this century have been five shot at Rosehaugh Farm, Elgin on 14 October 1969 (SB **6**:84), one at Findhorn late July 1970 (SB **6**:365), one at Alves 1–3 August 1972 (SB **7**:347), one at Mosstodloch late July 1976 (SB **10**:91), one at Alves 11 July 1981, one calling near Portgordon on several days in July 1984 (SBR 1984) and one near Forres on 18 June 1988 (SBR 1988).

During the 'Quail year' of 1989 unprecedented numbers reached Moray. The first birds arrived in early June and by late July at least 88 calling birds had been located. The great majority were in fields of growing cereals in the lowland strip below 50m altitude, between Brodie and Buckie. None was reported from Nairn District, where few observers were active. In 1990 Quail called briefly near Forres (three), near Nairn (two) and at Pitgaveny and Mosstodloch.

[Reeves's Pheasant

Syrmaticus reevesii]

Introduced.

An attempt to introduce this species as a game bird at Glenferness about 1886 was abandoned as the birds proved worthless for sport.[**17**]

Pheasant

Phasianus colchicus

Common resident breeder.

Pheasants are widespread and common in most parts of the lowlands where there is sufficient cover, usually agricultural land containing woods and copses. They penetrate as far up the river valleys as cereal growing is practiced. The size of the self-supporting feral breeding population is unclear as large numbers are reared for sport on many estates. Concentrations of birds are often present in the countryside adjoining release sites prior to the shooting season, conspicuously gleaning the autumn stubbles.

Water Rail

Rallus aquaticus

Scarce winter visitor, occasional in summer but no recent proof of breeding.

Water Rails were described in 1844 as 'not infrequent' along the sides of lochs and rivers but there is no indication of the season.[**6**] Breeding was first reported at Loch Spynie where a nest was found on 19 May 1851.[**3**] Chicks were seen there on 27 July 1852 [**32**] and a number of eggs were collected between then and 1857.[**4**] They were also present at the loch in summer between 1949–60, in 1969, 1985, 1987, 1989 and 1990. Breeding is extremely difficult to prove and may have taken place in some of these years, and also at Loch Loy in the 1950s and Cran Loch in 1989. Thomson noted breeding at Ardclach in the late nineteenth century.[**27**]

Winter records are more frequent and have come from at least seven lowland marshes in recent years. The largest number reported at one site was four at Loch Spynie on 4 January 1976, 26 March 1990 and 29 October 1990. One was killed by flying into a floodlight at RAF Lossiemouth on the night of 1 December 1988.

Spotted Crake

Porzana porzana

Rare visitor, mainly in summer.

St.John wrote of killing this species at Loch Spynie in autumn and winter e.g. 12 October 1849.[**3**] One was also killed there in summer, in 1843.[**4**] Eggs were reputedly collected in Darnaway in 1867 (I.S.Suttie). There are six more recent records:

1 calling at night Kinloss in late May–early June 1967 (B.Etheridge)
1 Findhorn Bay 1 Oct 1972 (SB **7**:348)
1 calling Loch Oire 16 June 1980 (SBR 1980)
1 calling Garmouth 7 July 1981 (SBR 1981)
1 dead at a Sparrowhawk plucking post near Forres 10 May 1983
1 long dead Netherton 11 May 1983 (SBR 1983)

Little Crake

Porzana parva

Accidental.

Edward gave a record of a Little Crake found dead by a girl tending cattle on the banks of the River Isla at Thornton (near Keith) on 12 March 1852.[**97**]

Corncrake

Crex crex

Rare summer visitor, formerly common.

Corncrakes were abundant in Moray and Nairn last century and Thomson wrote in 1900, of Ardclach parish, 'everyone knows the incessant nightly crake of this familiar bird'. He noted their arrival in May and thought that there was one or more pairs on every farm in the parish.[**27**] Soon a decline began [**44**] which accelerated in the early 1940s and after the Second World War they were almost extinct in Moray.[**45**] In the 1950s and 1960s there was a slow recovery with around 6–12 pairs annually. In the 1978–9 survey, however, no Corncrakes were recorded in the Districts.[46] Since then there have been only four definite reports:

1 heard Lochinver (near Miltonduff)	4 June 1982
1 near Loch Spynie	29 Sept 1982
1 calling for several days near Fochabers	July 1985
1 calling Aultahuish near Dallas	28 May 1989

Moorhen

Gallinula chloropus

Numerous resident breeder.

A widespread and common species breeding from sea level to 490m near Loch Builg. They occur in summer on freshwaters of all sizes from farm ponds and marshes to large lochs where these have dense marginal vegetation. They are also found, less commonly, along the margins of slower flowing stretches of lowland rivers and burns. Upland haunts are deserted in winter. Moorhen numbers are difficult to assess because of the birds' skulking habits but 10–20 can be seen feeding in the open in winter around several lowland lochs. The highest count was 33 at Gilston on 10 January 1989.

[Purple Gallinule

Porphyrio porphyrio]

Probable escape.

A specimen of this species which is on display in Forres Museum was captured by boys on Cluny Hill in summer 1881.

Coot

Fulica atra

Scarce resident breeder and winter visitor.

A widespread breeder on well-vegetated lochs, mainly in the lowland strip but inland to at least Loch Belivat where there were two pairs on 15 July 1986.

In winter the largest numbers are on Loch Spynie, where the breeding population is augmented by many immigrants in autumn. The highest counts are usually in December–January, when 100–150 are regular (max. 256 on 4 January 1976), declining thereafter. Elsewhere in winter up to 60 can be seen on Loch Flemington (best count was 200 on 31 October 1985) and 10–40 at Loch na Bo (max. 88 on 14 January 1990), Loch Oire and Cloddach. Birds occasionally appear in sheltered coastal waters, e.g. singles in Buckie harbour on 25 February 1979, Lossie estuary on 9 March 1986 and at Kingston on 27 August 1988.

A Coot ringed near Spalding (Lincolnshire) in August 1980 was shot at Loch Spynie five months later. Also found there, in February 1973, was a bird ringed at Loch of Strathbeg in March 1963.

Crane

Grus grus

Accidental.

Three were shot in Strathavon in 1875.[**7**] There were no further occurrences for over 100 years, until one was in the Bogmoor area between 12–21 April 1978 (BB **72**:518). A very tame bird near Lossiemouth on 7 June 1983 was almost certainly one of the two which left the Highland Wildlife Park at Kincraig in 1982. In 1987 two Cranes stopped briefly at Auldich, Ballindalloch in April and two (presumably the same birds) in second summer plumage remained in the Strypes–Teindland Mains area from 25 May until at least 28 July 1987, occasionally displaying. They were also seen at Millbuies on 13 August and at Kirkhill, near Elgin, on 12 October (BB **81**:553). In 1988 one returned to Teindland Mains in mid May and remained until at least 13 June. It was later seen over Millbuies on 23 September and then frequented fields near Lhanbryde from 6 October–19 November (SBR 1988).

Little Bustard

Tetrax tetrax

Accidental.

One was shot in a turnip field at Westfield, near Elgin, on 8 February 1861 and presented to Elgin Museum. A second bird was seen at the same place a few days later (*Zoologist* **19**:7,433–4).

Great Bustard

Otis tarda

Accidental.

One was shot at Oakenhead, near Lossiemouth, in 1803. Another was 'taken' at Inchbroom, 2 km to the south-east, a few years before 1844.[6]

Oystercatcher

Haematopus ostralegus

Numerous resident breeder, common winter visitor and migrant.

Oystercatchers breed extensively throughout the Districts with the exception of the highest uplands. They occupy agricultural land up to the moorland fringe, riverside shingles, coastal dunes and grassland and, infrequently, shingle beaches. Eggs are also laid on roadside verges and occasionally pairs will use the flat roofs of buildings such as at Elgin Academy, Forres Academy, Moray College and Baxters factory at Mosstodloch.

Inland breeding has taken place for well over 100 years and perhaps for as long as 200 years. Adults arrive inland in late February and early March, occasionally earlier in mild winters such as 1989 when first arrivals at Mundole were on 17 January. They gather in large flocks often in traditional areas close to rivers and lochs e.g. at Mundole (max. 399 on 20 March 1986) and at Craigellachie (max. 251 on 7 March 1985). Pairs disperse from these flocks to occupy breeding territories. After the young have fledged, mixed flocks of

PLATE 18 Oystercatchers on the shore in winter *(John Edelsten)*

juveniles and adults gather to feed beside water and in mown hay fields before deserting the breeding grounds in July and August. Only occasional stragglers remain inland after August, latest was one at Aberlour on 10 October 1987. Both young and adults from the inland population, together with juveniles and a few adults from the coast, move south for the winter, mainly to south-west Scotland and north-west England/north Wales. Immature birds appear to remain there for at least two years.[**47**] There have been over 50 ringing recoveries linking the Districts with these areas and small numbers have moved to east Grampian and Tayside. Another bird, ringed near Forres in late March 1984, was recaptured as far south as Vendée (France) in February 1989 and three birds marked at Mundole in March–April have been found during subsequent winter periods in Waterford (Eire), Jersey and Devon.

In recent years the counting of waders at main sites in winter has been co-ordinated on the same day and the highest numbers in the Districts have consistently been counted at the Nairn and Culbin Bars and in Findhorn Bay. Counts since 1985/6 are shown below:

		Oct	*Dec*	*Jan*	*Feb*
1985/6	Nairn/Culbin Bars	2,807	1,977	2,576	1,733
	Findhorn Bay	832	936	732	1,657
1986/7	Nairn/Culbin Bars	1,879	1,579	2,537	1,943
	Findhorn Bay	800	766	2,586	1,202
1987/8	Nairn/Culbin Bars	1,142	1,215	1,272	1,312

	Findhorn Bay	690	692	634	967
1988/9	Nairn/Culbin Bars	1,888	692	1,289	1,009
	Findhorn Bay	2,352	753	808	629
1989/90	Nairn/Culbin Bars	832	1,589	724	786
	Findhorn Bay	600	820	593	780
1990/1	Nairn/Culbin Bars	1,241	743	722	686
	Findhorn Bay	270	471	727	730

Between 100–300 usually winter around Burghead, with similar numbers at Lossiemouth and on the rocky shore between Portgordon and Portessie. Ringing has shown that the wintering population is composed of local breeding birds from the coastal plain with some immigrants from the Northern Isles. Evidence of winter immigration from abroad has been obtained on four occasions: two Norwegian chicks, one from Vesteralen to the north of the Arctic Circle, were found here in winter, while birds ringed at Culbin/Findhorn in January 1981, September 1981 and April 1987 were reported in the Faroes in subsequent summers. Counts in June/July at the Bars revealed 200 Oystercatchers in 1987 and 55 in 1988. These are mostly immature birds and non-breeding adults. In April 1989 there were 228 at the Bars and 696 in Findhorn Bay. Some passage of more northerly birds through the Districts also takes place in spring and autumn.**[47]**

Avocet

Recurvirostra avosetta

Rare visitor.

There is one old record of a skull found in marshy ground near the sea in the 'Moray area' in 1887.[4] Although no locality is given the finder was O.A.J. Lee who stayed at Kincorth House near Findhorn Bay in 1887 and the skull probably originated in this area.

There are five more recent records, all in spring:

1 Lossiemouth	17 May 1969 (SB **6**:93)
1 Culbin Bar	1 April 1973 (SB **8**:245)
2 Lossiemouth	25 March 1984 (SBR 1984)
6 Findhorn Bay	28–29 March 1984 (SBR 1984)
1 Findhorn Bay	6 May 1986 (SBR 1986)

Stone Curlew

Burhinus oedicnemus

Accidental.

One was on upland sheep pasture between Tomcork and Berryburn (Dunphail area) from 4–7 June 1987 (SBR 1987).

Pratincole

Glareola sp.

Accidental.

A pratincole was watched for an hour at Loch Spynie on 17 August 1923 but was not specifically identified (SN **145**:8).

Ringed Plover

Charadrius hiaticula

Scarce resident breeder and common migrant.

A common breeder last century, it was described as abundant on suitable coastlines and widespread but local along rivers as far inland as the glens of the Glenlivet area.[**4**]

Today the breeding population is greatly reduced. A survey in 1973–4 revealed an estimated 40 pairs in Moray and Nairn [**48**] and a comparable follow-up survey in 1983–4 showed around 45 pairs.[**101**] In some areas such as Findhorn/RAF Kinloss (where there were nearly 20 pairs in the early 1980s) and the Lein at Kingston, human disturbance has undoubtedly affected breeding success. At the latter site eight nests were found in 1978, but there were none in 1988. It seems likely that the present breeding population is somewhat lower than it was in 1983–4. The main surviving concentration is on the coast between Nairn and Findhorn Bay where 10 pairs were located in 1991. Only a few pairs now breed inland, on riverside shingles or around gravel workings. Five pairs were at Cloddach quarry in 1988 and seven pairs

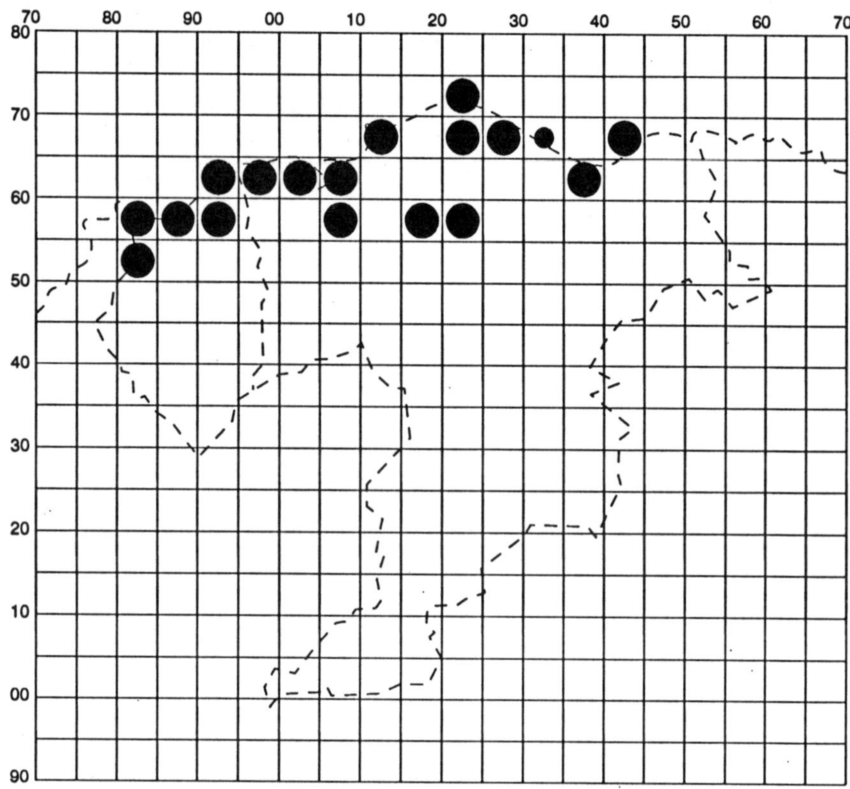

Figure 10 Ringed Plover summer distribution 1981–90 (April–July, excluding migrants)

from 1989–91, but success there is very low due to disturbance. Movement inland usually takes place in March but sometimes earlier, e.g. one pair at Cloddach on 19 February 1989. Two birds at 1,130m on the Cairngorm plateau near Lochan Buidhe on 12 June 1979 were probably of the northern race *C.h.tundrae*.[**49**] Other individuals visited the plateau on 19 May and 28 July 1987.

Large numbers of probable northern birds pass through on migration, especially in spring in Findhorn Bay where the brief May peak reached 1,500 on 8 May 1987 and 1,400 on 23 May 1991. Evidence that some of these spring passage birds winter well to the south is provided by the individual ringed on the Algarve (Portugal) on 24 August 1984 and caught in Findhorn Bay on 19 May 1986, and another, ringed in the Bay on the same May day, was dead in Morbihan, France on 29 August 1989. Two others, ringed on spring passage in May in southern Scotland, were found at Lossiemouth (August) and Findhorn Bay (May) in later years. Autumn passage is more protracted but is most marked in August. Over 100 regularly occur at Findhorn Bay (max. 400

on 18 August 1991) and Lossiemouth (max. 240 on 15 August 1991).

Wintering flocks of variable size are found around the Nairn and Culbin Bars (usually 20–70), in Findhorn Bay (20–50), at Burghead (15–40), Lossiemouth (10–40) and around Portgordon (30–80). A bird ringed as a chick at Cloddach in June 1989 was found wintering at Balintore, Ross & Cromarty, in January 1991.

Kentish Plover

Charadrius alexandrinus

Accidental.

One was watched at Culbin Bar on 12 June 1975 (SB **9**:197).

Dotterel

Charadrius morinellus

Scarce summer visitor and breeder.

Dotterel occur regularly in Moray only on the Cairngorm/Ben Macdui plateau around Loch Avon and on the highest hills surrounding upper Glen Avon. Here they nest on windswept, barren and sparsely vegetated ridges, mostly above 1000m. Survey work by the NCC between 1987–9 located breeding birds on seven hills with densities of one to five cocks/km^2 in suitable habitat. Annual variations in the length of snow lie are a contributory factor to wide fluctuations in population on the same hill from one summer to the next (R.Smith).

The nesting grounds are usually reoccupied in May, but when snow cover is extensive this may be delayed and birds wait on lower ridges such as the Ladder Hills. After the breeding season, gatherings of 50 or more are not infrequent on the high montane heaths, perhaps consisting of both local and passage birds. Most have left by late August.

Dotterel very rarely occur in lowland Moray. Apparently a few were shot near Forres last century and four were seen there on 5 August 1887.[4] A male near Buckie on 9 May 1903 (ASNH **13**:214) was the only spring bird. There is no record of Dotterel in Nairn.

PLATE 19 Dotterel, male incubating in the Cairngorms *(John Edelsten)*

Golden Plover

Pluvialis apricaria

Numerous breeder and common migrant.

Golden Plovers are generally distributed in summer over the moorlands and hills, up to at least 1,000m around Ben Avon. Exceptionally, in 1989, a pair bred on set-aside farmland at only 40m near Tarras, Forres. Although breeding densities are low over many moors, they can be locally much higher, up to nine pairs/km². A survey in 1980 found 95 pairs in 26 km² of south Nairn moorland around the Tomlachlan Burn.[**91**] In 1989 160 km² of moorland were surveyed, mostly in 10 km squares NJ 15, 04, 14 and 33. Sixty-nine pairs were located at an overall density of 0.43 pairs/km². There were between one and five pairs in each occupied 1 km², a density in occupied squares of 1.57 pairs/km².[**92**] In some areas suitable habitat has declined in the face of recent afforestation but numbers appear to be lower in other areas too. In the same 24 km² of south-west Moray there were 16 pairs in 1980 and seven pairs in 1989. In 4 km² around Carn na Cailliche there were 17 pairs in 1980 but only five in

1989.[**91,92**] Inland haunts are reoccupied in February and March when flocks appear on short grassland in the glens. As weather permits, pairs move up to the higher ground, temporarily returning to low pasture if conditions deteriorate. The breeding season is protracted with the first juveniles leaving the moors in early July and the last not until late August.

In late summer flocks form on farmland, often in association with Lapwings, and by early autumn they have moved to the coast. Throughout the winter flocks are usually to be found in traditional areas. October–February counts since 1980–1 have been as follows:

	Average max. flock size 1980/1–1990/1	*Range*
Findhorn Bay	296	151–583
Burghead	49	20–274
Lossiemouth	130	41–271
Portgordon/Buckpool	144	27–300

In the past larger flocks have occurred, e.g. 1,000+ at Kinloss airfield on 23 September 1966 and 900 at Buckpool on 18 December 1971.

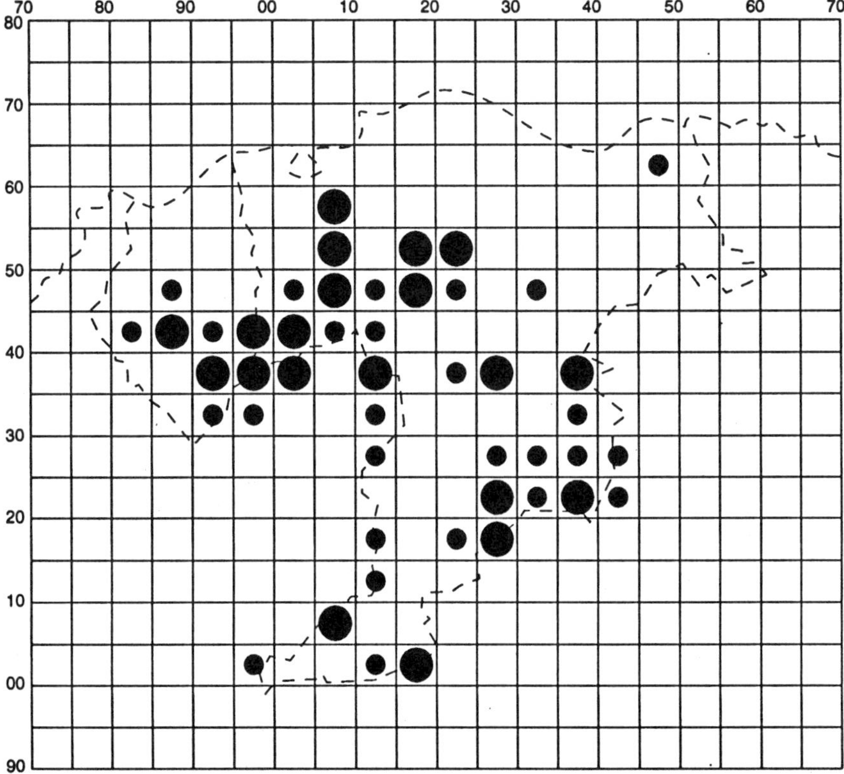

Figure 11 Golden Plover summer distribution 1981–90 (April–July, excluding coastal migrants)

Grey Plover

Pluvialis squatarola

Scarce autumn migrant and winter visitor.

Passage birds first appear on the coast in August; the earliest were three at Culbin Bar on 8 August 1984. Numbers very greatly; in some years there are very few while in others 40 or more may be seen together, usually around the Nairn and Culbin Bars or in Findhorn Bay. Peak counts there have been 130 on 14 October 1978 and 99 on 27 October 1985 but these are exceptional. Very small numbers also occur on the Lossie estuary (max. 25 on 16 October 1990) and at Speymouth (max. 13 between 23–28 September 1989).

In winter a small flock remains around the Bars; the highest recent count was 36 on 12 January 1986. These have usually left by April. There are five summer records, one at Nairn Bar on 12 June 1976, two at Nairn on 1 July 1978, one at Covesea on 30 May 1990, one at Nairn Bar from 1–11 June 1991 and four there on 30 June 1991, but no spring passage is apparent.

They have been seen inland on three occasions: one at Loch Spynie in 1906, *c.*10 there (of which two were shot) on 5 October 1967 and one at Gilston on 10 April 1988.

Lapwing

Vanellus vanellus

Numerous resident breeder and common migrant.

Last century Lapwings were variously described as 'plentiful',[6] 'very numerous'[3] and present in 'great numbers'.[27] Some idea of their abundance can be gauged from Harvie-Brown and Buckley's note of one small Banffshire town which dispatched 140 dozen eggs to London in mid April 1893.[4]

Today they are still familiar breeders up to *c.*450m where suitable habitat of short damp grassland or marshes remains. However, numbers are undoubtedly much reduced due, at least in part, to 'improvement' of marginal agricultural land. Lapwings usually appear inland from mid February (March in the higher glens) although occasionally earlier in mild weather, e.g. 35 at Craigellachie on 30 January 1983, and are sometimes in large flocks (max. 400 at Keith on 27 February 1982). Territories are established on the breeding grounds in March but birds move back into flocks in adverse weather. Laying commences in April and chicks may be found from mid May until July. Fledged juveniles

PLATE 20 Lapwing settling onto its eggs *(John Edelsten)*

flock together in pastures in the glens and in late summer and autumn they gather in coastal areas on stubble plough and mudflats. Flocks of up to 500 are usual but may be much larger, e.g. 2,000 at Findhorn on 13 August 1978 and 1,500 there on 19 August 1984. There have been occasional records from the Cairngorm plateau in summer, including singles on Ben Macdui at *c.*1,250m in the 1920s and on 4 June 1971, three on Stac an Fharaidh (*c.*1,000m) on 9 June 1988 and one freshly dead on Garbh Uisge Beag (*c.*1,100m) on 1 April 1990.

Most birds have left by November but small numbers overwinter on the coastal plain, usually groups of 50–100 but occasionally more, e.g. 300 near Elgin on 7 December 1975. In severe weather very few remain. Ringing of Lapwing chicks in the Districts has revealed movements to spend the winter in Ireland (five recoveries), France (three), Spain (three, one as far south as Cadiz) and Portugal (one). The earliest of these recoveries resulted from a chick ringed near Archiestown in June 1910 and shot in County Cork four and a half years later.

Knot

Calidris canutus

Common migrant and winter visitor.

The first migrants, often summer plumage adults, return from their high Arctic breeding grounds in July and 100 or more may be present in Findhorn Bay by the end of the month (max. 200 on 30 July 1985). Numbers continue to increase through autumn as young birds arrive in September and adults move into the Moray Firth during October from moulting grounds on the Wash and Dutch Wadden Sea. In midwinter flock sizes are very variable as Knot are highly mobile around the Firth, but they are usually to be found on both muddy and rocky shores in the following areas:

	1980/1–1990/1 regular numbers	*Maximum count*
Nairn and Culbin Bars	50–250	1,660 on 11 March 1988
Findhorn Bay	50–150	630 on 27 Oct 1985
Burghead	50–300	900 on 4 Oct 1982
Lossiemouth	50–250	270 on 9 Jan 1986
Buckie	10–100	300 on 23 Dec 1981

During the 1970s much larger flocks were sometimes recorded in the west of the Districts, e.g. 3,000 at Nairn on 24 December 1972.

By April numbers are generally low except in Findhorn Bay, where a marked pre-migration build-up can take place, often including birds moulting into adult summer plumage. Several hundred are regular at this time with over 1,000 counted in 1976, 1982, 1983 and 1988; peak counts were 1,500 on 23 April 1976 and 17–26 April 1988. Most have left by early May.

On 5 June 1988 there was a summering flock of 153 Knot at the Bars with a further 201 in Findhorn Bay. These were not in summer plumage and were presumably non-breeding immatures which had not migrated. It is uncertain whether similar flocks are present every year.

There have been over 40 ringing recoveries involving the Districts. Ten resulted from a catch of Knot in Findhorn Bay on 4 April 1980. Six of these were retrapped in Fife (and another at Teesmouth) in December–February of the following or subsequent winters. These recoveries, together with sightings of dyed birds, suggest that many of the Knot present at Findhorn during the spring peak have moved up from estuaries in south-east Scotland or north-east England. An example of onward movement in autumn comes from a young bird ringed at Portgordon on 11 September 1987 and shot at Somme (north France) five and a half weeks later; another bird from this catch was caught on the Wash in October 1989. Twenty-five Knot ringed at Burghead on 17 September 1989 were retrapped in Nigg Bay, Ross & Cromarty in November–December 1989, indicating that many of the birds present on rocky shores in autumn move into the inner firths later in the winter. Another bird from the same Burghead catch was at Holme, Norfolk on 4 November 1990.

Sanderling

Calidris alba

Scarce migrant and winter visitor.

Autumn passage begins in July, the earliest being two at Lossie estuary on 6 July 1989, and peaks in August. Because of the species' preference for sandy shores, few are seen in Findhorn Bay and only the coast between Nairn and the Culbin Bar regularly holds significant numbers. The Lossie estuary often holds birds during autumn passage, but only very few during winter. Since 1980 counts at these sites have been as follows:

	Autumn (July–Sept) 1990/1		*Winter (late Oct–March) 1980/1–90/1*	
	Av. peak	*Max. count*	*Av. peak*	*Max. count*
Nairn/Bars	38	95 (23 Aug 1991)	44*	78 (3 Jan 1990)
Lossie estuary	23	61 (11 Aug 1991)	11	19 (11 Feb 1991)

* The exceptional flock of 173 on 8 November 1986 is omitted from this analysis.

In late July–early August 1990 a big group (max. 60 on 28 July) was at Kingston where very few are normally seen, and a strong autumn passage at Delnies in 1991 peaked at 70 on 22 September.

Little spring passage is evident, although a few Sanderling are seen in May in most years with stragglers into June; the latest were eight at Delnies on 9 June 1991 and three at Lossiemouth on 26 June 1991. A dyed bird seen at Findhorn in May *c.*1986 had been marked on the Solway Firth a few days earlier.

Little Stint

Calidris minuta

Scarce autumn migrant.

Little Stints are usually scarce visitors to the muddy estuaries, averaging 5–10 birds in a normal autumn. On four occasions since 1960 much larger numbers have passed through. The table below shows maximum flock sizes counted at each site in the best years:

	Findhorn Bay and Nairn/Culbin Bars	*Lossie estuary*	*Kingston*
1960	106 (18–21 Sept)	?	?
1970	11 (12 Sept)	12 (13 Sept)	?
1978	21 (24 Sept)	6 (23 Sept)	9 (13 Sept)
1988	39 (9 Sept)	51 (5 Sept)	11 (5 Sept)

The great majority are seen between mid-August and late September as shown below. Extreme autumn dates have been 17 July 1983 (one at Kingston) and 31 October 1989 (one at Delnies). The only spring records concern a single bird in Findhorn Bay on 21 May 1990, two there two days later and one at Kingston from 2–9 June 1991. None has been seen inland.

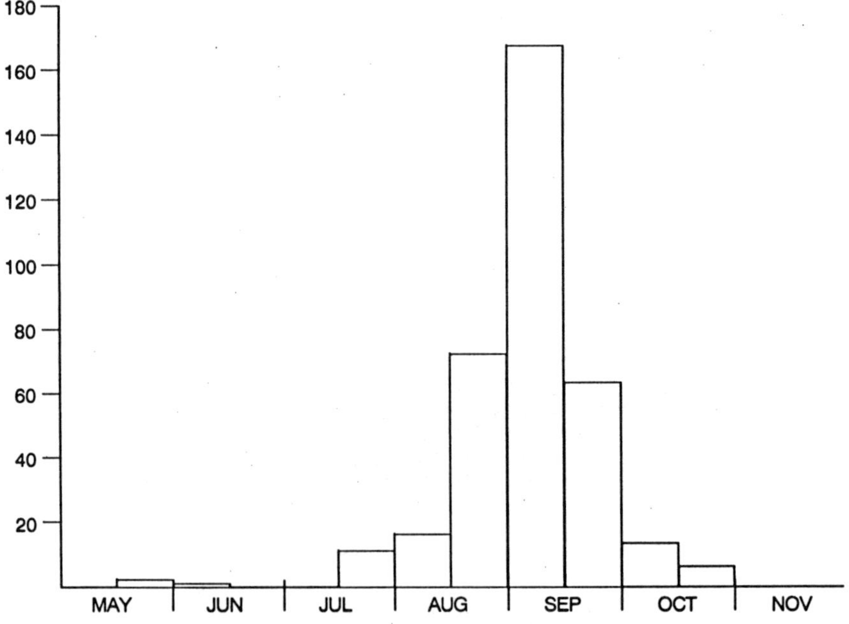

Figure 12 Little Stint half-monthly totals 1970–91

Temminck's Stint

Calidris temminckii

Rare summer visitor and migrant.

In summer 1979 a pair was present at one Moray site from at least 30 May–16 June. Song and display were frequent but no nest was found. They returned annually until 1982 but breeding was never proved. Two adults were present there again on 7 July 1986 but were not seen subsequently. Single migrants were at Lossiemouth on 17 October 1983 (SBR 1983) and at Kingston from 3–16 July 1991.

Baird's Sandpiper

Calidris bairdii

Accidental.

The only record is of a juvenile on the saltmarsh on the eastern side of Findhorn Bay on 5–6 October 1982 (BB **76**:493).

Pectoral Sandpiper

Calidris melanotos

Accidental.

There have been four occurrences:

1 Findhorn Bay	15 July 1967 (SB **5**:284)
1 Lein, Kingston	22 Oct 1986 (SBR 1986)
1 Lossie estuary	7–11 Sept 1988 (SBR 1988)
1 Findhorn Bay	16–21 May 1990

Curlew Sandpiper

Calidris ferruginea

Scarce autumn migrant.

Numbers of Curlew Sandpipers visiting the estuaries in autumn are very variable as shown on the histogram below. A few birds may appear in late July (the earliest being two at Findhorn Bay on 20 July 1990) but most pass through between mid August and late September with small numbers

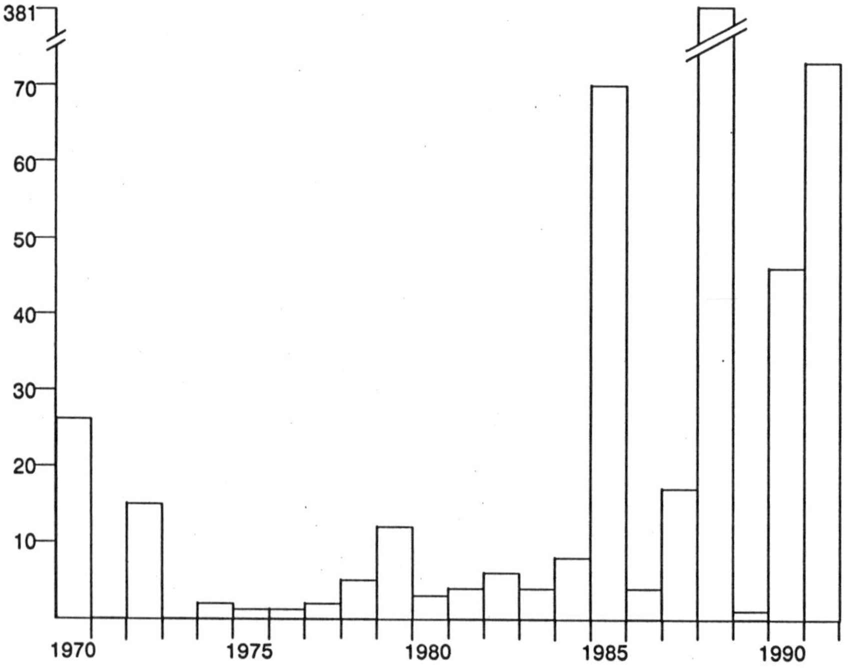

Figure 13 Curlew Sandpiper annual totals 1970–91

in October (the latest being one at Findhorn Bay on 4 November 1984). The highest ever single counts at each major site (all in 1988) were 285 at Findhorn Bay 10–11 September, 40 at Lossiemouth on 8 September and 35 at Kingston on 3 September. There are three spring/summer records, of singles in Findhorn Bay on 19 April 1987, 8 June 1981 and 22–25 May 1990. The great majority have been at Findhorn Bay, Culbin Bar, Lossiemouth or Kingston. Elsewhere there were four in Portgordon harbour on 11 September 1988, three remaining until 24 September.

A passage migrant ringed in More og Romsdal (Norway) on 26 August 1988 was trapped in Findhorn Bay three weeks later.

Purple Sandpiper

Calidris maritima

Common winter visitor.

Purple Sandpipers inhabit the rocky shores of the Districts in winter. Three main flocks are present each year and there is probably little movement between them. Peak winter counts in these areas since 1970 have been as follows:

	Av. winter max. 1970/1–1990/1	*Peak count*
Burghead/Hopeman	102	250 (3 April 1977)
Lossiemouth	151	300 (27 March 1986)
Portessie (Buckie)	273	332 (15 Feb 1980)

A smaller flock of 25–50 is regular on the foreshore at Nairn.

The first arrivals are usually seen in August (the earliest being two at Burghead on 18 July 1990) and good numbers are still present in late April with stragglers until mid May (the latest were three at Burghead on 19 May 1973).

Measurements suggest that a small proportion of the birds in the winter flocks are from the population which breeds on the Hardangervidda in southern Norway but the majority belong to the larger high Arctic race. A bird ringed at Buckie on 17 April 1988 was seen in the Netherlands on 25 November 1989 and one ringed in the Netherlands on 16 November 1987 was caught at Buckie on 3 January 1991. Two others in the April 1988 Buckie catch had been marked at Rosehearty (Aberdeenshire) on 24 November 1984 and 6 December 1986.

Dunlin

Calidris alpina

Scarce breeder, common migrant and winter visitor.

Dunlin are scarce breeders in the Districts. They are found in pockets such as the wet moorlands of the Lochindorb area, the Ladder Hills (seven pairs between Lecht and Carn Mor in July 1986) and the Carn Kitty/Carn Shalag area (four pairs in 1980 [**91**] and three in 1989 [**92**]). Most nest between 300–800m, but they occasionally penetrate to much higher ground; one pair nested at 1,100m near Lochan Buidhe in 1961 and 1962 and a pair was seen on Cairn Lochan at 1,215m in 1971.[**76**] Last century they bred in rough pasture near the coast,[**3**] but the only recent coastal nesting was an unsuccessful attempt at Findhorn in 1970.

Autumn passage on the muddy estuaries begins in late June and continues until late September. First to arrive are mostly adults of the southern race *C.a.schinzii* with the proportion of juveniles increasing in August. These birds pass through the area rapidly. Usually about a month later Dunlin of the larger northern race *C.a.alpina* start to appear with the peak movement of juveniles sometimes well into September. Main autumn passage sites are shown below:

	Av. June–Sept max. 1980–90	*Range*
Findhorn Bay	484	189–1,144
Lossie estuary	134	28–552
Kingston (Speymouth)	80	26–471

In autumn 1988 *alpina* passage was exceptional and peak counts at each site were 1,144 at Findhorn Bay on 20 September, 552 at Lossiemouth on 19 September and 471 at Kingston on 18 September.

In late October/November further influxes take place, of adult *alpina* which have moulted on the Wadden Sea or the Wash, and peak numbers are present in midwinter. The wintering population varies widely from year to year but highest counts at the main sites in recent years are shown below:

	Av. Dec–Feb max. 1984/5–90/1	*Range*
Nairn/Culbin Bars	1,342	516–1,921
Findhorn Bay	2,227	860–5,000
Lossiemouth	185	134–234

Most of these birds are of the race *alpina*. Exodus from the estuaries takes place in March but a variable spring passage uses Findhorn Bay in late April and May;[**90**] the peak count was 700 on 5 May 1989.

There have been about 35 ringing recoveries involving Moray and Nairn. The only movement certainly originating from our small local breeding population relates to a chick ringed near Dava in June 1959 and found (long dead) at Gironde, France in October 1967. Onward movement of autumn-ringed *schinzii* birds, destined for north-west Africa, has produced recoveries in Norfolk (after eight and 36 days), Gironde, France (four days), Portugal (eight days) and Morocco (six weeks). Evidence of the presence of northern (*alpina*) Dunlin in autumn is provided by birds ringed in Finnmark (Norway) and near Murmansk (Russia) in late summer and retrapped in Moray seven and 17 days later, respectively. Two other same-autumn immigrants onto local estuaries were from passage sites in southern Norway. Three recoveries have indicated onward movement of adults into Moray from the autumn moulting area on the Wash, albeit not in the same year. Birds ringed in Findhorn Bay between September and early April were later in eastern Germany, Sweden (two) and Poland (two) in the July–October period, on migration through the Baltic. A July-ringed Polish bird was in Findhorn Bay in January 1989. A spring-returning *alpina* was retrapped in Findhorn Bay in April 1984, having been ringed in Finland in July 1976.

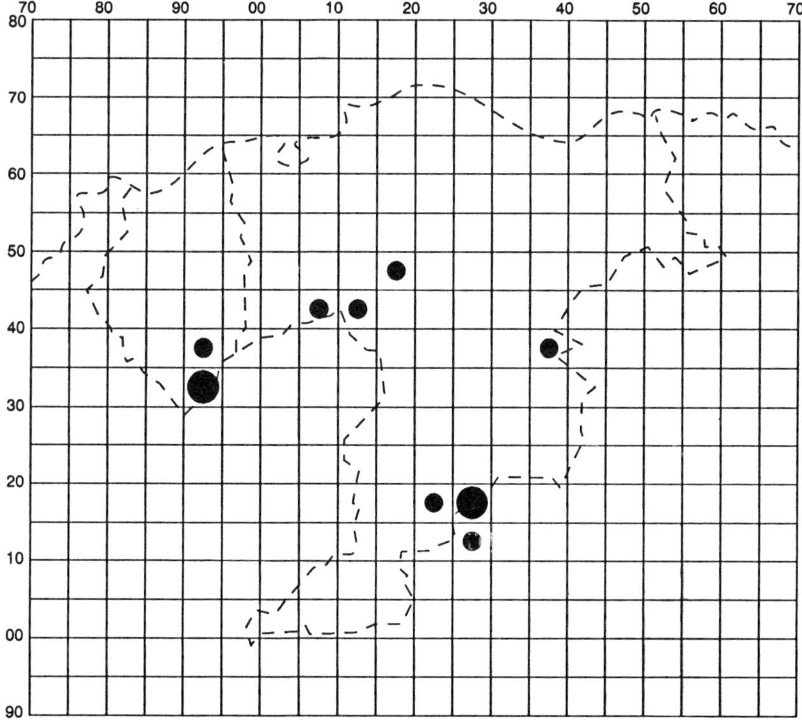

Figure 14 Dunlin summer distribution 1981–90 (April–July, excluding coastal migrants)

Broad-billed Sandpiper

Limicola falcinellus

Accidental.

There have been three occurrences:

1 Lossiemouth	29 Aug 1967 (BB **61**:342; SB **5**:216–217)
1 adult Kingston	11–14 July 1988 (BB **82**:524)
1 adult Kingston	17–19 June 1990 (BB **84**:470)

Ruff

Philomachus pugnax

Scarce autumn migrant.

Ruff are seen annually on autumn passage, usually in very small numbers. Most records come from Findhorn Bay, Lossie estuary or Kingston. The pattern of occurrence is shown in the histogram below. The April records were in 1974, 1979 and 1980, and the only Ruff to have been seen in winter was at Nairn Bar on 8 January 1987.

In August 1978 passage in Findhorn Bay was exceptional, peaking at 51 on 21 August. Other large flocks in recent years were 19 on floodwater near

Elgin from 1–4 September 1957, 24 at Kinloss on 23 August 1970, 15 at Findhorn on 2 September 1974, 15 at Lossiemouth on 31 August 1977 and 19 at Lossiemouth on 24 September 1980.

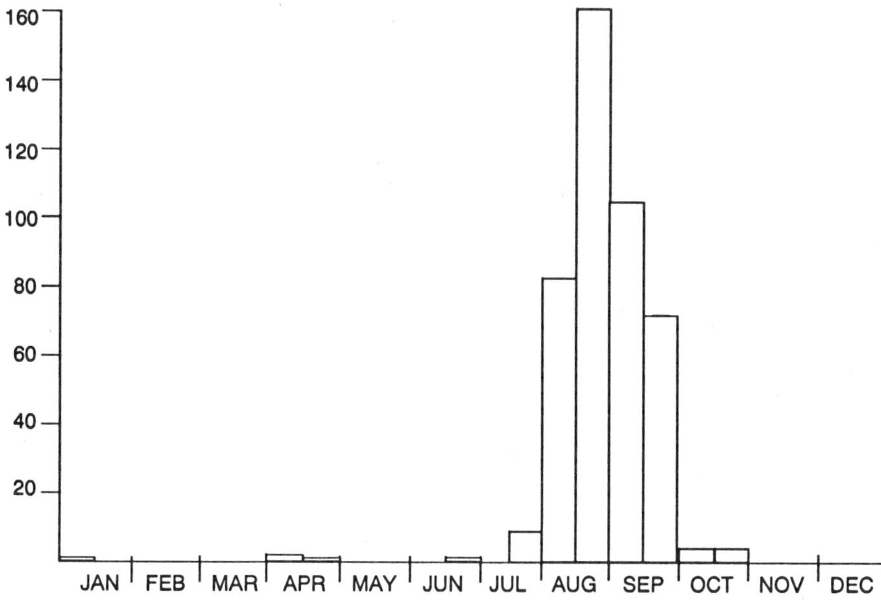

Figure 15 Ruff half-monthly totals 1970–91

Jack Snipe

Lymnocryptes minimus

Scarce migrant and winter visitor.

Since 1970 there have been 44 Jack Snipe reported in Moray and Nairn. Their monthly distribution has been as follows:

Jan	Feb	Mar	Apr	May	Jun	Jul	Aug	Sep	Oct	Nov	Dec
8	4	7	1	0	0	0	0	0	19	4	5

The only multiple sightings were of at least 10 at Findhorn from 15–30 October 1975, three at Kingston on 16 March 1985 and two there on 13–14 October 1990, otherwise all records relate to single birds. Most occur in the saltmarshes bordering Findhorn Bay (20) and the Spey mouth at Kingston (9). There have been six inland records, at Loch Spynie (two), Loch Flemington,

Loch Loy, Darnaway and (the only upland occurrence) at Aldunie, Cabrach, where one was found dead on 17 January 1991. There is one old summer record, of one shot near Loch Spynie on the unusual date of 10 August 1906 (ASNH **15**:245). It seems likely that the species is considerably under-recorded in the Districts due to its secretive nature and reluctance to be flushed.

A migrant ringed on North Ronaldsay, Orkney on 18 October 1977 was found dead at Darnaway on 19 February 1978.

Snipe

Gallinago gallinago

Numerous breeder and migrant.

A common breeder in marshes and low altitude wet moorlands to at least 400m. Densities in western Moray have been assessed at 31 pairs between Carnach and Johnstripe in 1988 and 21 pairs in 32 km^2 of moorland between Lochindorb and Cairn Eney in 1989.[**92**] Snipe are one of the breeding waders most at risk from drainage of marginal grazing land.

In autumn upland haunts are deserted and sizeable congregations may build up in low lying wetlands, e.g. 44 at Loch Flemington on 19 October 1989 and 42 at Kingston on 27 October 1990. These flocks contain an unknown proportion of immigrants. Large assemblies are also met with in midwinter in unfrozen marshes during severe weather, e.g. 48 on an island in the Spey near Fochabers on 4 January 1985. Return inland takes place mostly in March.

There is one ringing recovery, of a bird marked near Leeds in July 1960 and shot at Glenferness in September 1965.

Great Snipe

Gallinago media

Accidental.

Two birds have been shot in autumn in the Spynie area:

1 Pitgaveny	15 Oct 1898 (ASNH **8**:51)
1 Spynie marshes	20 Oct 1915 [**53**] (SN **48**:357)

Woodcock

Scolopax rusticola

Numerous resident breeder and migrant.

Breeding was first recorded in Moray in 1837 [**50**] and in Nairn in 1860.[**27**] By 1895 they were abundant and still increasing.[**4**] In 1934–5 many estates reported a further increase; one pair per 100 acres of suitable habitat was the estimated density at Pitgaveny.[**50**] Today the Woodcock is a widespread and numerous breeding species. Although many overwinter inland, others move up-country in early March when their evening territorial roding flights begin around plantations and deciduous woodlands throughout the Districts. Open woods with clearings and damp patches are preferred.

Many Woodcock chicks have been ringed in Moray and Nairn, particularly in the mid-1930s, and December–February recoveries indicate that some move towards the coast in winter or else migrate out of the area in a south-westerly direction; there have been recoveries in Wigtown, Northern Ireland (two) and Portugal. Others remain in the inland woods, even around Tomintoul, only moving to the coast if freezing conditions become severe. Occasionally in the past they have been exceptionally numerous at the coast, even feeding on the foreshore. In December 1878 as single gun bagged 378 around Covesea [**51**] and in February 1889 a 'considerable number' was shot on the shore between Lossiemouth and the lighthouse.[**52**] In 1927 a Woodcock was found dead at 1,230m on Ben Macdui (BB **20**:234). An unknown number of Continental birds is present in the area in winter; a Woodcock caught by a cat on the shore at Findochty on 16 October 1989 was probably a tired migrant, and another ringed on Helgoland in March 1939 was found dead at Kinloss in March 1940. One shot near Elgin in September 1913 had been ringed as a chick in Dumfries and Galloway the same summer.

Black-tailed Godwit

Limosa limosa

Scarce migrant.

Black-tailed Godwits are mostly seen alone or in small groups in autumn. There is another, much smaller, passage in spring. The pattern of occurrence is shown in the histogram below. The early November total is composed mainly of one flock of 14 birds which stopped briefly in Findhorn Bay in

1984. The great majority of records are from Findhorn Bay with a small number at Lossiemouth and a scattering elsewhere. There are five inland records, from the Spynie area in autumn 1878, 2 May 1976 and 29 April 1979 (two), at Cloddach on 24 July 1989 (three) and at Loch Flemington on 31 August 1989. In 1987 there was an unprecedented autumn influx in Findhorn Bay, peaking at 26 on 15 September. Most had left by the end of September but two birds remained until 17 January 1988. Twenty-four were in the bay from 22–26 August 1991.

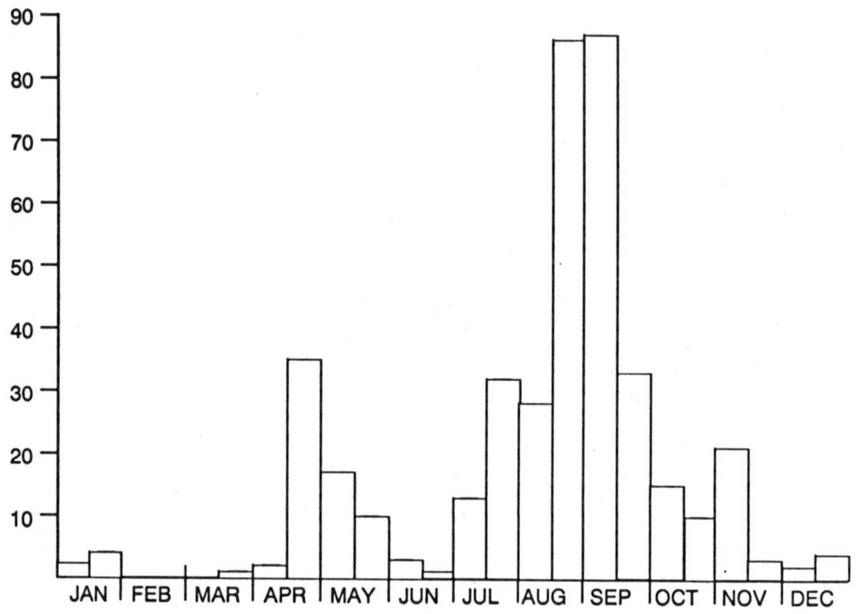

Figure 16 Black-tailed Godwit half-monthly totals 1970–91

Bar-tailed Godwit

Limosa lapponica

Common winter visitor and migrant. Small numbers in summer.

Flocks of Bar-tailed Godwits are seen mainly on the western coasts of the

Districts in winter where they feed on the sandy shores between Nairn and Burghead. On passage small flocks occur more widely, although 236 at Lossiemouth on 27 August 1988 was an unusually high count. Arrivals in the Whiteness–Culbin area begin in mid July, when adults in summer plumage may be seen. Numbers continue to build up through the autumn, many birds apparently arriving from the Siberian breeding grounds indirectly, having moulted elsewhere. A remarkable number was counted at Nairn on 2 September 1956 when 3,500 flew in to join a further 1,500 already on the beach (SB **1**:35). Largest flocks are present in midwinter but their mobility within the whole Moray Firth may result in wide fluctuations at any one site. Winter counts at the main roosts in recent years have been as follows:

	Av. Dec–Feb peak	*Range*
Nairn/Culbin Bars	800 (1985/6–1990/1)	390–1,860
Findhorn Bay	404 (1980/1–1990/1)	78–1,500
Burghead	142 (1980/1–1990/1)	42–250

Most leave by late March but in some years considerable numbers are still present at the end of April, although 2,000 at Findhorn on 5 May 1982 was exceptional. A small flock (50–250) usually summers around the Bars and Findhorn Bay; they were first noted there in June 1891.[**4**] On 5 June 1988 there were 67 at the Bars and 168 in Findhorn Bay, all in non-breeding plumage, so presumably immatures. There were 166 at Burghead on 13 June 1990 and 253 at the Bars on 11 June 1991. The only recent inland record is of one flying over Elgin on 15 March 1991. They were described as 'occasional' at Loch Spynie last century [**4**] and one was shot near Fochabers on 27 November 1903.[**54**]

Two birds ringed at Fort George were found at Nairn and Findhorn Bay in later winters. Another, ringed at Whiteness Head in August 1986, was caught at Burghead in January 1987 and on the Cromarty Firth in November 1989, illustrating the fact that Bar-tailed Godwits are very mobile around the Moray Firth.

Whimbrel

Numenius phaeopus

Scarce migrant.

Whimbrel are mostly seen or heard in coastal districts on autumn passage between mid July and mid September. A much smaller spring passage also takes place, usually in late April and early May. In 1978 one was off Culbin on the extremely early date of 11 March and two were there on 25 March. The annual pattern of occurrence is shown in the histogram below.

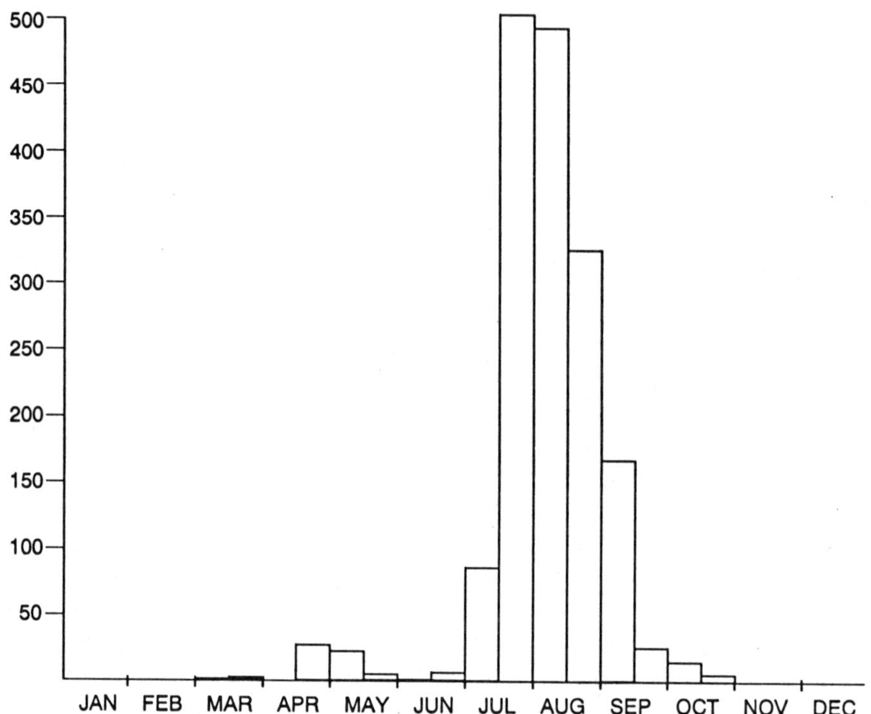

Figure 17 Whimbrel half-monthly totals 1969–91

The distribution of flock sizes (1969–91) is as follows:

Birds in flock	1	2	3	4	5	6	7	8	9	10
Number of flocks	138	46	23	14	14	4	4	6	6	2
Birds in flock	11	12	13	14	15	16	17	22	27	28
Number of flocks	4	5	5	4	4	4	2	1	1	1
Birds in flock	30	36	39	40	44	47	58	70	71	83
Number of flocks	1	1	1	1	1	1	1	1	1	1

The largest flocks were 83 at Kingston on 2 August 1990, 71 at Findhorn on 31 July 1969 and 70 at Kingston on 23 July 1989.

Surprisingly there have been only two records more than 10 miles from the coast, a single bird flying north over Bridge of Brown on 24 April 1978 and another over Cairn Gorm on 10 May 1989.

Curlew

Numenius arquata

Numerous breeder, common migrant and winter visitor.

Curlews are widely distributed breeders on low altitude moorland, damp grassland and open clearings in sparsely wooded country. They nest from sea-level to at least 500m around Tomintoul. In 1989 28 pairs were located in 25 km^2 of moorland in the Glen Latterach area between Pikey Hill and Meikle Hill, with a further 23 pairs in 32 km^2 in south-west Moray between Lochindorb and Cairn Eney.[**92**] A lone bird once spent several days at 1,080m near Lochan Buidhe in the Cairngorms [**76**] and singles were on the plateau on 27 June and 3 July 1988.

Spring return to the upland territories takes place in February and March, the earliest being seen near Ballindalloch on 10 February 1972. The breeding season is comparatively short, with birds moving back to the coast in July and very few left inland by August. At this time flocks of several hundred may build up in coastal areas; the largest was 1,200 at Findhorn on 13 August 1978. In autumn many local birds move out of the Moray Firth to winter in Ireland as evidenced by the chick ringed near Buckie in June 1971 and killed in South Munster in December 1975. Another local chick was dead in Argyll in October. Other Curlews remain on our coasts where they are joined by immigrants from the north and Scandinavia. Birds ringed as chicks further north and found wintering in Moray in December–March had originated from Fetlar (Shetland), Finland and Norway (just north of the Arctic circle).

The true size of the winter population is hard to assess because, particularly at high tide, many Curlews move to fields a short distance inland to continue feeding and are therefore not counted at coastal roosts with other waders. The main shores where flocks have been regular in recent winters are the Nairn and Culbin Bars, Findhorn Bay, Lossiemouth and Buckie, with up to 300 at each site. In the past bigger counts have included 2,000 at Findhorn on 27 November 1977 and 650 at Lossiemouth on 24 October 1978. A sizeable inland wintering flock is regular around Cloddach except during hard frost; 334 were there on 26 December 1988. Prolonged severe weather can cause serious mortality, even at the coast. Over 100 were found dead around Gordonstoun early in 1947.

Spotted Redshank

Tringa erythropus

Scarce migrant.

Spotted Redshanks occur mostly on autumn passage, usually singly or in groups of up to three. Largest gatherings, both in Findhorn Bay, were nine on 5 September 1968 and ten on 15 September 1974. The pattern of occurrence is shown in the histograms below. The great majority have been seen in Findhorn Bay (77) with a few on the Lossie estuary (17) and at Kingston (10). Two singles at the Nairn Bar, on 8–11 September 1956 and 25 October 1988, were the only records for Nairn District. There have been two inland sightings, one near Elgin on 25 August 1956 and another over Loch Spynie on 9 July 1989.

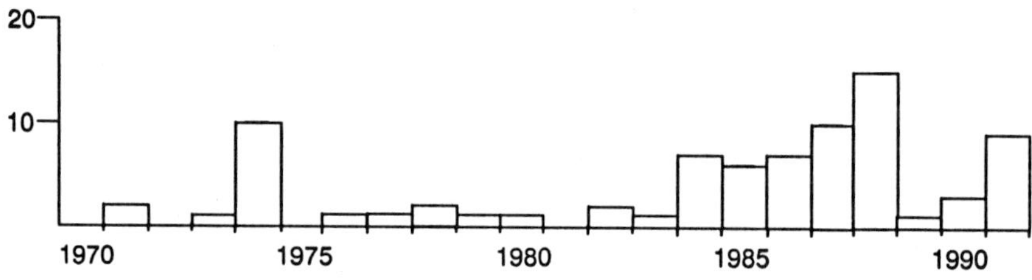

Figure 18 Spotted Redshank annual totals 1970–91

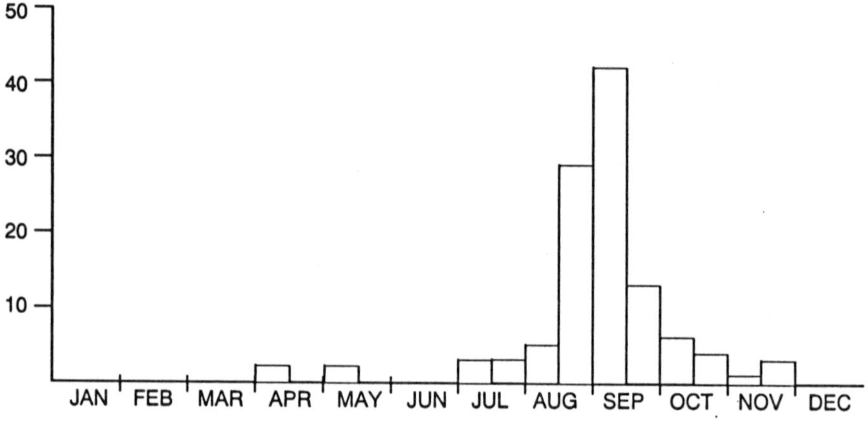

Figure 19 Spotted Redshank half-monthly totals 1970–91

Redshank

Tringa totanus

Scarce breeder, common migrant and winter visitor.

Breeding Redshanks are widely but thinly spread through the Districts from sea-level estuarine saltings to marshes and wet grassland in upland glens. Drainage of marginal farmland has doubtless contributed to a substantial decline; they are certainly no longer 'unusually abundant' in Glenlivet and Glen Fiddich as there were in 1892.[4]

Inland breeding grounds are reoccupied in March and the season is over by late July. Birds then return to the coast to join adults arriving from Iceland so large moulting flocks build up, especially in Findhorn Bay where 500–800 are regularly counted (max. 2,000 on 28 August 1988 and on 18 August 1991). The influx of Icelandic Redshanks continues through September and October and numbers in Findhorn Bay remain high, e.g. 2,200 on 29 October 1989. Soon, however, this immigrant population largely deserts the bay and flocks are established on muddy and rocky shores all along the coast. Midwinter maxima at the main sites since 1981/2 have been as follows:

	Av. Dec–Feb max. 1981/2–1990/1	*Range*
Nairn/Culbin Bars	528*	259–839
Findhorn Bay	292	170–434
Lossiemouth	60	39–136
Portgordon/Strathlene	56	26–93

* counts only available since winter 1985/6

Most native birds apparently leave the area in winter, while ringing has shown that Redshanks from south-eastern Scottish estuaries may move into the Moray Firth at this time.

In early spring numbers in Findhorn Bay increase once more as a premigration build-up takes place. Recoveries of ringed birds have shown that this build-up is the result of Redshanks from the local wintering population moving into the bay and others from the south stopping off on their northward journey, the furthest coming from Bangor (north Wales). The highest numbers are usually present in April, usually 1,000–2,000 but at least 3,000 were counted on 4 April 1980. Few Redshanks are seen on the shore in summer as both adults and immatures travel to the breeding grounds.

There have been three summer recoveries in Iceland, of birds ringed in Findhorn Bay in April 1980 and September 1988 and at Buckie in January 1987. A chick marked in Iceland in July 1987 was caught in Findhorn Bay in September 1988. Another bird, ringed in the bay in autumn, was caught at sea in the Rockall area in April 1984, presumably *en route* to Iceland. The only movement certainly relating to a native-bred bird involved the chick ringed near Dava in June 1977 and caught in Norfolk in July 1978.

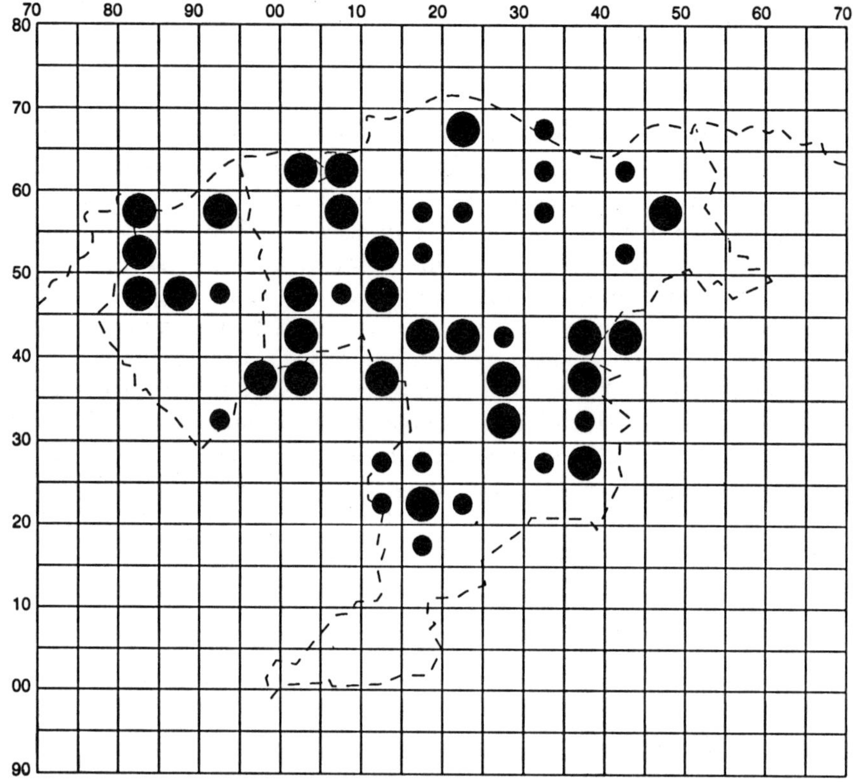

Figure 20 Redshank summer distribution 1981–90 (April–July, excluding coastal non-breeders)

Marsh Sandpiper

Tringa stagnatilis

Accidental.

One stayed on the Lossie estuary from 20–23 April 1984 (BB **78**:550).

Greenshank

Tringa nebularia

Scarce migrant and winter visitor. Has bred.

There is no recent record of nesting in the Districts but Nethersole-Thompson watched a breeding pair near Inchrory in 1935.[**93,95**] Single birds were present in suitable habitat near Loch Builg on 19 April 1970, near Inchrory on 14 May 1972 and close to Lochindorb on 23 May 1980.

Autumn passage at the coast begins in early July and lasts until late September with the peak in most years between early August and mid September. It is unusual to see more than three together in most areas but in Findhorn Bay there are often up to ten or more at this time; the highest counts were 25 on 25–27 July 1985 and 24 on 12 August 1989. A few have overwintered in the bay since at least the early 1970s, usually up to four but there were six in 1977/78 and 1980/81, seven on 17 January 1988 and 17 December 1989, and nine on 17 February 1991 and 6 December 1991.

Little spring passage is evident, although there is a slight increase during March and April. The highest count was eight in Findhorn Bay on 9 April 1989.

Lesser Yellowlegs

Tringa flavipes

Accidental.

The only record is of one watched on the Carse of Delnies on 15 September 1974 (BB **68**:317).

Green Sandpiper

Tringa ochropus

Scarce migrant.

Green Sandpipers pass through the Districts in very small numbers, mostly in autumn. The annual totals since 1970 and half-monthly pattern of occurrence are shown in the histograms below. All records have involved one or two birds with the exception of six at Findhorn Bay on 4 August 1970, three there on 17 December 1989 and from 21–27 August 1991 and three at Kingston on 20 August 1978 and 18 August 1990. The only midwinter records have been in Findhorn Bay, on 20 February 1988 (one), December 1989–March 1990 (three on 17 December, two staying until 14 January and one until late March) and December 1990 (one on 16 December, staying until 11 March 1991). They feed along muddy creeks at the edge of the estuaries or at the margins of lochs and rivers, the furthest inland being singles at Glenlatterach reservoir on 13 July 1975 and at Cloddach Quarry on 27 July 1991.

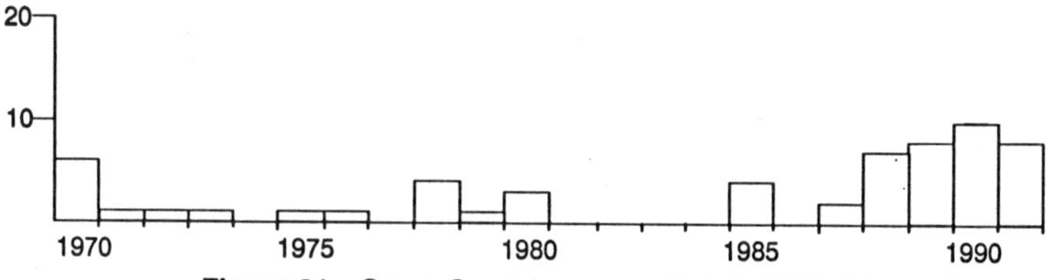

Figure 21 Green Sandpiper annual totals 1970–91

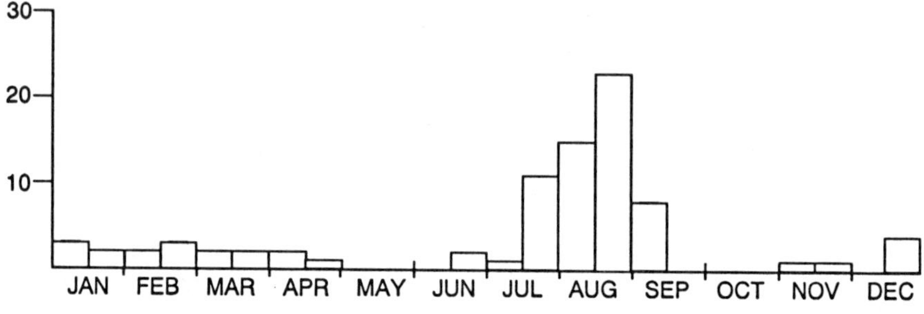

Figure 22 Green Sandpiper half-monthly totals 1970–91

Wood Sandpiper

Tringa glareola

Rare migrant.

Fifteen have been seen in Moray but there is no record for Nairn. All birds have occurred singly except for three near Lossiemouth on 21 May 1980. Five dates were in spring (25 April–31 May) while the rest relate to autumn passage (25 July–9 October). Eight were on small freshwater pools in lowland Moray with seven at the coast (four at Findhorn Bay, one at Lossie estuary and two at Kingston).

An old claim that a Wood Sandpiper's nest with four eggs was collected in 'Elginshire' on 23 May 1853 (ASNH **8**:14–16) was later dismissed as probably relating to Common Sandpipers (BB **4**:54).

Common Sandpiper

Actitis hypoleucos

Numerous summer visitor and breeder.

The Common Sandpiper is a familiar feature in summer on the stony margins of lochs of all sizes, along river shingles and up the larger burns high into the glens. Breeding has occasionally taken place at much higher altitude, e.g. one pair by a stream west of Loch Etchachan at 1,100m in 1961.[**76**] Their nests are often at some distance from the water's edge, perhaps on a grassy bank or even among trees.

Spring arrival takes place in the second half of April, the earliest being one in Glenlivet on 14 April 1991. They arrive directly onto the breeding grounds and no coastal spring passage is evident. The breeding season is short and by late June birds are moving to the coast. During July and early August small numbers are present on the estuaries, feeding in the river beds at low tide, and in the muddy creeks. In July 1970 there were 25–60 daily in Findhorn Bay, but recent counts have not exceeded 25. Few remain by early September; the latest birds were one at Findhorn on 29 September 1982 and one at Speymouth on 16 October 1969.

An adult ringed in breeding habitat at Tomintoul on 7 July 1977 was found near Arcachon (south-western France) on 23 September 1981. A bird ringed at Findhorn in July 1969 was found dead in Perthshire four years later.

Turnstone

Arenaria interpres

Common winter visitor, a few remain in summer.

Turnstones are common in winter on all the rocky shores of Moray but there are few in Nairn where little suitable habitat exists. The first returning adults are usually seen in mid July but it is late August before any substantial influx takes place. Young birds arrive in September and peak winter numbers are present from October onwards. Maximum counts on the main rocky shores during the six winters since 1985/6 have been as follows:

	Av. peak count	*Range*
Burghead–Hopeman	110	52–204
Lossiemouth	217	125–270
Portgordon–Strathlene	337	246–424

Smaller numbers are found at Findhorn (30–50 regular, max. 81 on 14 December 1986) and between Findochty and Cullen (57 on 30 December 1984). There is a regular flock of *c*.20 around Nairn harbour, the only flock in the District.

Most birds leave during April with a few lingering until mid May. During summer a small flock of Turnstones usually remains around Speymouth, often 10–50 with highest counts of 56 on 11 June 1982 and 70 on 30 June 1985.

The only truly inland record concerns a Turnstone in summer plumage at Lochindorb on 15 May 1985. Five were more than 2 km up river from Speymouth on 15 December 1991.

Wilson's Phalarope

Phalaropus tricolor

Accidental.

Two have been seen in recent years, both in Findhorn Bay. A juvenile associated with Dunlin from 8–13 September 1987 (BB **81**:561) and an adult female made a brief stop on 16 May 1990.

(Red-necked Phalarope

Phalaropus lobatus)

There is an old record of one 'obtained' near Forres on 8 December 1890.[4] In view of the date, confusion with Grey Phalarope seems possible, although the bird was apparently seen by George Gordon.

More recently a phalarope, probably of this species, was seen at Findhorn on 22 August 1974 (SB **8**:438).

Grey Phalarope

Phalaropus fulicarius

Accidental.

There is a single record from last century, of a female found at Nairn in December 1879.[7] On 19 January 1991 one was seen on the sea off Lossiemouth (MNBR 1991).

Pomarine Skua

Stercorarius pomarinus

Scarce migrant offshore in summer and autumn, rare in winter.

The earliest record relates to two birds obtained near Innes House (presumably at the coast) on 13 October 1910. These were presented to Elgin Museum. There are no further coastal records for 54 years until one was seen off Lossiemouth on 22 July 1964. Doubtless this reflects a lack of observers and unawareness of weather conditions which might lead to an observable passage. Since 1970 a few have been seen almost every year, usually during on-shore gales. Annual totals are shown below:

Total birds seen	*No. of years (1970–91)*
0	6
1–5	10
6–10	2

11–15	1
16–20	2
21–25	0
26–30	1

Best years were 1977 (20, including 15 off Lossiemouth on 27 August), 1985 (18, including nine off Lossiemouth on 11 October) and 1991 (29, including nine off Lossiemouth on 4 November). The main passage takes place between mid August–mid October (98 birds seen). Outwith this period, totals are three in June (on 24 June 1984), two in July, 20 in November, four in December and one in January (on 21 January 1979).

There is one inland record, a bird shot while feeding on a hare carcass at Dallas on 21 November 1922 (SN 1923:84).

Arctic Skua

Stercorarius parasiticus

Scarce migrant in summer and autumn.

Described as 'not uncommon' on the coast last century,[**3,6**] Arctics remain the most frequently recorded skua species today. The table below compares the pattern of occurrence offshore for the three common skua species:

	% Birds seen			
	1 May–15 July	*16 July–31 Aug*	*1 Sept–15 Oct*	*16 Oct–31 Jan*
Pomarine	3.6	34.9	41.0	20.5
Arctic	2.5	54.7	36.7	6.0
Great	1.4	49.8	46.2	2.7

It appears that autumn passage of Arctics is earlier than that of Pomarines and there are substantially fewer late autumn and winter records, the latest being one at Burghead on 25 November 1985. Although sometimes seen harrying gulls around the estuaries in fine weather, most Arctic Skuas are seen from projecting headlands such as Lossiemouth, when they are forced to pass close to land by onshore gales, especially from the north-east. The heaviest passages off Lossiemouth were in 1991 on 5 September (50), 10 September (52) and 18 October (56). The only inland record is of one shot on Aultmore on 25 October 1902.[**54**]

Long-tailed Skua

Stercorarius longicaudus

Accidental.

Four were killed in the Districts in the last century:

2 'obtained' near Forres	*c.*10 Aug 1868 [4]
1 shot Nairn sands	July 1882 [4]
1 'obtained' Findhorn	11 Aug 1897 (ASNH **6**:254)

No others were seen until 19 September 1988 when an adult with tail streamers was watched close inshore off Delnies (MNBR 1988). On 19 September 1990 a group of two adults and one juvenile (possibly three) passed Lossiemouth (MNBR 1990). In 1991 two adults passed Lossiemouth on 11 September and one juvenile was on the Lossie estuary on 17 October (MNBR 1991).

Great Skua

Stercorarius skua

Scarce migrant in summer and autumn.

The first report of a Great Skua in the Moray Firth does not appear to have been until 15 October 1897 when one was shot at the Buckie Loch, Culbin (ASNH **7**:118). Since the 1960s they have been recorded much more frequently, due to an increase in both observers and the Scottish breeding population. Ninety-six percent of all sightings are between late July and early October. The heaviest passage recorded was on 18 October 1991 when 32 passed Lossiemouth in one hour. Of the three common skuas, Greats are seen least often in winter. There have been three inland records, birds found dead at Ardclach on 2 October 1962 and Clochan on 29 October 1990 and another, very much alive, flying over Lochindorb on 4 June 1990.

Four chicks, all ringed in Shetland, were subsequently found dead in the Districts, three near Nairn in August (two) and October, and the bird at Ardclach in October.

Mediterranean Gull

Larus melanocephalus

Accidental.

A bird of this species, moulting into first-summer plumage, was watched on the Lossie estuary on 2 April and 11 May 1989 (MNBR 1989).

Little Gull

Larus minutus

Scarce visitor.

Usually only two or three Little Gulls are seen each year. They have occurred in nearly every month, but 79% were during the period May–September:

Jan	Feb	Mar	Apr	May	Jun	Jul	Aug	Sep	Oct	Nov	Dec
0	3	0	3	9	10	12	6	13	2	3	2

Totals for 1970–91 are shown in the histogram below. Single birds account for 71% of all records; the largest groups were five first-summer birds at Speymouth on 31 May 1976 and up to five there from 2–16 July 1991. Most are seen at the Lossie estuary, Speymouth or Findhorn Bay. There have been four inland records, three at Loch Spynie (one shot in April 1847 [**3**], and singles seen on 28 September 1987 and 7 September 1991) and one juvenile at Cloddach on 24 July 1989.

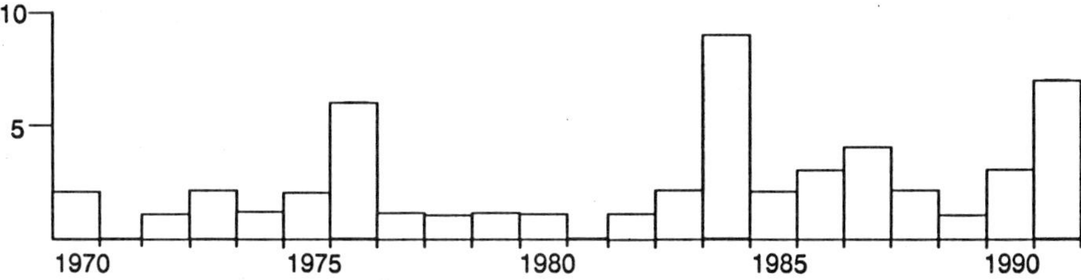

Figure 23 Little Gull annual totals 1970–91

Black-headed Gull

Larus ridibundus

Common resident breeder and winter visitor.

There are numerous Black-headed Gull colonies scattered through the Districts in marshes, on moorland and lowland lochs and on river islands. The following colonies are known to have held in excess of 20 pairs:

Achavraat: 1989 — 50–80 pairs
Archiestown: 1958 — *c.*20 pairs
Ardclach: 1989 — 30–40 pairs
Auchlochan: 1989 — 20+ pairs
Loch Belivat: 1847 — 'large colony'; 1900 — 'fairly large'; 1958 — *c.*130 pairs; 1989 — colony extinct
Loch of Boath: 1900 — bred; 1986 — 21 pairs; 1988 — 2 pairs
Bogmoor island: 1976 — 35–40 pairs; 1986 — 70 pairs; 1990 — 250–300 pairs; 1991 — 50 pairs
Brokentore: 1988 — 100 pairs
Cloddach: 1991 — 65–70 pairs

PLATE 21 Black-headed Gull with newly hatched chicks *(John Edelsten)*

Loch of Cotts: 1938 — 150 pairs; 1958 — 4–5 pairs; now drained
Loch of the Cowlatt: 1982 — 20 pairs; 1987 — 30–40 pairs; 1990 — 55 pairs
Loch Dallas: 1986 — 80 pairs; 1988 — 112 pairs; 1991 — 45 pairs
Darnaway Castle (Black Loch/Tearie): 1958 — 1,375 pairs; 1970 — 900–1,100 pairs; 1989 — 80 pairs; 1990 — 40 pairs
Dava lochans: 1958 — *c.*200 pairs; 1986 — 200+ pairs; 1990 — 315 pairs
Drumlochan: 1988 — 85 pairs
Loch Dubh: 1988 — 42 pairs; 1990 — 52 pairs
Fleenas: 1991 — 40 pairs
Loch Flemington: 1989 — 50–60 pairs
RAF Kinloss: 1960s — up to 500 pairs were discouraged by the RAF
Loch of Little Benshalag: 1987 — 30–40 pairs; 1990 — 45 pairs
Maverston: 1991 — 40 pairs
Mortlach Hills: 1978 — 'scores'; 1985 — 150 pairs; 1988 — 100 pairs
Muir of the Clans: 1991 — 80 pairs
Loch Noir: 1969 — 70 pairs; 1979 — 600 pairs; 1987 — 40–50 pairs; 1988 — 6 pairs
Speyslaw: 1938 — 100 pairs; 1989 — colony extinct for many years.
Loch Spynie: 1863 — 'great numbers'; 1885 — 'thousands'; 1938— 500 pairs; 1958 — 100 pairs; 1988 — 20 pairs

Other smaller colonies of a few pairs exist, especially along the river shingles of the lower Spey. The Loch Spynie colony appears to have been vast last century: in 1885 over 1,200 eggs were collected in one day, only two days after it was last robbed.[4]

Upland colonies are reoccupied during March/April and those nearer the coast in February or early March. Young fledge in June and colonies are largely deserted by mid July. In late summer birds sometimes visit the highest mountain plateaux, e.g. four on Ben Avon summit on 5 July 1984.

In early autumn, northern immigrants start to arrive on the coast where they mingle with native birds, many of which, in turn, disperse out of the area. Immigrant numbers continue to increase through autumn into winter, when roost counts can be huge, e.g. 20,000 at Findhorn on 22 March 1976. Many move inland to feed on farmland during the day, flight lines back to the coast being a familiar sight on winter evenings. Black-headed Gulls are absent in winter from inland areas out of daily coastal commuting range.

The origin of our winter immigrants is indicated by the presence here of birds ringed as chicks in Norway (14) Iceland (six), Caithness (four), Shetland (three) and Orkney (three). Dispersal of locally ringed birds, mostly marked as chicks, has resulted in over 30 recoveries of which the majority were in Grampian Region but others moved, in their first year, to Inverness, Orkney, Northern Ireland, Tayside, Cumbria and Cheshire. A second-year bird was seen in Glasgow in February.

Ring-billed Gull

Larus delawarensis

Accidental.

There have been three records, probably relating to only two individuals:

1 adult Lossiemouth	5 Feb 1979 (BB **73**:512)
1 adult Kingston	29 Dec 1985 (BB **79**:553)
1 adult Lossiemouth	9 Jan 1986 (SBR 1986) (was probably the same as the Kingston bird)

Common Gull

Larus canus

Common resident breeder and winter visitor.

Common Gulls nest in colonies ranging from a few to many hundreds of pairs. Currently the largest colonies are among the hills to the east of Dufftown. Recent estimates of the number of pairs in this area are shown below:

	1977 [**56**]	*1988*
Tips of Corsemaul	*c.*1,000	3,385 (±745)
Craig Watch (south-west)	*c.*1,000	1,207 (±554)
Ben Main	?	1,785 (±725)
Auchindoun hut circles	?	*c.*100

The 1988 counts are the result of a detailed NCC survey. They estimated a further 1,000 pairs in nearby unsurveyed areas. Other sizeable colonies are on the Moss of Dunphail (340 pairs in 1988), Clunas Reservoir (120 pairs in 1989), on Spey islands near Bogmoor (50 pairs in 1991) and Fochabers (35 pairs in 1990), and at Elfhill near Buinach (40 pairs in 1989) and at Maverston (40 pairs in 1991). Elsewhere there are numerous smaller colonies, mostly less than 20 pairs, on moorlands, river shingles and in quarries and gravel pits. Very few breed at the coast. Formerly there were large colonies around Keith on the Gow Moss, Hill of Towie and Meikle Balloch Hill. The latter colony held 1,000 pairs in 1971 but was deserted during the 1970s as forestry spread over the hill. In 1977 there were *c.*370 pairs on the moors around Mill Our and Pikey Hill but these were gone by 1980, although 15–20 pairs remain on nearby Carn na Cailliche.

Young fledge in June/early July and can often be seen in flocks on newly-mown hay fields through July. By late August few remain in the uplands but large assemblies sometimes build up at the coast, e.g. 6,000 at Findhorn Bay on 21 August 1970 and 5,500 there on 26 August 1988. Doubtless arriving northern immigrants mingle with local gulls in these flocks. In midwinter large numbers roost at the coast and daily commute inland to feed on arable land, at least as far as Dufftown. Nearly 4,000 were counted heading inland over Clochan in the early morning of 11 December 1984. In March birds move further inland and start to reoccupy breeding colonies.

Forty-seven recoveries have resulted from ringing Common Gulls, mostly chicks, in the Districts. Of these 19 showed only local dispersal, another 19 showed movement within Scotland (mostly southward in winter) and six went to northern England (in October–February). Two were in Ireland in winter, the furthest being a first-year bird in Wexford in November 1980. The origin of our winter immigrants is indicated by the presence here of birds ringed as chicks in More og Romsdal (Norway), Orkney and Shetland. A first-winter bird ringed at Kinloss in October 1981 was shot near Tromso in arctic Norway (presumably its country of origin) in August 1986.

Lesser Black-backed Gull

Larus fuscus

Numerous summer visitor and breeder.

Lesser Black-backs are scarce breeders on moorland, river shingles and coastal dunes and cliffs. Precise historical data on breeding numbers is sadly lacking. In 1889 'hundreds' were nesting on a ridge near Pluscarden,[**52**] and in the 1960s/early 1970s there were *c.*50 pairs on the Meikle Balloch Hill at Keith but encroaching forestry caused desertion of the colony by the mid-1970s. Gow Moss near Keith also formerly held a sizeable colony. More recently, in 1969–70, 50 pairs were estimated on the Moray coast,[**57**] mostly at Kinloss, and in 1977 'some' were breeding on the hills east of Dufftown.[**56**] Today the population of the Districts is probably between 120–150 pairs. Most of these are on the Tips of Corsemaul near Dufftown (110 pairs in 1988) with a few others on the lower Spey shingles (*c.*five pairs), at RAF Kinloss (two to five pairs), on Carn na Cailliche (one pair), Moss of Dunphail (one pair) and sporadically along the coast (5–10 pairs maximum). In 1990 a pair raised three young on the flat roof of a garage salesroom near Elgin station. Occasionally birds are seen high on the Cairngorm plateau: there were singles at Feith Buidhe on 9 and 22 July 1989 and three over Cairn Lochan on 13 May 1990. Summer and early autumn flocks at the coast are small; 16 at Lossiemouth on 7 June 1987 is the largest group reported recently.

Spring arrival of birds of the race *L.f.graellsii*, which breed in the Districts, takes place in March or occasionally late February (earliest were singles at Elgin on 16 February in 1987 and 1989) and most leave again in early autumn. A few are seen later and there is one winter record, a bird at Nairn from 28 December 1990–18 February 1991. The exceptional 86 adults at Findhorn on 22 October 1966, may well be migrants from the *graellsii* populations in Iceland and the Faroes. Birds of the darker-backed Scandinavian races, *L.f.fuscus* or *L.f.intermedius* have been seen on eight occasions at all seasons of the year. The two mid winter records were of six in Findhorn Bay on 2 February 1967 and one at Elgin on 19 January 1987.

Return of adults to their natal colony was shown by two birds dead at Kinloss in May 1987 which had been ringed there as chicks in 1980 and 1981. There are two other recoveries, a chick ringed on Hoy, Orkney in July 1935 was found dead at Dunphail in November of the same year and an adult ringed at Aberdeen on 18 June 1949 had moved to Lossiemouth only two days later.

Herring Gull

Larus argentatus

Common resident breeder and winter visitor.

Herring Gulls breed commonly along the coast but only in small numbers inland. In 1969–70 there were 1,160 pairs on the Morayshire coast [**57**] but there are fewer today. Recent counts are shown below:

Covesea–Hopeman (1990)	134 pairs
Findochty–Portknockie (1987)	140 pairs
RAF Kinloss (1987)	70 pairs

The RAF Kinloss colony held 420 pairs in 1970 but is now almost extinct due to culling for aircraft safety. In 1978, 90 pairs nested on Nairn Bar but there are none there now. Inland there were 'a good many' in the hills east of Dufftown in 1977 [**56**] but only 37 pairs on the Tips of Corsemaul in 1988. In the 1960s/early 1970s there were up to 400 pairs on the Meikle Balloch Hill, Keith. In 1971 this colony was still persisting despite afforestation of the area, many nests being surrounded by trees three metres tall. There were none left in the late 1970s. In 1978 20 pairs bred on the Spey shingles at Bogmoor. Elsewhere inland, occasional small groups nest e.g. 20 pairs on the Moss of

Dunphail (1988), three pairs at Cloddach quarry (1988) and three pairs on Mill Our in the late 1970s.

In the late 1950s Herring Gulls were first noticed nesting on roofs in Lossiemouth and in 1969 there were *c.*eight pairs, also one pair in Nairn.[58] By 1976 there were nine pairs in Nairn but only one in Lossiemouth.[59] The habit has persisted with at least six pairs in Lossiemouth in 1983.

Even during the summer months large flocks of immatures and non-breeding birds collect on the shore, e.g. 1,120 at Lossiemouth on 20 June 1984 and 3,000 there in mid July the same year. During autumn and winter, coastal concentrations can also be very large, although few are seen inland beyond daily commuting distance from the coastal roosts. Continental immigrants swell the local flocks to an unknown degree but their presence is evidenced by the bird found at Findhorn on 24 April 1948 which had been ringed as a chick near Murmansk, Russia, in 1947. A yellow-legged adult was at Lossiemouth on 5 April 1989.

Hybrid Herring × Glaucous (or Iceland) Gulls were seen at Lossiemouth on 11 January 1986 (MNBR 1986), 31 May 1988 (MNBR 1988) and 5–22 April 1989 (MNBR 1989).

Local ringing, mostly of chicks, has produced a total of 81 recoveries, 72 of them within the Districts. The furthest travelling of the others went, in their first winters, to the Netherlands (April) and Donegal, Eire (long dead in August). Eleven and one and a half year old birds were found in winter in Northumberland and on Merseyside. Ringing elsewhere in Britain, again principally of chicks, has resulted in 181 recoveries in Moray and Nairn. Most of these represent post-breeding dispersal from other Scottish colonies, often from the north or west coast. Eight came from northern England and two from Ireland.

Iceland Gull

Larus glaucoides

Scarce winter visitor.

The first documented occurrence of Iceland Gull in the Districts was one which was shot at Dallas on 6 May 1892.[4] There are no further records, probably reflecting the lack of observers, until 1971 when one was at Garmouth on 12 December. Yearly totals since then are shown below.

Since 1970 at least 37 individuals have been seen, a few staying for several months, e.g. one at Burghead harbour between 26 December 1985–12 May 1986. As shown below, they are most frequent in late winter/early spring with very few records in autumn. Earliest arrival was one at Lossiemouth on 10 October 1982 and latest stayer was an adult at Lossiemouth on 28 July 1986. Of the 29 birds whose age was determined, five were adult and 24 were immature.

Apart from the old Dallas record there have been five inland occurrences, at Loch Spynie (two), Elgin, Duffus and Loch Flemington.

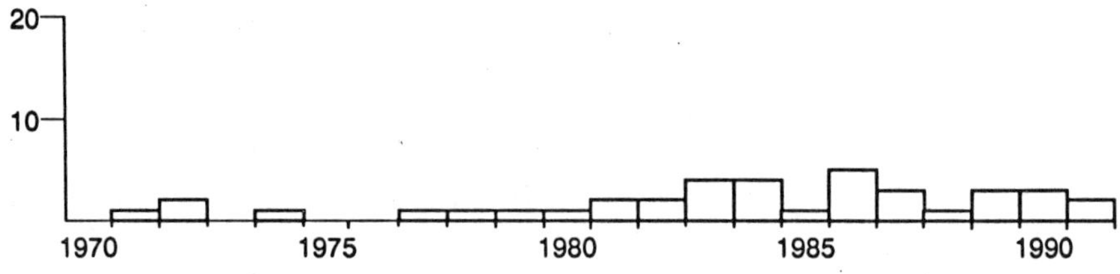

Figure 24 Iceland Gull annual totals 1970–91

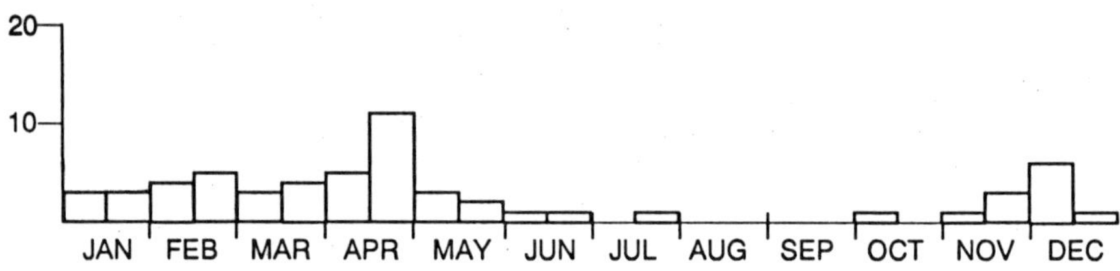

Figure 25 Iceland Gull half-monthly totals 1970–91

Glaucous Gull

Larus hyperboreus

Scarce winter visitor.

Glaucous Gulls are seen annually in very small numbers along the coast. The half-monthly pattern of occurrence between 1968–90 is shown in the histogram below.

Although there is some influx of birds in autumn, most arrivals take place in December and numbers are highest in the first third of the year. Most records concern single birds (89%) but two are sometimes seen together and there were three at Findhorn on 18 February 1983. On 14 February 1976 five were seen between Burghead and Spey Bay, but not together. There have been only two inland records, a lone bird at Keith on 11–14 January 1978 and another at Clochan on 25 April 1983.

Gulls thought to be hybrids between Glaucous and Herring were seen at Lossiemouth on 11 January 1986 (MNBR 1986), 31 May 1988 (MNBR 1988), and 5–22 April 1989 (MNBR 1989).

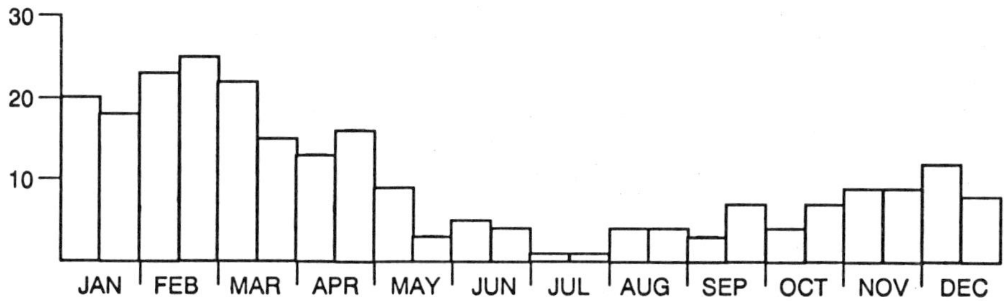

Figure 26 Glaucous Gull half-monthly totals 1970–91

Great Black-backed Gull

Larus marinus

Scarce resident breeder, common autumn and winter visitor.

The present breeding population is unlikely to exceed 20–30 pairs. Most are on the coast at Kinloss (*c.*five pairs), Covesea (one or two pairs) and between Findochty and Portknockie (three to five pairs). They no longer breed on the Nairn and Culbin Bars where there were about 30 pairs in the 1960s–70s. Inland, in 1988, there were four pairs on the Moss of Dunphail and another four pairs on the Tips of Corsemaul. St.John claimed that they nested regularly at Lochindorb in the mid nineteenth century [**3**] and in May 1881 a clutch of eggs was collected near Ardclach.[**27**]

An annual influx takes place on the coast in late summer and autumn, sometimes resulting in huge flocks, particularly at Lossiemouth where the highest count was 2,300 resting on the estuary on 31 August 1986. Other localities regularly holding 500–1,000 birds are Speymouth and the Nairn and Culbin Bars. There were 1,800 in Findhorn Bay on 18 September 1990. During May–July flocks contain mostly non-breeding immatures but by autumn there are often up to 90% adults. Numbers are much reduced in midwinter, typically 50–100 at Lossiemouth.

Great Black-backs are the only gulls commonly occurring far inland in winter, where they can be seen in small groups along the river shingles scavenging dead salmon, e.g. 16 at Strathavon on 18 December 1983.

Ringing of chicks at Culbin in the 1960s resulted in ten recoveries. Six of these were found dead on the local coast in the same autumn or winter and one was shot inland on the River Divie at Edinkillie two and a quarter months after ringing. Longer movements were shown by the birds found in the Lothians (after five and three quarter years) and at Loch Hourn (after three years). Fifty-three recoveries in the Districts of birds ringed elsewhere, mostly as chicks, indicate that our autumn and winter immigrants originate in a number of northern Scottish colonies especially in Orkney.

Kittiwake

Rissa tridactyla

Numerous breeder and common migrant.

In 1895, and also in the early 1950s, there were no known Kittiwake colonies in the Districts.[**2,4**] However, although the Covesea colony was not documented until 1968 it was clearly in existence for at least several years previously. Today Kittiwakes breed on the cliffs between Hopeman and Covesea and also on the Bow Fiddle Rock at Portknockie. The number of apparently occupied nests at these colonies has changed as follows:

	1959	*1968*	*1979*	*1982*	*1983*	*1985*	*1986*	*1987*	*1988*	*1989*	*1990*	*1991*
Hopeman/ Covesea	-	*c.*300	-	16	17	70	109	130	161	250	231	249
Bow Fiddle Rock	*c.*90	-	22	-	-	-	1	10	13	31	45	43

After the breeding season, large congregations of birds can be seen loafing at low tide on the three main estuaries, peak counts at each site in recent years being 1,900 at Findhorn Bay (10 August 1988), 7,000 on Lossie estuary (24 August 1978) and 4,400 at Speymouth (21 September 1991). Offshore passage in autumn can also be heavy in stormy weather with onshore winds, e.g. 6,000/hour flying east past Buckie on 14 October 1982. Only small numbers of Kittiwakes are seen in midwinter, most juveniles having dispersed far into the Atlantic. Adults reoccupy the colonies in March. The only inland record concerns a bird whose remains were found in a Peregrine eyrie in the Cabrach in early June 1988.

A chick ringed in a colony in northern France had dispersed north to Buckie where it was found dead on 20 September 1983. Four other Kittiwakes, dead on local beaches in autumn, originated in colonies at the Farne Islands (two), Berwick-on-Tweed and Dunbar.

Ivory Gull

Pagophila eburnea

Accidental.

An adult was seen on the coast between Burghead and Hopeman on 17 January 1934 (SN **212**:54). Another, less satisfactory, record given by Harvie-Brown and Buckley concerns one on the shore at Culbin in late June 1888.[4]

(Caspian Tern

Sterna caspia)

Two large terns on the Old Bar, Findhorn on 2 June 1887 were well described by the observer who noted their size as a little less than Lesser Black-backed Gull. Harvie-Brown and Buckley were reluctant to accept the record because the birds were not shot.[**4**]

Sandwich Tern

Sterna sandvicensis

Common summer visitor, has bred.

Sandwich Terns no longer breed on the coast, although they once did so in considerable numbers at Culbin. On 2 June 1887 32 nests were found on Culbin Bar, 20–25 was the usual number around this time. In 1888 there was also one pair at the mouth of the Findhorn.[**4**] In 1936 there were three nests on the Bar and breeding was again confirmed there in 1947.[**2**] Eleven years later, in 1958, the colony was very much larger with 267 pairs,[**60**] but by the 1960s there were none. In 1970 150 pairs were found on Whiteness Head, just outside the Nairn boundary, on 3 July but they failed completely. On 6 July 1970 a single pair was nesting in the Arctic/Common Tern colony on the River Spey above Garmouth viaduct (SB **6**:380). Since 1970 Sandwich Terns have not bred but continue to be common summer visitors.

The first arrivals are usually seen around the beginning of April or occasionally in late March, the earliest being one at Spey Bay on 18 March 1990. Numbers then build up rapidly and in some years large flocks accumulate in Findhorn Bay, e.g. 600 on 22 April 1970 and 1,000 on 3 May 1984. Following the breeding season, adults and juveniles from east coast colonies move into the Moray Firth to feed and several hundred can sometimes be seen resting on the shore; peak counts in recent years were 400 at Kingston on 7 August 1985 and 337 at Lossiemouth on 13 August 1987. Ringed birds recovered in Moray and Nairn at this time include first-year birds from colonies on the Farne Islands (six, the earliest on 5 August), Coquet Island (Northumberland) and Salthouse (Norfolk). There have been several older birds from the Farnes and from the Sands of Forvie (Aberdeenshire). Offshore passage may be heavy in late summer; on 28 August 1977 511 flew east past Lossiemouth in two hours. Usually most Sandwich Terns have left the area by the end of September, although there were still 300 at Findhorn on 30 September 1967. Most years a few remain until early October; the latest were two at Covesea on 31 October 1968. There have been two winter records, one at Nairn Bar on 21 February 1984 and one at Nairn from 15–22 February 1987.

Roseate Tern

Sterna dougallii

Rare summer visitor.

St.John wrote, in 1863, that Roseate Terns were sometimes seen in tern flocks but gave no more details.[3] A single bird was seen at Culbin in 1867. In 1887 there were seven pairs on the Culbin Bar and five nests were found on 26 May. The eggs were collected by the finder and no further breeding there is recorded.[4]

There are a few more recent records:

1 Findhorn	4 Aug 1967
2 Findhorn	29 July 1969
3 Nairn	9 July 1970
1 Findhorn	23 Aug 1970
1 Lossiemouth	24 Aug 1986

Common Tern

Sterna hirundo

Common summer visitor and numerous breeder.

Records of breeding in the last century begin with a colony on the sands between Burghead and Findhorn in 1844.[6] In 1895 they were abundant on Culbin Sands and inland breeding was noted well up the rivers as far as Glenlivet.[4]

In recent years there have been only two main colonies. On the lower Spey Common Terns breed on a shingle island on the Bogmoor–Garmouth reach. Counts since 1972 have been as follows:

1972	500 pairs
1975–80	200–300 pairs
1981–5	100–150 pairs
1986	250 pairs
1988–9	100 pairs
1990–1	30–35 pairs

An increasing colony of Black-headed Gulls is currently taking over the island at the expense of the terns. Another colony at Findhorn held 200 pairs in 1970 and 140 pairs in 1981 but fewer breed in the area today, among the Arctic

Terns at Kinloss.

Very small numbers continue to nest inland, mostly on the middle reaches of the Spey but also on some smaller stony upland rivers, e.g. six pairs on the River Deveron near Cabrach about 1970 and one pair there in 1987. On 23 July 1977 at least three birds were behaving anxiously in the Tips of Corsemaul gullery but there was no proof of breeding.

Spring arrival takes place in the second half of April; the earliest was one at Spey Bay on 14 April 1979. When the young have fledged, mixed flocks of Common and Arctic Terns frequent the river mouths resting on shingles or mudflats. Largest flocks have been 1,320 at Lossiemouth on 1 August 1989, 1,180 at Culbin Bar on 9 August 1988 and 585 at Speymouth on 28 July 1972. These flocks clearly contain many birds on passage from colonies outwith the Districts. Most Common Terns have left by October, although one was off Findhorn on 16 November 1985 and there is a late winter record of one at Lossiemouth on 25 February 1980 (not 2 February as in SBR 1980).

Ringing of local chicks has revealed that our Common Terns spend their first winter and summer off the coast of West Africa. There have been recoveries in Ghana (one on 30 August only *c.*eight weeks after fledging, others in November, March and May), Ivory Coast (April) and Sierra Leone (June). Another was in Portugal by 7 September. Interesting longevity was shown by the individual ringed as a chick near Nairn on 9 July 1951 and found dead in Easter Ross on 15 July 1974, 23 years later.

Arctic Tern

Sterna paradisaea

Common summer visitor and numerous breeder.

Nesting was first reported on Culbin Bar where nine pairs bred in 1887;[4] the colony was still present in 1936.[2] In 1969 25 pairs nested on Nairn Bar but there have been very few pairs there since then, and no certain breeding since 1978. St.John wrote, in the mid nineteenth century, that Arctic Terns breed generally by loch and river margins,[3] but this statement probably reflects confusion with Common Terns. In recent years the furthest inland breeding Arctic Terns have been only 3 km upstream on the Spey.

Only one moderately large colony exists today, on the dunes at RAF Kinloss. In 1978 there were 100 pairs, 50 pairs in 1979, 500 pairs in 1980 and 350 pairs in 1981. In 1987 there were *c.*100 pairs, *c.*275 pairs in 1990, and *c.*140 pairs in 1991. On the Spey there are often 5–10 pairs on the shingles at the river mouth (max. 17 pairs in 1984). Upstream at the Common Tern colony in the Bogmoor area there were 50 pairs in 1976, 40 pairs in 1983, under 20 pairs in 1986–1989 and an increase to 60 pairs in 1990.

Arrivals are usually in the second half of April (the earliest being one at Findhorn Bay on 7 April 1990) but in some years few are reported before May. In August and early September large groups can sometimes be seen resting on the shore, e.g. 400 at Lossie estuary on 12 August 1985. Most have left by late September, the latest were two at Lossiemouth on 3 October 1976.

There are three foreign recoveries of locally ringed Arctic Tern chicks showing movement to African waters in their first winter. They were found in Morocco (17 September), off Guinea (13 December) and Ghana (20 March). Another was in Denmark on 7 September.

Little Tern

Sterna albifrons

Scarce summer visitor and rare breeder.

Little Terns have a long history of breeding in Moray and Nairn but are now perilously close to extinction in the Districts. In 1844 an unknown number bred on the sands between Findhorn and Burghead [6] and there is a similarly vague record for Nairn Bar in June 1847.[32] In 1887 there was a colony with 19 nests in the Findhorn area.[4] In 1895 pairs bred 'all along the suitable portions of the coast-line' between Findhorn and Speymouth. The largest colony was at Findhorn with a smaller one on Nairn Bar.[4] Both localities held breeding Little Terns in 1936 — figures are only given for the Bar where there were four nests.[2] In 1958 the Findhorn colony held 40 pairs but a rapid decline ensued with 10 pairs in the early 1960s, three pairs in 1967 and only one pair in 1969.[61] There were three to four pairs in 1971 and occasional breeding continued there until 1980. In 1978 there were three pairs on Nairn Bar where breeding has not been proved since, although one or two pairs are sometimes seen. In 1986 a new site with two nests was located in east Moray, one pair bred there from 1987–9 but they were seen only briefly in 1990 and 1991.

Little Terns are occasionally seen feeding in shallow coastal waters away from breeding sites. The earliest spring arrival date was 5 May 1984 and the latest in autumn was one at Portgordon on 7 October 1979 (not 7 September as in SBR 1979).

Black Tern

Chlidonias niger

Scarce visitor in summer and autumn.

The first record was not until 16 August 1962 when one was seen at Speymouth. Altogether, until the end of 1991, there have been 19 records, 16 involving singles and three of two birds together. Eleven sightings were at Speymouth, two at Findhorn and Loch Flemington, and one each at Loch Spynie, Lossiemouth, Culbin Bar and Delnies. The monthly distribution of birds and annual totals are shown below and in the histogram.

April	May	June	July	Aug	Sept	Oct	Nov
0	2	3	0	5	8	3	1

The earliest was one at Speymouth on 5 May 1967 and the latest was one at Loch Flemington from 2–10 November 1985.

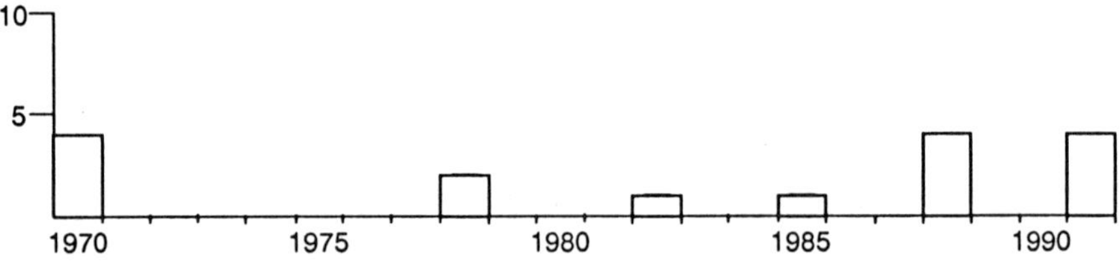

Figure 27 Black Tern annual totals 1970–91

White-winged Black Tern

Chlidonias leucopterus

Accidental.

An adult between Whiteness Head and Carse of Delnies on 14 July 1970 was watched on both sides of the Nairn/Inverness boundary (BB **64**:354, SB **6**:203).

Guillemot

Uria aalge

Common offshore.

Guillemots can be seen swimming offshore in small parties at most times of the year, although usually only flights of passing birds are seen in summer. Breeding has never been attempted and only sickly or storm-driven birds come ashore. Numbers visible from the coast vary widely from year to year but they are most numerous when large shoals of sprats or herring provide good feeding in the Firth. Greatest concentrations are usually in October, especially in 1980–2 when there were several hundred in Spey Bay. On 15 October 1988 there were 851 off Findhorn and 250 off Kingston. Normal rates of visible passage seldom exceed 200/hour but on 14 October 1982 *c.*1,400 flew east past Lossiemouth in one hour. A mid-winter count between Whiteness Head and Spey Bay on 11 December 1982 revealed 480 Guillemots.

During prolonged spells of stormy weather in late winter considerable numbers of dead birds are sometimes washed up on the beaches. These are usually unoiled and starvation appears to be the main cause of death. In late February–early March 1983 44 were picked up between Spey Bay and Findochty, and on 15–16 February 1986 *c.*150 were found between Findhorn and Lossiemouth.

There are no recent inland records but after severe gales in January 1885 many storm blown birds were found up to five miles from the sea between Burghead and Nairn.[**4**]

Twenty-one ringed Guillemots have been found dead on beaches in Moray and Nairn in autumn and winter and four in summer. They originated from seven Scottish colonies, the furthest two from the west coast island of Canna. The oldest was found at Lossiemouth 12 ½ years after it was ringed as an adult on Handa island.

Razorbill

Alca torda

Common offshore.

Razorbills are usually less numerous than Guillemots but small groups can be encountered swimming offshore in all but the early summer months. Much larger numbers sometimes congregate off west Moray in autumn; the best year was 1986 when there were 320 off Findhorn on 25 September and 778 off Burghead on 27 September. On 26 February 1989 there were 410 in Burghead Bay, an unusually large mid winter count.

Prolonged storms can cause substantial wrecks of Razorbills. In January 1885 many storm-driven birds were found up to five miles inland between Burghead and Nairn.[4] More recently a wreck in late February/early March 1983 left 117 dead on the beach between Spey Bay and Findochty.

In 1974 a single Razorbill was on a cliff ledge at Covesea on 11 May but was not seen subsequently.

Six ringed Razorbills have been found dead on local beaches. Four were marked in Scottish west coast colonies: Shiant islands (two), Handa and St Kilda (found 14 ½ years after it was ringed as an adult). Another was from Fair Isle.

Black Guillemot

Cepphus grylle

Scarce offshore, rare breeder.

Described as infrequent visitors in the 1860s,[3] they probably remained that way for the next 100 years. In the last 20 years records have increased enormously but it is unclear to what extent this increase reflects the greater number of observers and popularity of sea-watching. Breeding first took place about 1982 when one pair nested unsuccessfully near Portknockie. In 1986 another nest was found nearby and two young were reared. Successful breeding has continued at the same site in 1987 (one young), 1988 (two), 1989 (two), 1990 (two) and 1991 (two). In 1989 and 1991 a second pair of adults was present nearby but no other nest was found.

Offshore records increase from August onwards with a large peak in October. Until 1990 highest single counts were 12 off Buckie on 17 October 1970, 11 there on 21 October 1969, ten at Burghead on 6 January 1972 and ten at Spey Bay on 8 December 1973. On 19 October 1991 a remarkable 41 flew west past Lossiemouth in one hour. In most years an apparent decline from January onwards may be genuine or reflect a paucity of sea-watchers in cold weather. In spring also very few birds are seen, only five in April–July 1969–89, away from the nesting locality.

One of the young birds reared and ringed at Portknockie in 1988 was found dead at Banff two and a half weeks later. Another chick ringed on Fair Isle in August 1975 was dead at Burghead in September 1976.

Little Auk

Alle alle

Scarce winter visitor, occasionally common.

When severe weather conditions to the north drive many Little Auks into the North Sea large-scale movements can be seen offshore and some may even be picked up inland. Prior to the mid 1980s, this was exceptional; between 1970–86 the number of birds seen each winter never exceeded three (no records in four winters). More recently, however, there were good numbers in 1987/8 (2,500+), 1989/90 (693) and 1990/1 (718).

In the mid nineteenth century St.John wrote that Little Auks visited Moray at irregular intervals and generally in great numbers; in January 1847 many were found dead along the shore.[**3**] Another wreck took place in 1879 when storm-driven birds were found at Pitgaveny, Hopeman and Duffus.[**4**] In January 1895 17 were found dead between Nairn and Burghead with a further three at Portgordon.[**4,62**] In December 1896 several were dead at Roseisle and another was four miles from the sea near Forres. The following year one was found alive at Findhorn (ASNH **7**:53). In winter 1906/7 there was one well inland at Craigellachie following a storm (ASNH **16**:117) and another storm-driven bird was near Elgin on 21 December 1914.[**54**] There

follows a gap of 36 years until the next documented occurrence, again inland, of one exhausted at Bridge of Marnoch, on the east Moray border, on 1 March 1950.[**63**] Between 1965–86 one or two were seen or found dead on the shore in most years, usually between November and April but there were two summer records, one freshly dead at Findhorn on 4 July 1969 and one flying east off Lossiemouth on 27 August 1977.

The most spectacular influx of Little Auks to date took place in late November/early December 1987. Following two off Findhorn on 16 November the main passage began on 27 November when 15 passed Lossiemouth. Peak movements were detected on 29 November when 968 flew past Lossiemouth in two hours, with a further 341 in two hours on 30 November. On 3 December 205 passed Findhorn in 20 minutes and on 5 December 758 were counted off Lossiemouth in one and three quarter hours. Small numbers continued to be seen inshore until February 1988; one was inland at Alves on 24 January. Comparatively few corpses were washed ashore, but one of these had wing and tarsus measurements indicating membership of the Franz Josef Land race *A.a.polaris* (MNBR 1987). Only two were seen in autumn 1988, one off Burghead on 25 October and one in Spey Bay the next day. Another strong, but very brief, passage took place in autumn 1989 when 678 Little Auks passed Lossiemouth on 25 November. There were 15 the following day and no further sightings. In 1990 mostly small numbers were seen offshore on 10 dates from 10–31 December, best counts being 45 at Burghead on 13 December and 82 at Lossiemouth on 26 December. In 1991 400+ passed Nairn Bar on 9 January and between one and 23 were seen on 15 dates in January–February. On 7 January one was found exhausted in Morinsh Forest, Glenlivet, 35 km from the sea. In autumn, at Lossiemouth, there were 72 on 18 October, 25 on 8 November and up to six on six other dates. The earliest three were on 2 September.

Puffin

Fratercula arctica

Scarce offshore.

Puffins are rarely seen off the Moray and Nairn coast as there are no nearby breeding colonies and they spend the winter months far out to sea. Last century they were apparently seen 'several times' in Findhorn Bay in winter [4] and four were killed off Lossiemouth on 25 May 1859.[7] There is an inland record, undated but pre-1895, of two found in the Cabrach in a snowstorm.[4] Since 1974 only 50 have been seen offshore, in September (10), October (16), January (nine), May (five) and one or two in every other month between June and February. During the serious auk wreck in February/March 1983, 11 were found dead, unoiled, between Spey Bay and Findochty. On 24 November 1975 one was found alive far inland at Dunphail.

Three ringed Puffins have been found dead on Moray beaches. They were ringed in summer on Fair Isle, the Farne Islands and Skomer (south Wales).

Pallas's Sandgrouse

Syrrhaptes paradoxus

Accidental, has bred.

This central Asian species reached Moray during two of its periodic eruptions last century.

The 1863 invasion provided two records, one killed at Lossiemouth and another shot by the Duke of Richmond on 23 October. The latter bird came from a flock of seven or eight flushed from river shingles beside the Spey between Gordon Castle and the river mouth.[100]

In 1888 a much larger invasion took place. The first birds were seen on 15 May at Findhorn and numbers rapidly increased until there were hundreds along the shore. They were especially abundant on the dunes each side of Findhorn Bay, and between Loch Spynie and Speymouth. At least one was reported as far inland as Ben Rinnes. In late June breeding was confirmed when young were found on Culbin Sands. Another brood was found there on 8 August 1889.[4]

Rock Dove/Feral Pigeon

Columba livia

Common resident breeder.

In the mid nineteenth century true wild Rock Doves apparently bred on the cliffs at Covesea and perhaps elsewhere.[**6**] Since that time the wild population has lost its identity through extensive interbreeding with domestic doves. The resulting Feral Pigeons are today common in towns, around farms and maltings and along the coast. When food is abundant, large flocks may assemble; 410 at Burghead Maltings on 31 January 1982 is the highest count.

Stock Dove

Columba oenas

Numerous resident breeder, formerly common.

Following its spread into Scotland in the 1860s–70s, the Stock Dove was first recorded in Moray *c.*1879 in the Forres area. The first breeding took place near Pitgaveny in 1883 and there were four or five pairs there by 1885, the same year in which upland breeding was first noted, in Glenlivet. In 1887 a big increase was noticed on Culbin Sands, where they were nesting in rabbit holes, and up the Findhorn valley. By 1892 Stock doves were 'literally swarming all along the sandhills, rabbit wastes, heathery and gorse-covered portions of the Plain of Moray, over the Culbin Sands, penetrating up the Findhorn and Nairn, and populating the hardwoods around these rivers in their lower straths, . . . '. They were also up the Lossie, Spey and Avon rivers, breeding on rocky and heathery hillsides up to 600m on the summit of Cairn Dregnie in Glenlivet, where nests were also found on Carn an t-Suidhe and The Bochel.[**4,64**] By 1936 they were breeding fairly commonly but probably less abundantly than in the 1890s.[**2**] By the early 1960s they were decreasing inland [**45**] but were still numerous on sand dunes and in coastal woods. During 1968–72 breeding was proved in only three 10 km-squares, although presence was recorded in 15 others, mostly coastal.[**65**] Furthest inland, by far, were eight in the Ailnack gorge near Tomintoul on 25 April 1971; one pair was still there on 20 April 1975.

Stock Doves are now seldom seen outside the Laich of Moray and lowland Nairn where most occur on farmland in the vicinity of plantations. On 30 November 1975 an exceptional flock of 95 was near Urquhart (SB **9**:214),

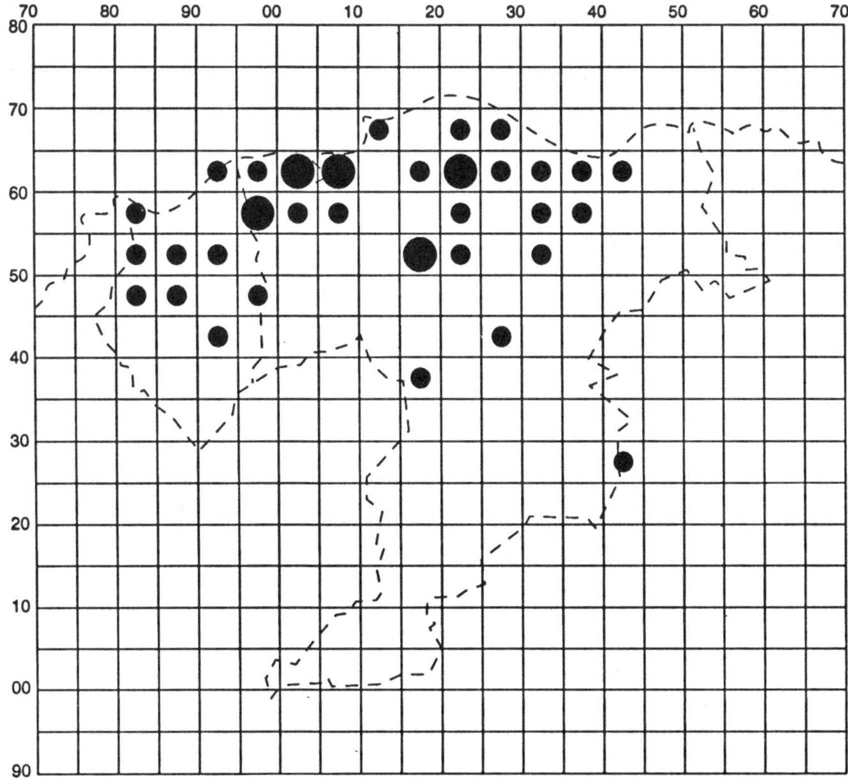

Figure 28 Stock Dove summer distribution 1981–90 (April–July)

but since then the largest flock has been 30 near Kinloss and groups of more than 10 are now rare. The Nairn Bar remains a stronghold; 18 were seen there on 7 July 1978 and there were 23 birds in seven scattered groups on 18 June 1988. An unusual upland report concerned two in the Cabrach at 390m on 14 April 1987.

Woodpigeon

Columba palumbus

Common resident breeder.

Woodpigeons were scarce at the start of last century but had increased greatly by the 1860s. In 1895 they were described as 'often abundant', breeding widely over the lowlands and well up the glens, these birds moving to lower ground in winter.[**3,4**] The great proliferation of forestry in the last 50 years has doubtless lead to further expansion of the breeding population. Today they are common in suitable habitats throughout the Districts, nesting in scrub and woodlands of all types. More unusual nesting sites have included gorse bushes on the heaths near Hopeman, a cliff cave at Covesea and a niche in the wall of Lochindorb Castle. The breeding season is very long with young in the nest as late as 3 October.

In winter, especially in hard weather, huge flocks assemble on lowland farmland, often in brassica fields or snow-free stubbles. Flocks of 1,000–2,000 are not unusual, 5,000–6,000 were at Duffus on 24 December 1988. At this season large movements of Woodpigeons sometimes take place as birds flee severe weather conditions or seek alternative food supplies.

A bird ringed on the Black Isle in September 1986 was shot near Elgin in March 1988.

Collared Dove

Streptopelia decaocto

Common resident breeder.

The first Scottish breeding by Collared Doves took place at Covesea in 1957, when one young fledged on 30 July (SN **69**:188–189). In 1958 one pair reared two broods of two young there and seven were seen on 17 September. The following year they spread to Duffus. In 1960 they bred at Duffus House and Gordonstoun and the first birds were seen in Elgin and Forres.[**66**] On 1 September there were 17 at Covesea.[**67**] In 1961 they arrived in Nairn where breeding probably took place (SB **2**:491) as well as in Forres. Autumn counts elsewhere revealed 35 at Covesea, 27 at Forres, 24 at Gordonstoun and 23 at Duffus. In 1963 there were 67 in Forres and 60 at Covesea, where over 200 were counted the following year.[**60**] Breeding populations in 1964 were estimated at 50–70 pairs at Elgin, 16–25 pairs at Forres, 15–17 pairs at Covesea and at Duffus, 10–12 pairs at Gordonstoun and six to eight pairs at Hopeman. Single pairs were found in Lossiemouth and Alves.[**66**] Other localities colonised in the late 1960s included Keith (present 1965, five to six pairs 1969), Kinloss (first nested 1966, 20 on 23 October 1967) and Buckie (present 1968). By 1970 breeding was noted in Fochabers, Burghead, Mulben and probably Cullen. In the late 1960s/early 1970s large numbers were to be found congregating at favoured feeding areas, e.g. 65 near Elgin, 63 at Urquhart and a remarkable flock of 328 at Covesea on 6 February 1972 (SB **7**:364).

By the late 1970s the population increase had slowed down and even decreases were being reported. During the Winter Atlas period, 1981–4, flocks of more than 13 birds were seen in only five of 33 10km-squares surveyed.[68] Today they breed commonly throughout the Districts as far inland as the Tomintoul area, where two were on the moorland edge at 400m at Glenmullie on 3 June 1989. They almost invariably stay close to human habitation where they can feed around farms, distilleries and on bird tables. Autumn and winter flocks seldom exceed 30; a group of 41 at Keith in February 1988 was the first flock of over 40 to be seen for 11 years.

Ringing indicates that immigration of Collared Doves from the south continued until at least the early 1970s. Birds marked as adults in Hampshire, Cambridgeshire and Perthshire were found dead in Moray between 1972–4. Another, ringed at Newburgh (Grampian) in November 1963, was dead at Hopeman five months later.

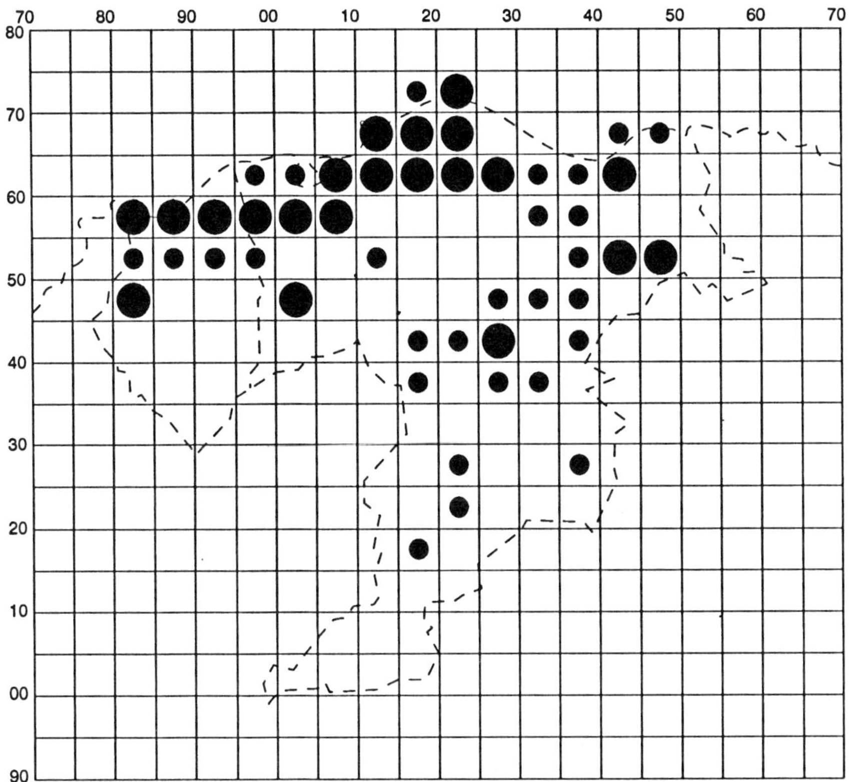

Figure 29 Collared Dove summer distribution 1981–90 (April–July)

Turtle Dove

Streptopelia turtur

Rare visitor on passage.

There have been 17 records; three involved two birds and the rest were singles. Eight of these relate to the period 1844–1887 and seven of the others have been since 1968, most recently one at Mosstodloch on 17 May 1988. The monthly pattern of dated records is shown below:

May	June	July	Aug	Sept	Oct	Nov
3	4	0	2	4	1	1

The occurrences are spread almost evenly between spring (earliest 17 May) and autumn passages. The latest were two (one shot) near Elgin on 6 November 1885.[4] All have been within 7 km of the coast but scattered between Cawdor and Cullen.

Cuckoo

Cuculus canorus

Summer visitor and numerous breeder.

Cuckoos are generally first heard in the Districts during the last week of April or first week of May (the earliest being on 25 April in 1985 and 1987). Their familiar calling quickly becomes a feature of the moorlands and birchwoods in spring and early summer. Here the ubiquitous Meadow Pipit is frequently parasitised and the Cuckoo population can be high, e.g. about 20 adults were seen along 5 km of the Findhorn valley between Banchor and Drynachan on 17 June 1989. Thicker broadleaf and coniferous woodlands, together with agricultural land, hold Cuckoos at a much lower density.

By midsummer when adults have stopped calling they are far more elusive. Most have left the Districts by early August, although young birds are occasionally seen until the end of the month. An adult at Findhorn on 3 September 1978 was unusually late.

Yellow-billed Cuckoo

Coccyzus americanus

Accidental.

One was picked up exhausted in a garden at Caskieben, Nairn on 5 October 1953. This bird, a first-year female, is preserved in the Royal Scottish Museum.[**89**]

Barn Owl

Tyto alba

Scarce resident breeder.

Barn Owls were apparently unknown in Moray and Nairn before *c.*1824 when one was caught at Craigellachie.[**4**] In 1836 one was killed at Pluscarden [**6**] and a pair was introduced at Kilravock, near Cawdor, *c.*1840.[**3**] By 1863 they were still rare but established as breeders in hollow trees, church towers and ruins such as Elgin Cathedral.[**3**] By 1895 they were more widespread though still not common.[**4**]

Today Barn Owls remain very scarce breeders. During the summers of 1968–72 they were reported in only six 10 km-squares [**65**] and proof of breeding was obtained only at Broadley, near Buckie. In winters 1981/2–1983/4 birds were again seen in only six 10 km-squares.[**68**] In 1989 seven nests were found and birds were seen in six other localities; it seems unlikely that the present breeding population much exceeds 25 pairs. Recent nest sites have all been close to agricultural land, mostly in castle ruins or disused farm buildings from sea level to 250m in Glenlivet. In 1938 and 1948–1949 one bird regularly roosted in a coastal cave at Covesea but did not breed. The high proportion of current records which relate to road casualties must reflect a serious strain on a precariously small population.

A chick ringed at Pluscarden in June 1986 was found at Beauly in September 1987 and another, ringed in May 1989 in Nairn District, was dead in Tayside on 23 October 1989.

[Eagle Owl

Bubo bubo]

Probable escape.

St.John was satisfied that an owl described to him, having been seen in woods near Brodie, was of this species.[**3**] Unfortunately no date or supporting evidence is given.

In 1984 a pair was found breeding. One egg was laid but it was later broken and the pair moved to another site nearby. Here they nested again in 1985 and a chick was fledged in June. One of the adults was killed in October but the remaining adult was seen at the nest site on 10 April 1986. This bird continues to survive and has laid an infertile clutch of eggs in 1987 and in each year since then.

Snowy Owl

Nyctea scandiaca

Scarce visitor.

A Snowy Owl was shot on Culbin Sands in spring 1833 and there was another around 1840 on the shore 'near Innes House', presumably close to the Boar's Head Rock.[**6,13**] In December 1892 one was shot at Cawdor [**4**] and another was killed near Covesea lighthouse on 18 June 1917 (SN 1918:274).

Since 1940 there have been summer records from the plateau between Cairn Gorm and Ben Macdui in at least 14 years. Occurrences in this area have been as follows:

1940	1♂ in summer [**76**]
1952	1♂ 19–29 June (SN **64**:176–177)
1953	1♂ 19 July–13 Sept (SN **69**:57)
1963	1 1 June (BB **57**:271)
1964	1 5 June (BB **59**:301)
1965	1♂ 23 April–19 Aug, different bird 8 Aug, 1 stayed until 17 Oct (BB **59**:291)
1966	1 25 June–3 July (BB **60**:322, **61**:362)
1967	1 3 July (BB **61**:362)
1979	1♂ 25 July–29 Aug (BB **74**:479)
1980	1♂ 13 July–31 Aug (BB **74**:479)
1981	1♂ 2 April (SBR 1981)

1984	1 immature ♂ 21 June–1 Oct (BB **78**:561)
1987	1 ♀ 21 June–4 Sept (SBR 1987)
1990	1 ♀ 27 May–18 Aug and 16 Dec (R.Smith)
1991	1 ♀ 15 April (R.Smith)

Elsewhere an adult male was on Corsemaul near Dufftown on 7 January 1953 (SB **2**:99–100). In the mid 1960s one or two Snowy Owls were frequently seen on the moors above Archiestown. Following a single there on 15 November 1964, a male was present on 21 November and a female on 23 November, both staying until 7 February 1965, and the female until 15 March (one bird on 17 March). The male was seen again between 29 August–30 October 1965 (BB **59**:291,301) and the following year one was present between 23 January –3 March (BB **60**:322) and 20 August–23 October (BB **61**:362). In winter 1968/9 one was regularly seen around Roy's Hill near Knockando and presumable the same bird was at Loch Noir on 10 June 1969. In the Cabrach a Snowy Owl was present from 11–25 February 1965 (BB **59**:291) and between 28 October 1965–12 January 1966 (BB **60**:322). A female was there from 24–26 November 1974 (BB **68**:322) and another female between December 1984–April 1985, and again in February–March 1986 (D.Balharry).

Analysis of pellets from the owls on the Cairngorm plateau in 1980 and 1987 showed that 96% of their diet (by weight) was composed of Mountain Hare leverets and Ptarmigan. Other food items recorded were Short-tailed Field Vole, Dotterel chicks and Red Grouse.[**103**]

Tawny Owl

Strix aluco

Numerous resident breeder.

The Tawny was a common owl last century [**4**,**6**] and remains so today. They are found throughout the Districts where suitable woodlands exist including up larger glens, to 400m at Inchrory. Mature deciduous and mixed woods are preferred where ageing trees provide ample holes for nesting. Nest sites are often a limiting factor in plantations and here pairs have been found using old crows' nests, a shelf in a hut and even the floor of a deer-stalking tower. When nest boxes are provided breeding density can be high, e.g. four pairs along a 2 km forest ride in Lossie Forest in 1988. The nesting season usually lasts from late March until June; an exceptionally late nest at Gordonstoun in 1959 contained two small young on 2 October.

The furthest movement shown by ringing is only 11 km, from Ferness to Auldearn, by an owl in its first autumn.

Long-eared Owl

Asio otus

Numerous resident breeder.

Long-eared Owls appear to have been more numerous last century than they are today. In 1844 they were described as 'by far the most abundant owl',[6] they were still common and widely distributed by 1895 [4] and were plentiful around Ardclach in 1900.[27] During the five summers from 1968–72 they were located in 13 out of 33 10 km-squares,[65] suggesting a considerable decline.

Today they appear to be widely but thinly distributed through the Districts as far inland as Tomintoul, where breeding was proved in 1986. Little is known of their true status due, in part, to their strictly nocturnal lifestyle, but young were heard calling in six woods within 6 km of the coast between Forres and Lossiemouth in June/July 1989. Most recent broods have been on the margins of conifer plantations and in relatively isolated small pine woods. Eggs are usually laid in the disused nests of other birds, most commonly crows. In 1936 a pair was found nesting in a hole in the bank of a ditch.

Short-eared Owl

Asio flammeus

Scarce breeder and migrant.

Although there appears to be no published record of breeding before 1939, Short-eared Owls were regular autumn migrants last century, arriving in October on the low ground in the Districts.[**3,4**]

In late May 1939 a nest with six eggs was found at Birkenhill near Elgin (SB **1**:38). Today they are widespread but scarce breeders in heather moorland, young plantations, marshes and occasionally in open country near the coast. Breeding numbers vary from year to year, as vole abundance fluctuates, and from area to area as moorland is ploughed and plantations mature. Between 1968–72 breeding was confirmed or probable in 15 10 km-squares out of 33 surveyed, with birds present, and possible nesting, in a further 12 squares.[**65**] Coastal breeding took place, unsuccessfully, at Kinloss in 1967 and a brood was raised near Hopeman in 1984.

In late summer Short-eared Owls disperse widely from the breeding grounds. In July 1972 one was hunting at 1,200m on the Cairngorm plateau at Cairn Lochan.[**49**] During winter most inland areas are deserted; birds are still seen near the coast but it is uncertain whether these are local birds, northern immigrants or both. Usually only one or two are seen at one time but four were at Loch Spynie on 9 November 1969 and 19 January 1975. Inland breeding territories are reoccupied in March; the earliest were two in the Cabrach on 2 March 1985.

Two siblings from a brood ringed in east Moray were found in quite different directions. One was in Orkney in its first October while the other was dead at Newburgh (Grampian) two autumns later.

(Tengmalm's Owl

Aegolius funereus)

St.John wrote that a bird seen near Elgin and described to him 'could be scarcely of any other species'.[**3**] As there is no further evidence to support this record it is best disregarded.

Nightjar

Caprimulgus europaeus

Former summer visitor and breeder.

In 1844 Nightjars were 'found in summer months about all the larger woods and plantations'.[**6**] In 1895 they still occurred over 'all the area'[**4**] and in Ardclach parish in 1900 they could be heard churring in the evenings 'in most fir woods over the district'.[**27**] Numbers declined in the first half of this century but they were still breeding in coastal heathlands and younger pine plantations, especially Culbin, in the late 1950s. Two pairs were near Fochabers at this time.[**69**] By the late 1960s the decline had accelerated. During the five summers 1968–72 birds were found in only four localities, two in Nairn District (including one at Kildrummie on 28 June 1970) and two in Moray where breeding was proved at Monaughty and may have taken place near Fochabers.[**65**] Since then there has been only one report, of a churring bird near Forres on 25 June 1975 (SB **9**:215).

Swift

Apus apus

Summer visitor and common breeder.

Parties of screaming Swifts dashing around the houses on summer evenings are a familiar feature of towns and villages all over the Districts. They breed from the coast up to 350m altitude in Tomintoul and Chapeltown, Glenlivet.

The first spring arrivals are seen in early May, between 8–14 May in 16 of the last 22 years, earliest on 5 May 1988. Most nests are in the roofs of older buildings such as houses and churches, and occasionally in bridges and other man-made structures. Coastal cliff nesting was also reported in the 1950s. During and after the breeding season, especially in bad weather, large numbers may gather to feed low over fresh water, particularly at Loch Spynie where there were 220 on 18 June 1987. On 12 August 1991 500 were hawking insects over newly-mown fields at Mosstodloch. In fine weather they may feed high over the mountains, e.g. 10 over Ben Macdui on 31 August 1973.[**49**] Most depart in late August but a few remain until mid September. The latest records are of one near Elgin in October 1904 [**53**] and two in Buckie on the remarkable date of 6 November 1985 (SBR 1985).

Alpine Swift

Apus melba

Accidental.

One was seen over Buckie harbour on 27 May 1972 (BB **66**:344).

Kingfisher

Alcedo atthis

Scarce visitor and occasional breeder.

Since the middle of last century there have been occasional reports of Kingfishers wandering to Moray and Nairn. The first recorded occurrence was at Forres, prior to 1845,[**13**] and there was another around the mouth of the River Findhorn about 1863.[**3**] In the same year, on 18 August, one was seen on the Black Burn, Pittendreich near Elgin.[**7**] In 1874 one was on the River Nairn at Newton of Budgate [**7**] and there was a sighting near Moy in the late 1870s.[**4**] Two birds were reported in 1884, one on the River Fiddich near Craigellachie in May and one, shot on the Moy Burn at Dalvey in summer, whose skin was subsequently used to adorn a hat![**4**] In 1891 one was caught in a tennis net at Brodie and there was a record from Cullen around this time.[**4**] In 1893 there was a single on the Spey at Boat o' Brig [**4**] and one was shot on the Findhorn in July 1896.[**27**] There follows a dearth of records for much of this century, except for one at Fochabers and Rothes in late October/early November 1921 (SN 1922:120). Doubtless others were seen but records were not kept.

Since 1974 Kingfishers have occurred almost annually, usually singly and one or two per year. It seems likely that, in some instances, the same individual has been involved in more than one record so the total number of birds is unclear. Reports have come from the following areas (singles unless indicated):

River Findhorn (Darnaway–Findhorn Bay)	Sept 1974, March 1976, Oct–Nov 1977, May 1979, May–July 1985 (2), Oct 1986–Feb 1987, Jan 1989, Sept 1990.
River Spey (Rothes–Kingston)	Nov 1975, Sept 1981, Dec 1984, Sept–Oct 1986, Sept 1989–Dec 1990 (at Aberlour in April 1990), Jan–Feb 1991.
River Deveron (Rothiemay)	Oct 1975, Aug–Sept 1990
River Isla (Grange)	Pair summered 1977 and 1978 and may have attempted to breed (SB **10**:140). Single, autumn 1990.
River Nairn (Nairn)	Sept 1981
River Fiddich (Dufftown)	2 for 2–3 years in the mid 1980s, 1 until at least 18 June 1986.
River Lossie (estuary)	Aug 1986
(Elgin)	July 1990
Portknockie harbour	15 Oct 1988

In 1991 a pair nested beside the River Spey at Craigellachie and reared at least one young (MNBR 1991).

(Bee-eater

Merops apiaster)

Baxter and Rintoul gave a record of a Bee-eater killed at Lossiemouth in October 1853.[**2**] This, however, appears to be an error as Gordon, writing in 1889, made no mention of it and included instead a Hoopoe killed at Lossiemouth in that month.[**7**]

Roller

Coracius garrulus

Accidental.

One was shot at Ballindalloch Castle on 30 August 1831 and placed in Elgin Museum.[**7,53**] Another report, of a bird seen at Upper Manbeen (near Miltonduff) in summer 1857,[**7**] was considered to be unreliable by Harvie-Brown and Buckley.[4] In 1868 one was shot by a gamekeeper in the Elgin Oakwood.[**100**]

More recently one stayed at Garrowood, Grange from 29 May–3 June 1974 (BB **68**:323).

Hoopoe

Upupa epops

Rare visitor.

Twelve Hoopoes have been seen in Moray but only two in Nairn. All records are shown below:

1 killed Lossiemouth	Oct 1853
1 shot near Loch Spynie	26 April 1902 (ASNH **12**:149)
1 Drybridge	22 May 1975 (SB **9**:216)
1 Leuchars near Elgin	28 Aug–12 Sept 1977 (SB **10**:141)
1 Fochabers	14–16 Oct 1981 (SBR 1981)
1 Drybridge/Buckpool	9–late Oct 1982 (SBR 1982)
1 Covesea	12 May 1983 (SBR 1983)
1 near Buckie	summer 1983 (J.Legge)
1 Buckie	4 June 1984 (SBR 1984)
1 Auldearn	29–30 April 1987 (SBR 1987)
1 Westerfolds near Duffus	5 May 1989
1 Monaughty near Alves	12 Sept 1989
1 Elgin	29 Sept 1990
1 Nairn	18 Oct–14 April 1991

The overwintering bird in Nairn in 1990/1 was remarkable, even in a national context.

(Wryneck

Jynx torquilla)

There are two old records, neither of which is very satisfactory. St.John claimed to have seen a Wryneck in the woods at Dulsie but gave no date or further details.[**3**] A report of one shot at Gordon Castle, Fochabers on 12 January 1814 [**4**] seems highly questionable in view of the date.

Green Woodpecker

Picus viridus

Rare resident breeder.

Following their northward spread across Scotland in the last 30–40 years, Green Woodpeckers have been seen annually in the Districts since 1977. Before then there were only two records, a bird near Fochabers in winter 1949–50 and another at Pluscarden in early summer 1974. In the period 1977–90 they were reported in 14 localities, but regularly only around Loch Spynie (annually 1985–9), Pluscarden (1983, 1985–6, 1988–90), Burgie (annually 1978–83), Arndilly (1980–1, 1985, 1988) and the upper Spey valley between Blacksboat and Hill of Dalnapot (1978, 1984, 1989–90). The number of localities providing records each year since 1970 is shown in the histogram below. The sudden increase in 1988–90 may be due, at least partly, to fieldwork for the Breeding Atlas.

In 1985 breeding was proved for the first time, at Pluscarden. In 1989 two pairs bred, one raised a brood near Pluscarden and in the upper Findhorn valley birds were heard in two sites in May/June with a nest found in one of them, which unfortunately failed. Birds were seen or heard in six other areas during spring and summer 1989. At Pluscarden the 1989 nest hole was reoccupied in 1990 but soon taken over by Starlings. It seems likely that a small regular

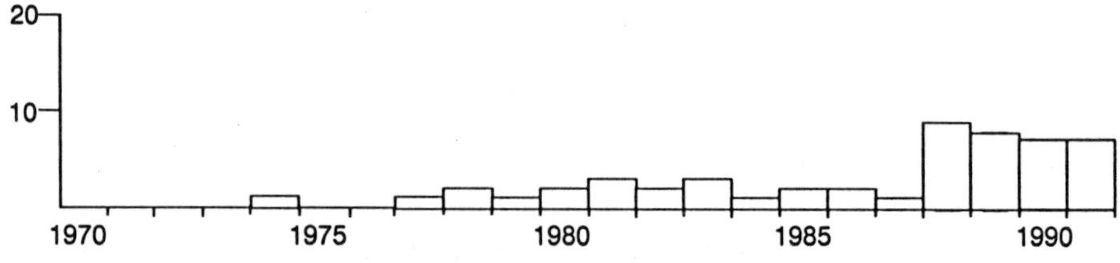

Figure 30 Green Woodpecker summer localities 1970–91

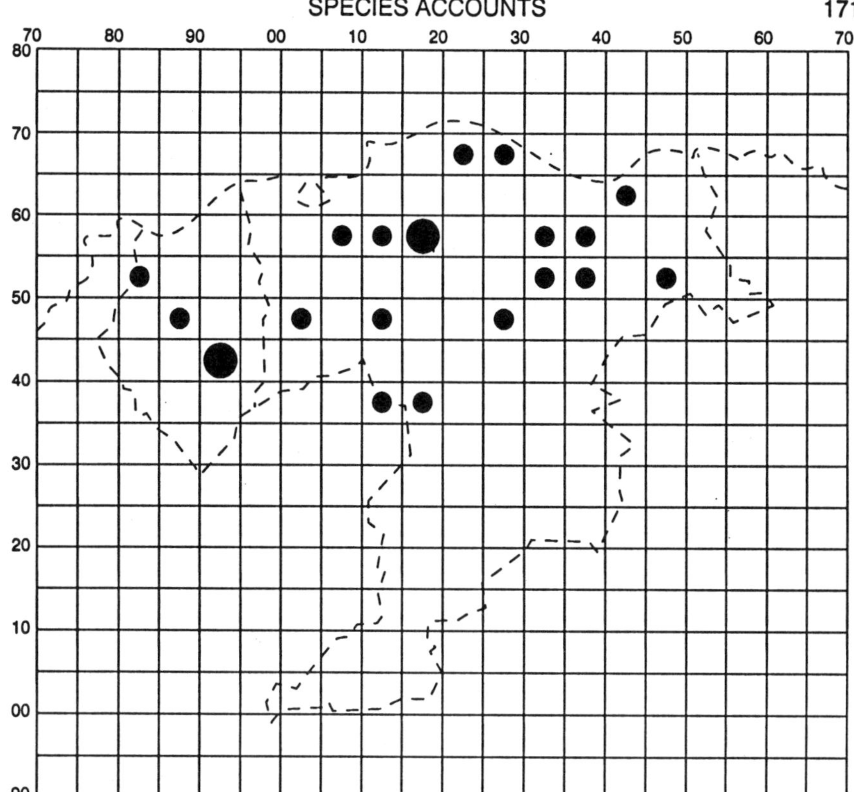

Figure 31 Green Woodpecker summer distribution 1981–90 (April–July)

breeding population has become established since the early 1980s.

Most Green Woodpeckers are seen in deciduous or mixed woodland, although a few have been reported passing through open agricultural land with only scattered trees. One of the 1989 nests was in a mature birchwood, the other among large deciduous trees on the edge of a mature conifer plantation.

Great Spotted Woodpecker

Dendrocopos major

Numerous resident breeder.

This was once a common species but declined in the first half of the last century. They still bred at Darnaway in the 1830s [2] but died out

PLATE 22 Great Spotted Woodpecker approaching nest hole *(John Edelsten)*

completely from Moray and Nairn during 1841–51.[70] During the next 50 years there was only one summer record, between Aberlour and Carron on 15 May 1884.[4] Winter birds were seen at Pluscarden in February 1862 and November 1898 and there were several in the Districts in 1868.[7,100] One was shot at Rothiemay in February 1903 and another near Fochabers on 12 December that year. There had been no further summer records by 1908 [71] but breeding took place once more in 1924 at Pluscarden and Altyre (SN 1925:76) and was proved in Nairn District in 1927 (SN 1928:109).

Today they are common breeders in larger tracts of mature woodland. In middle-aged plantations birds are often present in winter but leave to find nest sites in larger trees in the spring. Nest boxes may be used for roosting when natural holes are scarce, as in Lossie Forest, the birds enlarging the hole to gain entry.

(Lesser Spotted Woodpecker

Dendrocopos minor)

A pair was claimed to have been seen at Arndilly on 14–20 April 1922. Another observer, who apparently knew the species in England, also saw the birds in the second week of April. Between June–August they were lower down the Spey and there were four or five at Aikenway in September (SN 1923:68). Some caution must be attached to this series of records in view of the fact that Great Spotted Woodpeckers were only beginning to recolonise at the time and so would not have been familiar locally, possibly leading to confusion between the two species.

Skylark

Alauda arvensis

Common breeder and migrant.

Skylarks were abundant in the mid nineteenth century [6] but apparently became scarcer by 1900.[4,27] They are now common breeders once more throughout the Districts and one of the first species to commence song in the milder days of late winter. They breed in all types of open country such as coastal dunes and bars, arable land, moorlands and even high mountain plateaux. Upland areas are mostly deserted by October and reoccupied in the following February or March, the earliest noted return to the Cabrach being on 4 February 1988.

In midwinter significant numbers of Skylarks are seen only near the coast where flocks of 30 are not unusual; the highest count (on the ground) is 200 feeding near Findhorn Bay on 26 January 1984. In severe weather large-scale movements may take place, e.g. 1,500 flying west over Kinloss on 6 February 1970. These flocks may well contain many Continental immigrants; during freezing conditions on 12 February 1963 flocks of 220, 190, 95 and 35 Skylarks flew in off the sea from the north-east at Nairn in only ten minutes (SB **2**:381). The winter destination of local Skylarks is uncertain.

Shore Lark

Eremophila alpestris

Rare visitor in winter and on passage.

The only records are from the Moray coast in six years between 1972–80:

2 Lossiemouth	26 Nov 1972 (SB **7**:367)
1 Spey Bay	12 May 1973 (SB **8**:258)
1 Spey Bay	8–29 Feb 1976 (SB **10**:103)
1 Spey Bay	19 Oct 1977 (SB **10**:141)
3 Lossiemouth	21 April 1978 (SBR 1978)
1 Spey Bay	3–20 Jan 1980 (SBR 1980)

Sand Martin

Riparia riparia

Summer visitor and common breeder.

Sand Martins were very numerous last century; in 1895 they were the commonest hirundines 'swarming all along the valleys' in suitable sites. A colony with 823 occupied holes was counted on the Findhorn near Forres, and many other colonies were mentioned along the Spey, Avon and Fiddich.[**4**] They continued to be 'very abundant' in the 1950s [**2**] and 1960s; in 1965 there was a colony of 560 pairs on the Spey near Fochabers.[**72**] In the late 1960s, in common with the rest of Britain, Sand Martin numbers declined and many colonies became seriously depleted or vacant. By the late 1970s some recovery had taken place with colonies of 225 pairs in Glen Rinnes (1977), 92 pairs near Keith (1976), 86 pairs at Fochabers (1976) and 85 pairs near Forres (1981). In the early/mid 1980s a further decline was evident but since 1986 numbers have once again begun to improve. In 1988–91 there were 44 known colonies of the following sizes:

Apparently occupied holes	*Number of colonies*
100+	1*
50–99	3
20–49	13
10–19	15
less than 10	12

* the largest colony, beside the Spey 2 km above Rothes, contained 152 holes in 1989, before the bank became unsuitable and numbers fell.

The average first spring date for arrivals in recent years has been 15 April, the earliest being 29 March 1989, but in poor springs the main arrival may be delayed until the end of the month. The earliest ever record was on 14 March 1880.[**4**] Colonies are usually located in sand pits or river banks close to water, although 10 pairs near Urquhart in 1988 were 2 km from the nearest water. Colony altitude range from a dune cliff facing the sea at Kinloss up to at least 300m near Tomintoul. On 6 July 1990 three birds were flying over Garbh Uisge Beag in the Cairngorms at *c.*1,000m.

At the end of the breeding season flocks can be seen hawking low over lochs for insects, e.g. 200 at Loch Spynie on 7 August 1984. They often roost communally in reed beds with Swallows. Most leave during August with small numbers staying into early September. Latest were singles at Elgin on 8 October 1980 and at Fochabers on 12 November 1892 (ASNH **2**:155).

There have been 15 recoveries of Sand Martins ringed in Moray and Nairn. Those showing movement out of Scotland were in Humberside

(September), Cambridgeshire (August (two), September), Hampshire (July), Kent (September), northern France (July, August (two)) and Morocco (March). Ringing elsewhere in Britain has produced over 40 movements into the Districts including 24 from southern England and one from Wales.

Swallow

Hirundo rustica

Summer visitor and common breeder.

Swallows are common throughout the Districts where human habitation has provided suitable nesting sites, from the bothy on Nairn Bar to Loch Builg Lodge at an altitude of 490m.

The first spring arrivals are usually seen between 10–20 April but there are two March records, 23 March in 1968 (a bird ringed in Cape Province, South Africa on 17 March 1967)[**60**] and 24 March in 1982. The main arrival depends on prevailing weather conditions and may not be until late April or early May. Nests are mostly built in farm steadings, ruined houses and garages, although almost any kind of building may be used. In 1973 a thorough survey of 10 km-square NJ 46 (Buckie area) revealed a breeding density of 0.66 pairs/km^2 of land.[**73**] First clutches are laid in late May and second clutches in July with late broods in the nest until early September. Occasional birds visit the high mountain tops, e.g. singles in the Cairngorms at 1,200m in June 1964 and on 24 June 1977.[**49**] After the breeding season, Swallows gather prior to migration, often resting on telephone wires in groups of 100 or more. Large communal roosts form in reedbeds at this time, especially at Loch Spynie where 5,000–10,000 assemble each evening in late August/early September. By the end of September most Swallows have left but stragglers remain into October and there were November records in seven years during the period 1974–89; the latest were singles at Lossiemouth on 22 November in 1981 and 1987.

Ringing at the Loch Spynie roost in August and September has resulted in recoveries, in the same autumn, in Yorkshire (41 days later), Humberside (10 days) and Lincolnshire (21 and 37 days). Another was caught the following May on the Forties Delta rig in the North Sea. Birds marked at other local sites have been found in France (April), Spain (October) and South Africa (March). Eighteen ringed Swallows have moved into the area but (apart from the South African bird found in 1968) none came from further than Yorkshire.

House Martin

Delichon urbica

Summer visitor and common breeder.

Small groups of five to ten nests of House Martins are a fairly common sight under the eaves of buildings throughout the Districts up to 350m, in the Braes of Glenlivet where there were 15 nests on the Distillery in 1990. In 1989 the largest known colony, at Buckie High School, held exactly 50 nests and there were at least 30 occupied nests on a small bungalow near Aultmore. They also breed under bridges and on the coastal cliffs at Portknockie (max. 15 nests in 1986).

Earliest spring sightings are sometimes in late April (the earliest being 12 April in 1988) but in 13 of the last 19 years no House Martins were reported before May (average arrival on 5 May). The late start to breeding results in second brood chicks still in the nest in September; the latest was on 20 September 1984 in Aberlour. After the breeding season quite large gatherings can be seen feeding over freshwater (e.g. 200 at Loch Spynie on 16 August 1986) and resting on telephone wires, e.g. 190 at Clochan on 6 September 1987, where they do not even nest. They do not join with other hirundines to roost communally in reedbeds in late summer. Most have left by the end of September, but October reports are common and there are several November records, the latest being two at Burghead on 15 November 1984.

A pure albino martin at Loch Flemington on 27 July 1989 was either this species or Sand Martin.

Richard's Pipit

Anthus novaeseelandiae

Accidental.

There have been four records involving four or five birds:

1 Whiteness Head	16–21 Jan 1972 narrowly crossed the Nairn District boundary (SB **7**:378)
1 Findhorn Bay	4–9 Oct 1987 (SBR 1987)
2 Kingston	17–18 Nov 1988, one remaining until at least 22 Nov (SBR 1988)
1 Kingston	26 Feb–2 March 1989. In view of the remarkable

coincidence of locality it seems possible, although rather unlikely, that one of the Nov 1988 Kingston birds overwintered without being detected.

It is extraordinary that two out of four records should involve birds in January and February, a period when this regular vagrant to Britain is extremely rare nationally.

Tawny Pipit

Anthus campestris

Accidental.

One was seen on Spey Bay golf course on 22 August 1988 (SBR 1988).

Tree Pipit

Anthus trivialis

Summer visitor and numerous breeder.

Tree Pipits have colonised Moray and Nairn within the last 100 years. They were unknown in the 1860s but nests were found at Aberlour and Forres in 1885.[4] Since that time they have become locally common in inland areas.

Breeding today takes place in open deciduous woodlands, such as hillside birchwoods, and also in young plantations where a few mature pines or birches remain. Arrival usually takes place in late April or the beginning of May; the earliest was one near Dufftown on 9 April 1988. Most have left by early September.

Meadow Pipit

Anthus pratensis

Common breeder and migrant.

Over much of the uplands the Meadow Pipit is by far the commonest breeding passerine. They range up to the Cairngorm plateau where 150 were once seen feeding together on a 2,700m^2 snow patch near the summit of Ben Macdui in mid August. They are also abundant on the lower hills and heather moorlands, on rough pasture and in the youngest conifer plantations. They nest at much lower densities in the lowland agricultural belt and not uncommonly on wilder parts of the coast.

In late summer birds start to leave upland breeding areas and large passage movements may occur at the coast e.g. thousands at Kinloss 11–12 August 1970. Inland numbers decline further during autumn and very few remain after December. Most leave Moray and Nairn completely in mid winter, although some remain near the coast feeding along beaches and on salt marshes. A count of 300 at Nairn on 3 February 1983 was exceptional. Spring return to the moorlands begins in mid March and continues into April.

A nestling ringed at Kinloss in July 1979 was found at Kintore (Grampian) in August 1980.

Rock Pipit

Anthus petrosus

Scarce resident breeder.

A common coastal species whose main distribution coincides closely with the rocky shores of Moray, between Burghead and Lossiemouth and between Buckie and Cullen. Nests are situated among rocks and in crevices in cliffs and harbour walls. In 1986 one was built in a disused boat at Portgordon.

In winter birds forage along the tide line or in the intertidal zone. Recent counts revealed 57 between Portgordon and Strathlene on 16 December 1990 and 23 between Lossiemouth and Covesea on 31 December 1986.

Yellow Wagtail

Motacilla flava

Rare migrant.

A Yellow Wagtail was seen near Elgin in 1835 [**4**] and St.John reported seeing them two or three times but gave no details.[**3**] There are no further records until 1968; recent sightings have been as follows:

1 Covesea	24 April*, 7 May* and 19 Sept 1968
1 Speymouth	1–2 May 1970*
1 Buckpool	28 July* and 7 Aug 1973
1 Speymouth	19 May 1973
1 Forres	19 April 1976*
1 ♂ Speymouth	31 May–6 June 1976+
1 Speymouth	7 Aug 1977
1 ♀ Speymouth	26 May 1978
1 Speymouth	31 Aug 1980
2 ♂♂ near Lossiemouth	1 May 1983*

Birds marked * were of the British breeding race *M.f.flavissima*, the one marked + was of the Continental race *M.f.flava* (Blue-headed Wagtail). The others were not subspecifically identified.

Grey Wagtail

Motacilla cinerea

Summer visitor and numerous breeder. Scarce in winter.

Grey Wagtails, together with Dippers and Common Sandpipers, are one of the most characteristic species of fast flowing waters in summer. They inhabit rivers and stony streams from sea level to at least 500m altitude, sometimes breeding alongside small burns less than 1 m wide. Most unusual was the bird at 1,215m on Cairn Lochan on 21 May 1981.[**49**] Nests are usually built in banks, under bridges or in crevices in waterside stonework.

In late summer small flocks may feed together in favoured areas, the highest count being 15 at Garmouth on 15 August 1976, but during September most leave the Districts for the winter. November–February records inland are rare, although a few remain near the coast. Breeding territories are reoccupied from mid March, later in the uplands.

Two birds ringed here in summer have been recovered in Tayside, in April and July of later years.

Pied Wagtail

Motacilla alba

Common breeder and migrant.

Pied Wagtails are widespread and common in summer, breeding from sea level high into the glens at 500m or more. Nest sites include farm steadings, derelict buildings and rock crevices. They frequently use roadside walls and grassy banks, feeding on the road surface where insects are easily visible. In July 1989 individuals were seen on three dates on the Cairngorm/Ben Macdui plateau at *c.*1,100m and others were there in April, May and July 1990.

In late summer they congregate in communal roosts, using sites such as reedbeds, unharvested cereals, potato fields and trees. Often 100 or more birds may be present; the highest recent counts are 700 at Kinloss on 3 August 1981, 450 at Forres on 2 October 1987, and 325 at Garmouth on 12 August 1988. In September 1984 up to 140 roosted in a sycamore tree in the centre of Cullen. During September and October most Pied Wagtails leave Moray and Nairn. Their destinations are indicated by winter recoveries in southern Scotland and in England (Lancashire, Cheshire, Avon, Dorset and Buckinghamshire) of birds ringed at Kingston and at Pooltown, 1 km west of the Nairn District boundary. Others, marked in southern England (three), northern England (three) and Wales, have been found in the Districts during summer. Very small numbers overwinter locally inland, although more remain near the coast. Spring return is in March and early April.

Migrants of the Continental and Icelandic race *M.a.alba* (White Wagtail) occur in small numbers near the coast, mostly in late April (the earliest being 5 April in 1969) and early May (the latest on 13 May in 1987). The largest group was 18 at Strathlene, Buckie on 3 May 1987. On 6 May 1987 one was at 1,000m on Stac an Fharaidh, Cairngorm. Fewer are seen in autumn (max. four at Lossiemouth on 10 September 1987).

Waxwing

Bombycilla garrulus

Irruptive winter visitor, numerous in some years.

Waxwings visit Moray and Nairn irregularly. They may be quite numerous in one winter and then very few will be seen for several years. Since 1945 they have occurred in 29 out of 47 winters but in significant numbers only in 1946/7, 1957/8, 1959/60, 1961/2, 1963/4, 1965/6, 1966/7, 1970/1, 1972/3, 1974/5, 1975/6, 1988/9, 1990/1 and 1991/2. Biggest invasion years were 1946/7 (nearly 1,000 in the Districts) and 1965/6 (500–600 between Forres and Findhorn on 12 December). Arrival of the first Waxwings has varied between early October (the earliest were two at Buckie on 7 October 1970) and early December (1965). Flocks often feed in town gardens on Cotoneaster and hawthorn berries or rose hips although a wide range of other wild and ornamental fruits has been taken on occasion. Apples, including windfalls, sometimes prove attractive. Where food is plentiful a flock may linger for a week or more, the customary tameness of the birds affording excellent views. Three birds caught at Forres on 24 March 1987 had been ringed at Lossiemouth two months previously, but most pass through the Districts much more swiftly than this. Few are seen after the end of March, but there have been five April records and three in May (20 at Elgin on 5 May 1989, one at Forres on 8 May 1975 and one at Kinloss on 18 May 1971).

A Waxwing ringed at Oulu, Finland on 8 October 1972 was found in Forres on 1 December that year. In December 1980 a bird marked in Golspie was in Forres six days later.

Dipper

Cinclus cinclus

Numerous resident breeder.

Dippers occur widely on most fast flowing rivers and streams. They breed from sea level (even feeding on the beach near Portgordon) to an altitude of about 600m. During 1959–64 the behaviour and breeding of the species was studied by Raymond Hewson on the River Isla at Towiemore, near Keith.[**74,106**] He found that nest building started in February and eggs were laid from mid March until early April. Second clutches were started 5–14 days after the fledging of the first brood. Most nests were built on ledges and crevices below bridges, a common practice throughout the Districts. Overhanging banks and waterside rock faces are also common sites.

After becoming independent, young birds disperse from their parents' territories. They even appear on high altitude streams on the Cairngorm plateau, as high as 1,200m on Garbh Uisg Mor on 6 August 1983. When possible lowland Dippers remain on territory throughout the winter, but upland pairs move downstream if the water freezes over.

In the middle of the last century they were widely persecuted in lowland Moray for predating salmon and trout spawn and were almost wiped out in some areas.[**27**]

Wren

Troglodytes troglodytes

Common resident breeder.

Few parts of Moray and Nairn are without Wrens. Although densities are highest in woodland, including forestry plantations, they also breed commonly in mature gardens and on farmland where hedges and copses provide cover. They inhabit boulderfields and broken cliffs in the hills as well as gullies and scrubby banks on moorland. At the coast they can be watched foraging along the shore and among the rocks. Most birds appear to remain close to their breeding areas in winter, when severe weather causes population crashes. Numbers, however, can quickly recover in a run of good years. The number of pairs holding territory in 58 hectares of farmland at Clochan between 1977–85 is shown below:

1977	1978	1979	1980	1981	1982	1983	1984	1985
3	6	2	4	8	3	6	0	1

The highest count yet made was 31 in three hours in the Bin of Cullen pinewoods on 11 December 1983.

Dunnock

Prunella modularis

Common resident breeder.

Throughout the year Dunnocks can be found commonly in gardens, farmland, young plantations and scrub, wherever there is dense vegetation below which they can feed. They have been found nesting in juniper scrub up to 500m altitude near Loch Builg but are generally absent from moorland. Outwith the breeding season, they are normally encountered singly or in small groups but sometimes larger loose gatherings may occur where feeding is good, e.g. *c.*20 in a weedy field at Clochan in December 1981.

No locally-ringed Dunnock has been recovered more than 4 km from its place of ringing.

Robin

Erithacus rubecula

Common resident breeder and migrant.

The Robin is a familiar and common breeding bird in all types of woodlands, especially those with a well-developed shrub layer. They are scarcer in mature plantations and grazed birchwoods. They also nest in shrubby gardens and similar habitats around farms, villages and towns. Song can be heard throughout the year, especially in late winter and spring and again in autumn when both sexes establish separate winter territories. A huge variety of nest sites is used including holes in trees, vegetated banks and rock faces as well as disused buildings, garden sheds, nest boxes and many other man-made structures.

An unknown number of Robins move through the Districts in spring and autumn and doubtless some Continental migrants arrive on the coast in autumn. Unusually large numbers of Robins were at Speymouth on 31 October 1976. In 1989 20–30 were heard passing over Elgin on the night of 27–28 October and 13 were on the beach near Portgordon on 29 October.

There have been 28 recoveries of locally-ringed Robins but only one has moved out of the Districts, a first-year bird caught at Clochan on 2 September 1990 and retrapped on Caldey Island (south Wales) less than seven weeks later. Two immigrants have been found here, in July 1973 (ringed near Aberdeen in October 1970) and in April 1986 (ringed Kirkcolm, Dumfries and Galloway in September 1985), the latter possible a returning Continental migrant.

Nightingale

Luscinia megarhynchos

Accidental.

A juvenile was trapped and ringed at Loch Spynie on 10 August 1988 (SBR 1988).

Bluethroat

Luscinia svecica

Rare migrant.

There have been five records involving birds of both races:

1	Hopeman	15 Sept 1890 (ASNH **2**:113)
1 ♂	Orton	20 March 1975+ (SB **9**:224)
1 ♂	Miltonduff	late May 1987* (SBR 1987)
1 ♂	found dead Feith Buidhe, Cairngorm plateau (this bird was definitely in Moray contra SBR 1987)	23 May 1987*
1 ♂	Portgordon	14 May 1989

Birds marked * were of the Red-spotted race (*L.s.svecica*) and the individual marked + was of the White-spotted race (*L.s.cyanecula*). The other two were not subspecifically identified.

Black Redstart

Phoenicurus ochruros

Rare migrant.

There are a few doubtful reports from the last century but otherwise records are as follows:

1 ♀/immature	shot Aulthash (near Fochabers)	30 Oct 1903 [**54**] (ASNH **13**:55)
1 ♀	Covesea	16 April 1972 (SB **7**:373)
1 ♀	Lossiemouth	23 April 1977
1 ♀	near Nairn	19–23 Dec 1978
1 ♀/immature	Ben Rinnes	26 April 1984 (SBR 1984)
1 ♂	Kingston	8 April 1987 (SBR 1987)
1 ♂	near Dulsie Bridge	20 May 1989

Redstart

Phoenicurus phoenicurus

Summer visitor and numerous breeder.

Redstarts were considered to be rare breeders in the Districts in the mid nineteenth century [**3,6**] but were widely distributed in birch woods by 1895.[**4**] In 1891 they were especially numerous up the valleys of the Findhorn, Spey and Avon as far as Inchrory and Glen Builg, but in 1892 there were many fewer.[**4**] In 1900 they were 'pretty common' around Ardclach.[**27**] Between 1891–5 a pair nested in a roadside letterbox at Airdrie near Ferness.

Today Redstarts are rare in the arable lowlands but widely dispersed in the wooded uplands, although usually at low density. In eastern Moray they are very scarce but they become more numerous in the west of the Districts, e.g. along the upper Findhorn where they were found in at least 16 localities in 1988. A minimum of six males were singing between Banchor and Drynachan

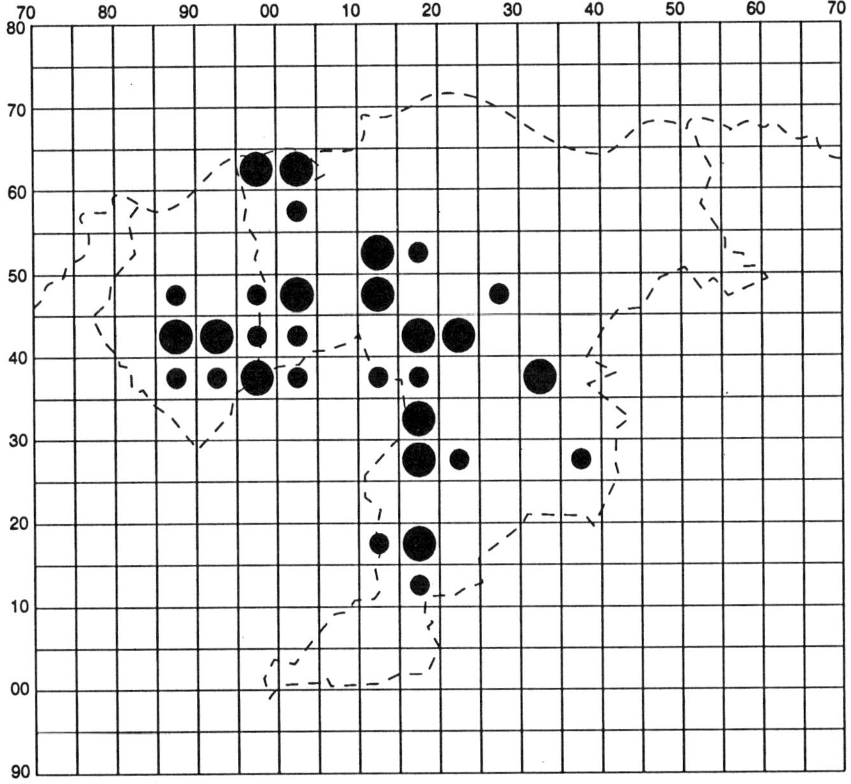

Figure 32 Redstart distribution 1981–90 (April–July)

in 1989. Most occupy open birchwoods and mixed deciduous woodland along river valleys where nests are usually in holes in trees. On 26 July 1991 a male was seen near Feith Buidhe on the Cairngorm plateau.

They arrive in late April or early May (the earliest was one at Fochabers on 23 April 1902) and few remain inland after August. Migrants are only occasionally seen at the coast; the most together were five at Findhorn on 13 August 1967, and the latest was a female at Kingston on 13 October 1988.

Whinchat

Saxicola rubetra

Summer visitor and numerous breeder.

An upland species, over much of its range, inhabiting open country usually with tussocky grass or sometimes heather, and with shrubs or small trees to provide prominent perches, Whinchats are generally only thinly distributed up the glens in gorse or juniper scrub, often in damp areas. In good habitat several pairs may breed close together e.g. four pairs in 1,500m of Glen Latterach in 1989.[**92**] They also occupy young plantations until the trees grow together. One male was singing on the Nairn Bar on 26 May 1989. One was seen at Garbh Uisg Beag on the Cairngorm plateau on 25 May 1991.

Most arrive in late April and early May (the earliest was one at Dulsie on 25 April 1987) and have left breeding areas by September. The latest on the coast was one at Spey Bay on 16 October 1981.

Stonechat

Saxicola torquata

Scarce resident breeder.

Formerly a widespread and locally common breeder, both at the coast and inland, Stonechats have recently become very scarce. At the end of the last century they were 'comparatively common' in Glenlivet and Glen Avon [**4**] and there were about six pairs in Ardclach parish alone.[**27**] On the coastal heaths between Hopeman and Covesea they were still very common in the 1930s, but the population fell to two pairs in 1945 before recovering to six or

eight pairs in the early 1960s. There were still six pairs there in 1985 and four in 1986–7. Only a single bird was seen in 1988 and 1989, but five pairs nested in 1990, and four pairs in 1991.

Between 1968–72 breeding was proved in every coastal 10 km-square except NH 85 and 95 and there were probably at least 30–40 pairs in the Districts. Their main habitat was the extensive gorse-covered heaths close to the seashore; most inland pairs also bred in gorse scrub, in gulleys and on the moorland edge. During the 1980s a marked decline took place, with last breeding probably occurring at Spey Bay and Kingston in 1984, Delnies in 1985 and Culbin Bar and Buckpool in 1986. The main cause of the decline appears to be severe winter weather, although in some areas clearance of gorse scrub may have played a part. Inland numbers declined much earlier, although seven pairs were located at four sites in 1977, including one pair at 305m in the Cabrach. Around Glen Latterach there were four pairs in 1976, three in 1977, two in 1979–81 and only one pair bred in 1983. During the next five years the only inland breeding took place at Auchness near Dallas (1980) and, probably, at Cairn Eney (1988). In summer 1989 came a remarkable, and very welcome, increase in inland Stonechats with at least 13 pairs located. A wide range of moorland scrub sites was occupied, ranging from Carn Ghiubhais to Glen Latterach and Ben Rinnes. Curiously there was no corresponding revival in coastal haunts; the only pair located bred successfully at Portknockie. In 1990 there were also thirteen pairs in inland localities and, encouragingly, at least eight pairs bred on the coast.

Most inland Stonechats appear to leave their territories in winter for unknown destinations, although some birds remain (e.g. one pair on Ben Rinnes on 27 December 1989).

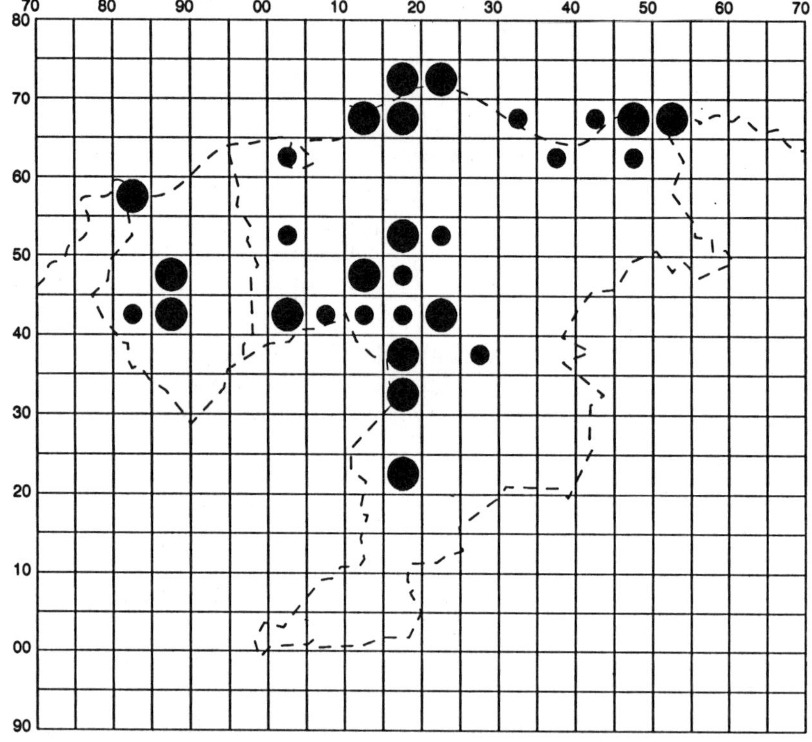

Figure 33 Stonechat summer distribution 1981–90 (April–July)

Wheatear

Oenanthe oenanthe

Summer visitor and numerous breeder.

A common upland breeding species which occurs more widely through the Districts on passage, especially in autumn. They are comparatively scarce on the eastern Moray moors, breeding thinly along the glens where close-cropped vegetation provides feeding areas. In western Moray and upper Nairn they are much more numerous, especially where rocky areas coincide with short turf. Their range extends high into the mountains up to the summit plateaux of

Ben Avon and the Cairngorms where, with Meadow Pipits, they are the only common breeding passerines. Formerly there were good numbers along the coastal dunes, nesting in rabbit holes, but suitable habitat is now much reduced by afforestation and only a very few pairs continue to breed at the coast, e.g. two pairs on Nairn Bar in 1987 and one pair at Strathlene in 1990.

Spring arrival of local breeders is mostly in early April with birds appearing directly on the breeding grounds; the earliest recorded was one at Edinkillie on 24 March 1989. Few are usually on the coast at this time (the earliest being one at Speymouth on 25 March 1989) but larger numbers are seen there in late April/early May and these are probably more northerly breeders passing through; peak counts have been 100 at Kinloss on 11 May 1976 and 40 near Hopeman on 13 May 1989. In autumn, breeding grounds are deserted in August and September (the latest were three at Loch of Boath on 6 October 1987) with coastal passage usually strongest in August and early September. Peak autumn counts were 73 at Kinloss on 6 August 1967 and 41 at Delnies on 18 August 1987. There are occasional October reports in most years; the latest was one at Lossiemouth on 10 November 1976, probably a bird of the Greenland race, *O.o.leucorrhoea*.

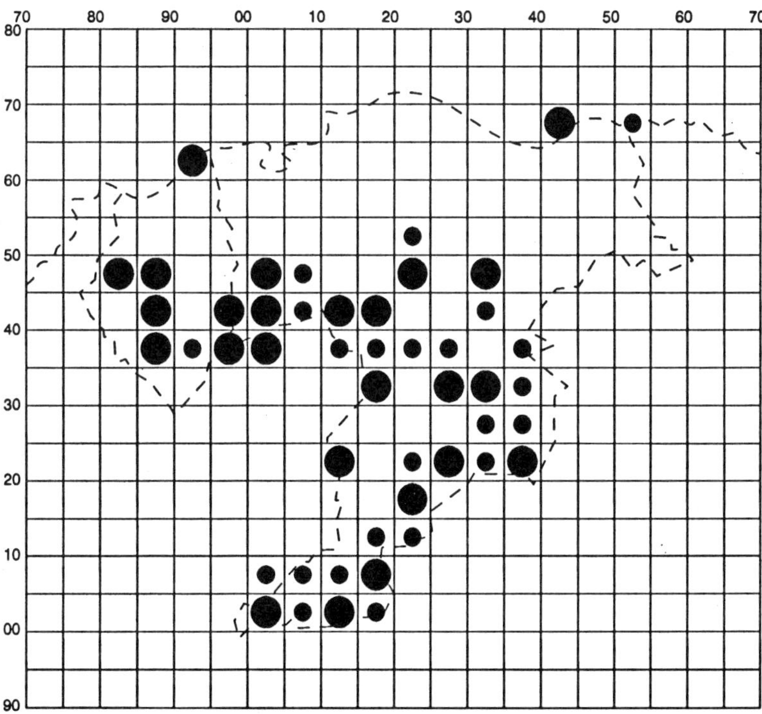

Figure 34 Wheatear distribution 1981–90
(May–July, excluding coastal migrants)

Grey-cheeked Thrush

Catharus minimus

Accidental.

One found dying at RAF Lossiemouth on 26 November 1965 was a first-winter male of the race *C.m.minimus* [**75**] (BB **59**:293).

Ring Ouzel

Turdus torquatus

Summer visitor and scarce breeder.

Late last century Ring Ouzels were common around Tomintoul, even abundant at Inchrory,[**4**] but apparently less numerous elsewhere in the uplands.[**6**] Today they are thinly dispersed on rocky hillsides, moorland gulleys and higher glens, mostly between 250–800m altitude. Glen Builg, south of Tomintoul, still holds by far the highest concentration: 16 pairs or singing males were located between Inchrory and Lochbuilg Lodge on 10 June 1989. A few widely scattered pairs breed much higher in the Cairngorms up to the plateau level. Nests are usually on crags or steep heather banks.

Arrival inland is usually in early April; the earliest was on 22 March 1844. The first eggs are laid in late April and the presence of fledged broods at the same time as nests with eggs in mid June suggests that some pairs at least are double-brooded. Most have left the breeding grounds by September, although one was still at Loch Builg on 28 October 1990. Occasional coastal migrants are seen in spring and autumn; the latest was one at Clochan on 6 November 1982.

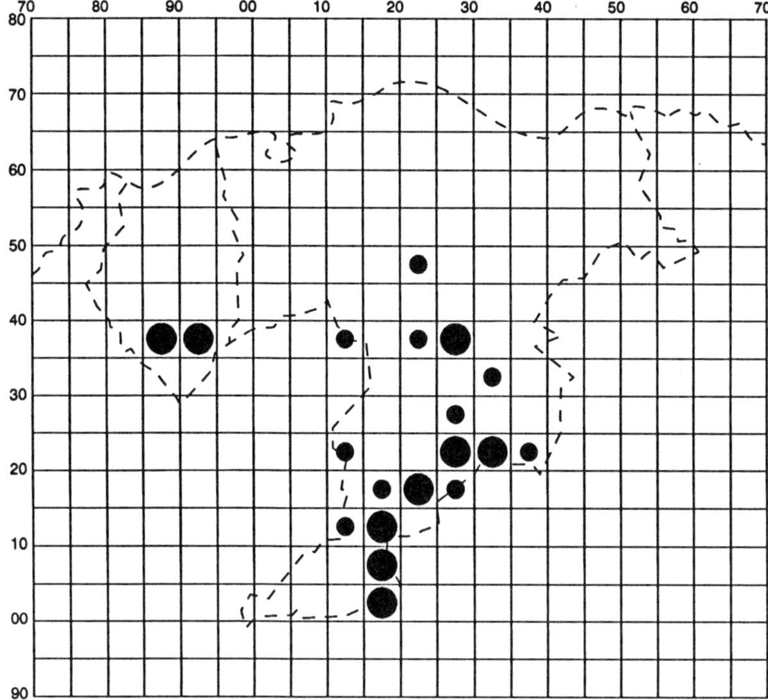

Figure 35 Ring Ouzel distribution 1981–90 (March–August, excluding coastal migrants)

Blackbird

Turdus merula

Common resident breeder, winter visitor and migrant.

Blackbirds are abundant breeders in gardens and woods throughout the Districts. Highest densities are found in open mixed deciduous woodland, with shrubberies and hedges for nesting, and also in mature shrubby gardens in towns and villages. Low numbers nest in mature plantations, hillside birchwoods and in juniper or gorse scrub on the moorland edge.

After the breeding season they gather in communal roosts often in thickets of evergreens such as rhododendron. In autumn large numbers of Continental immigrants, mostly from Scandinavia, join the local population. Some local birds, in turn, emigrate south from Moray and Nairn. Main arrivals are usually in late October and early November when flocks are sometimes seen coming in from the sea. In winter, Blackbirds feed in hedgerows, fields, around farms and in gardens where fallen apples are especially favoured.

There have been seven foreign recoveries of birds ringed in winter in the Districts, but unfortunately only one of these was found in summer, in Orebro (Sweden) on 10 July 1983. Others, perhaps all on migration, have been found in south Norway (September, October, November (two) and April) and north-western Germany (March). Another, ringed in the Netherlands in October 1984, was at Elgin on 1 January 1985. Of 89 other Blackbirds recovered in Moray and Nairn, 70 were local movements, 14 came from elsewhere in Scotland and five from England.

Fieldfare

Turdus pilaris

Common winter visitor and migrant. Has bred.

Fieldfares are usually most abundant in late autumn, when huge numbers may arrive in the Districts from Scandinavia. The main immigration in most years takes place in late October or early November, although a few are often seen in September and there are four August records, one near Nairn on

PLATE 23 Fieldfare seeking berries on a garden Cotoneaster *(John Edelsten)*

29 August 1968, one near Loch Spynie on 21 August 1983, one at Keith on 28 August 1988 and one at Clochan on 24 August 1991. Depending on weather conditions, large falls may take place on the coast e.g. October 1976 and especially October 1982 when there were thousands along the coastal belt from Findhorn to Buckie, stripping berries from the hedgerows. In other years most flocks drop directly into the uplands where rowans, together with crowberry and other ericaceous fruits, form the main diet. In December 1986 there were 7,500 at Ardclach and 6,000 near Dallas. If weather becomes severe or food supplies run low, many Fieldfares move on and only quite small numbers are often left in January–March. A few Fieldfares often move into country gardens where apples are available. Return passage in April and early May is usually small. Flocks of over 100 are unusual, the latest were five at Keith on 29 May 1988.

There are two certain breeding records: on 29 July 1972 a pair with at least two recently fledged young was found in the Tomintoul area (SB **7**:406) and in 1978 a pair nested successfully at Blackhills (I.S.Suttie). In 1988 a bird was seen carrying food into a dense spruce plantation in Glen Fiddich on 25 June, almost certainly indicative of breeding (J.J.C.Hardey).

Song Thrush

Turdus philomelos

Common breeder and migrant.

A common breeding species in scrubby woodland, younger plantations, farmland and mature gardens, they are also present, although less numerous, in the upland birchwoods and juniper scrub of the glens. In 1927 one was found dead at 1,230m on Ben Macdui (BB **20**:234).

In autumn almost the entire inland population moves south out of Moray and Nairn. The winter destination of our birds is indicated by recoveries of two, ringed locally, which were found long dead in May in Argyll and on Great Bernera (Lewis). Another, ringed at Duffus in October (perhaps on passage), was on Iona in February. A small number of Continental immigrants arrive in the Districts with other thrushes in October and November. A few Song Thrushes spend the winter along the coast; retrapping of ringed birds has shown that some of these are from the native population while evidence that immigrants may also be present is provided by a bird ringed in Orkney in October 1982 and found dead at Nairn in January 1984 and another marked in Elgin in December 1989 and recovered in Orkney in March 1991. The return to the breeding territories is surprisingly early, often in mid/late February when severe weather can still be expected.

Redwing

Turdus iliacus

Common winter visitor and migrant. Rare breeder.

Redwings were first proved to breed in May 1969 when a pair was found with a nest and eggs at Milltown near Elgin (SB **6**:111). Breeding took place again in 1971 (nest with four young near Tomintoul on 16 May (SB **7**:149)), 1976 (pair with fledged juveniles at Ferness on 22 July (SB **10**:106)) and 1980 (adult carrying food in Moray in June). Singing birds were also present in summer in suitable nesting habitat in 1973, 1974 (two), 1980 (two), 1981, 1988 (also one juvenile at a second locality on 2 August), 1989 (two) and 1990.

In autumn the first migrants sometimes appear in late September (earliest 27 September 1980) but the largest arrivals are usually not until mid/late October when nocturnal passage can be heard and thousands may descend on the hawthorns and rowans. In most years the immigrant flocks quickly pass through and only small numbers are left in midwinter, although 2,500+ were at Ardclach on 7 December 1986 and thousands more were near Dallas. Those which remain suffer badly in severe weather. Return passage in spring is light, with few birds seen after mid April.

A Redwing ringed on passage through Fair Isle on 1 November 1958 was found dead near Tomintoul 12 days later. Another, ringed at Clochan in October 1984, was wintering in Cantal, southern France, in February 1986.

Mistle Thrush

Turdus viscivorus

Common resident breeder and migrant.

The first record in the Districts was not until 27 February 1807 when several were found dead or dying in the snow at Gordon Castle, Fochabers. They first nested there in 1817,[**4**] had increased by 1851 [**7**] and were described as 'resident, abundant and spreading' over Moray and Nairn in 1895.[**4**]

Today Mistle Thrushes are widespread and common breeders, at low density, in all types of open deciduous and mixed woodland up to 400m in the birchwoods in the glens. They also nest in villages, large gardens and agricultural land with trees but are largely absent from pure conifer plantations. On 20 June 1989 one flew north over the Cairngorms at *c.*1,150m.

In late summer and autumn groups of 30–40 are not unusual, feeding on short grassland or berries up to the moorland edge. Largest flocks were 100 at Keith on 4 October 1977 and 84 near Loch Spynie on 11 September 1987. These flocks break up in winter when many birds leave the Districts, especially the uplands. One individual, ringed in Glenlivet in July 1977, was found as far south as Brittany (France) in October that year. Those which remain often aggressively defend a berry supply against other thrushes. Breeding territories are re-established early, with song from January and, in mild weather, the first eggs laid in late March.

Grasshopper Warbler

Locustella naevia

Summer visitor and scarce breeder.

Nests were found annually beside the River Lossie near Elgin between 1896–8 (ASNH 9:48), the first reported occurrence in the Districts. Since

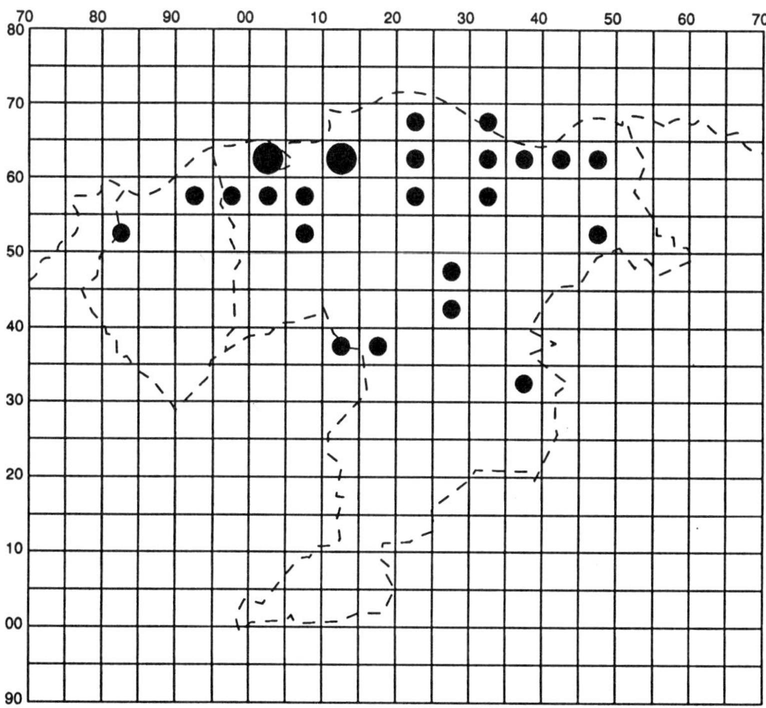

Figure 36 Grasshopper Warbler distribution 1981–90 (May–July)

then, breeding has only been confirmed on three occasions: at Clochan in 1978, near Moy in 1988 and at Alves in 1989. Singing birds are, however, heard in a scatter of sites in most years; 12 out of 33 10 km-squares were occupied during 1968–72. Many are doubtless overlooked and the species is probably a scarce but widespread lowland breeder in marshes, reedy ditches and, occasionally, young plantations with dense undergrowth. Occasional songsters are well inland: one was in a plantation in the Cabrach at 300m in 1991. Most arrive in early May; the earliest was one near Forres on 28 April 1961. The latest record is one at Loch Spynie on 13 August 1985 but they are hard to detect when not in song and some, no doubt, remain longer.

Sedge Warbler

Acrocephalus schoenobaenus

Summer visitor and common breeder.

A widespread breeding species in the lowlands but virtually absent from the uplands over 300m. Favoured habitats are reedbeds, marshes and pockets of young conifers where a dense undergrowth has developed. They can also be heard singing from damp thickets and overgrown ditches in farmland and waste ground. Loch Spynie marshes probably hold the greatest density of pairs, although no census work has been undertaken. The first arrivals usually appear in early May (the earliest was one at Kingston on 22 April 1984) but are later in poor springs. Most leave by early September (the last being singles at Loch Spynie on 25 September 1988 and at Kingston on 25 September 1991), but some have departed much earlier, e.g. a juvenile ringed at Loch Spynie on 30 July 1983 was caught in Cheshire 12 days later. Birds ringed further south (Tayside, Oxfordshire and Dorset) during August–September have been caught in Moray and Nairn during the following summer.

Marsh Warbler

Acrocephalus palustris

Accidental.

One was trapped and ringed at Loch Spynie on 23 August 1983 (SBR 1983).

Whitethroat

Sylvia communis

Summer visitor and common breeder.

Whitethroats are common only in lowland areas but penetrate further inland up the Spey and Findhorn valleys. They breed in drier scrubland, untidy hedgerows and young scrubby plantations. Numbers were much reduced in 1969, due to drought in their sub-Saharan wintering quarters in Africa. Recently their numbers have improved again and Whitethroats are once more a familiar roadside sight as they pop in and out of bramble and gorse patches, and the males perform their brief aerial song flights. First arrivals are usually in early May (the earliest was on 19 April 1850), but they are often scarce until mid May with no eggs laid until the end of the month.

In late summer they range more widely over the lowlands e.g. in country gardens and reedbeds. Most leave in August or early September; the latest record is one at Loch Spynie on 25 September 1988.

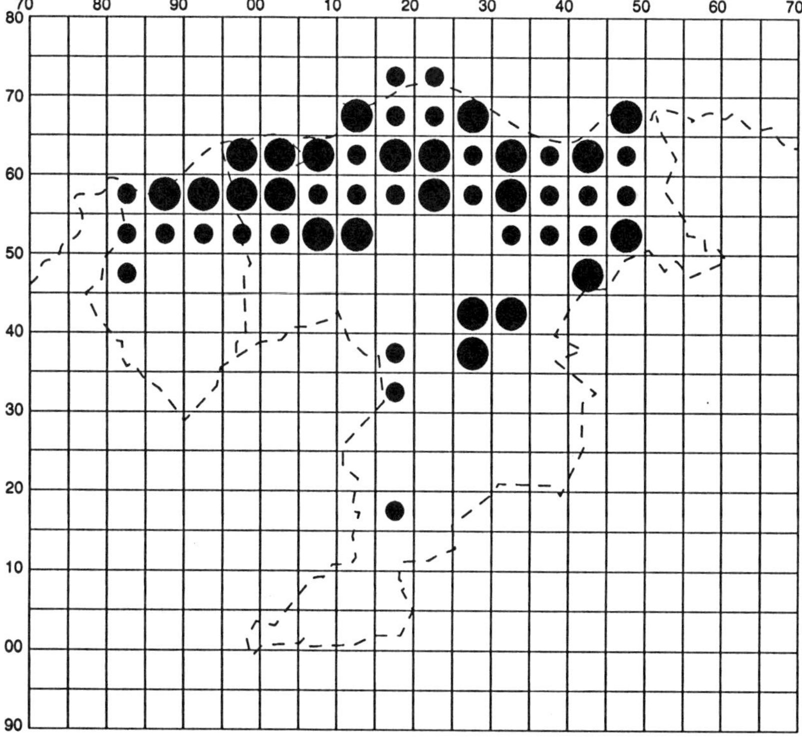

Figure 37 Whitethroat distribution 1981–90 (May–July)

Lesser Whitethroat

Sylvia curruca

Accidental. Probable summer visitor and rare breeder.

Reports that Lesser Whitethroats 'frequent whins in the neighbourhood of Elgin' in the early 1840s [6] lack any supporting evidence and must be considered unreliable. The first satisfactory record concerns two recently-fledged juveniles mist-netted together at Clochan on 14 July 1984. These birds were almost certainly reared in Moray (SBR 1984). The only other occurrences were in 1989, when a juvenile was mist-netted at Loch Spynie on 26 August, and in 1991, when one was singing on the Lein, Kingston in early June. The Cullen record given in MNBR 1987 was just outside the Moray boundary.

Garden Warbler

Sylvia borin

Summer visitor and scarce breeder.

Apart from a report of one seen at Birnie on 18 May 1871,[7] the Garden Warbler was not recorded in the Districts until 1951 when there was a bird at Findhorn on 28 May. Subsequent records were at Kellas (one on 31 May 1955), Findhorn (two on 13 August 1967), Cullen (one on 3 June 1968) and Gordonstoun (one on 22 October 1968). In 1969 a pair nested successfully at Kinloss, the first proved breeding in Moray and Nairn.

Over the last 20 years the species has increased considerably, although it remains scarce and its distribution is imperfectly known. Most singing males are heard in damp riverside scrub often with willows, particularly along the lower Spey (e.g. four between Ordiquish and Boat o' Brig in June 1984) and the lower Findhorn (three below the A96 bridge in May 1989). They are also occasionally found in open shrubby woodlands away from rivers, at five or six localities in recent years. The second proved instance of breeding was at Pluscarden in July 1986.

Spring arrival is in May; the earliest was on 11 May 1981. In late summer they occur more widely in deciduous woodlands, reedbeds and country gardens. Autumn departure is in August/September; a migrant was seen at Lossiemouth harbour on 19 September 1988. The latest migrants have been recorded at Clochan on 14 October 1976 and at Gordonstoun on 22 October 1968.

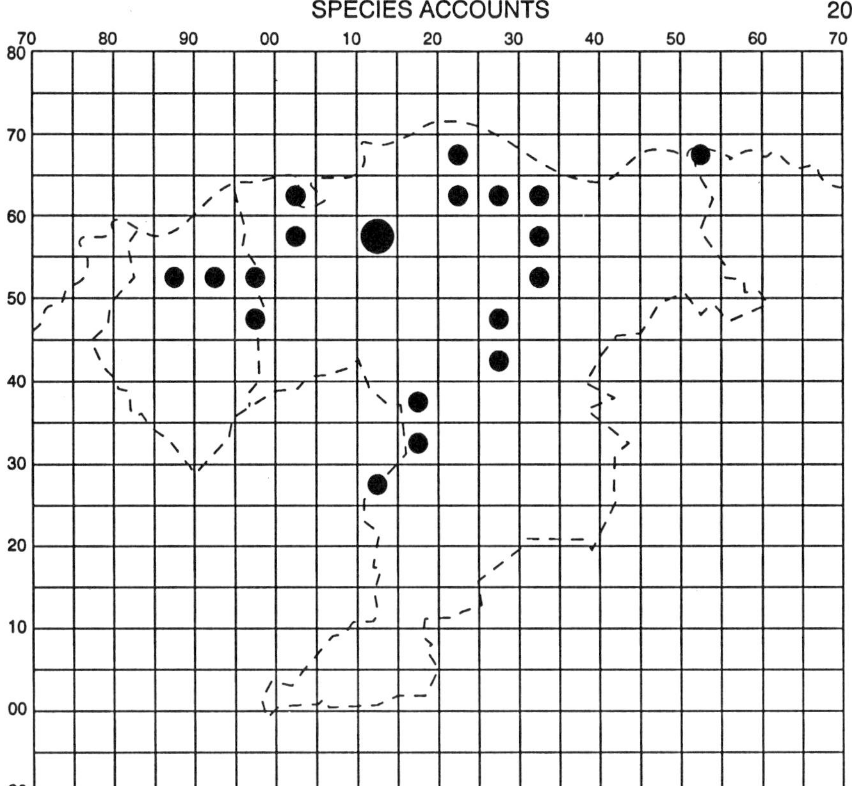

Figure 38 Garden Warbler distribution 1981–90 (May–July)

Blackcap

Sylvia atricapilla

Summer visitor and numerous breeder, scarce migrant and winter visitor.

In the last century Blackcaps were very rare winter visitors. A pair bred near Elgin in 1838 [**6**] and one sang there in 1852 and 1853.[**3**] In 1939 three young fledged from a nest at Birkenhill, New Elgin (SB **1**:40). Breeding was also proved in 1982 (near Buckie), 1983 and 1986 (at Cawdor, the first for Nairn District).

Blackcaps are now thinly distributed in mature deciduous woodlands with tall trees and a dense shrub layer such as rhododendrons. This habitat is scarce in the Districts, but where it occurs several singing males may be present, e.g.

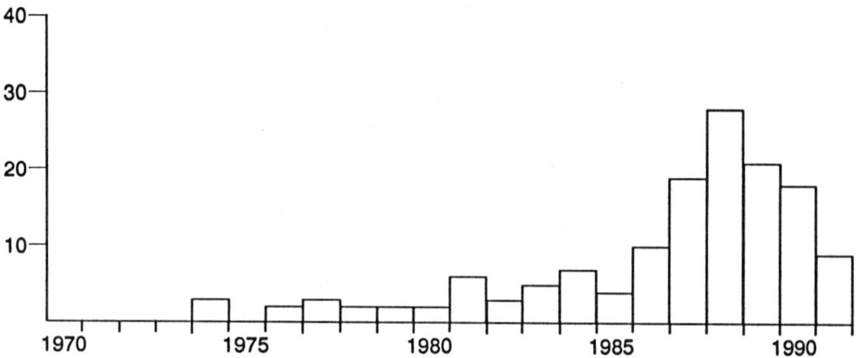

Figure 39 Blackcap annual total of singing males 1970–91

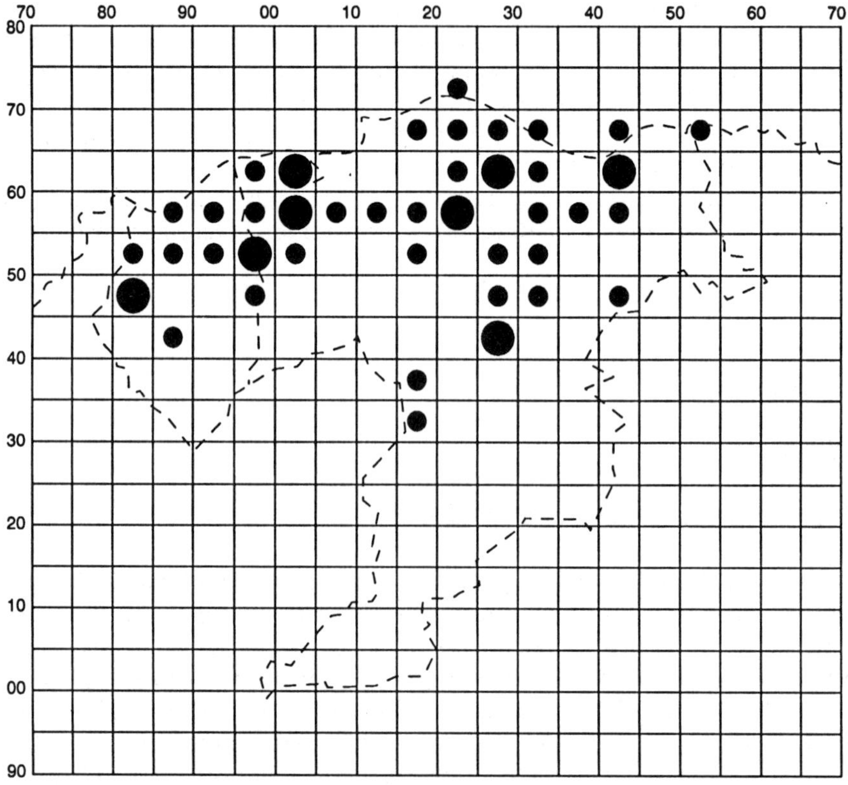

Figure 40 Blackcap summer distribution 1981–90 (May–July)

nine along the River Nairn between Nairn and Cawdor in 1988, six at Innes House in 1987 and two to four annually at Cairnfield, Buckie in recent years. Since 1976 song has been heard in 48 different localities; the best year was 1988 when 28 males were reported from 16 sites. The annual totals of singing males since 1970 are shown in the histogram opposite. The timing of spring arrival is confused by the presence of overwintering birds, although these are unlikely to sing in the Districts. The earliest song was heard at Forres on 24 April 1982 but early May is more usual. After the breeding season Blackcaps are also encountered in scrub, hedgerows, gardens and reedbeds. Most leave in August/September. Autumn passage is most obvious in October/early November when several may feed together on brambles or elderberries in coastal areas.

In recent years an increasing number of Continental migrants has overwintered in Moray and Nairn. The first records were of single males at Nairn from 29–31 December 1951 and in Craigellachie from 27–29 January 1952 (SN **64**:53–4). Since the early 1970s, the number of birds seen between December and March has risen greatly; 83% of reports are within 10 km of the coast; the furthest inland was one at Knockando in January 1985. The best winter was 1986/7, with at least 26 individuals; doubtless many others passed un-noticed. They often come to birdtables, especially in hard weather, taking a wide variety of foods.

One surprising ringing recovery relates to a Blackcap ringed in Devon on 25 October 1980 and found dead at Lossiemouth on 7 December that year.

Wood Warbler

Phylloscopus sibilatrix

Summer visitor and scarce breeder.

Wood Warblers are found very locally in mixed deciduous woodland, often where oaks are present and where there is little undergrowth. They have also been heard in mature birch woods. Despite their absence from Ardclach parish in the late nineteenth century,[**27**] the best locality today appears to be the Findhorn valley upstream from Darnaway. In the early 1960s there were several pairs, and eight singing males were heard in June 1980. During 1968–72 breeding was proved in four 10 km-squares and singing birds were present in two others. Away from the Findhorn valley the only recent reports concerned four in song at Glenlatterach in May 1984 (with two there in June 1986) and a single songster in Quarry Wood, Elgin in spring 1988.

Chiffchaff

Phylloscopus collybita

Summer visitor and scarce breeder. Rare in winter.

The Chiffchaff was first recorded near Elgin in the late 1830s [6] and in 1887 a nest was found near Forres on 21 May.[4] One was heard near Ballindalloch on 8 October 1891 (ASNH **1**:135) but there are no further records until one near Forres in 1956. Since 1960, reports of singing birds have increased greatly as shown below:

Years	*Number of singing birds*
1960–4	2
1965–9	5
1970–4	3
1975–9	11
1980–4	20
1985–9	87

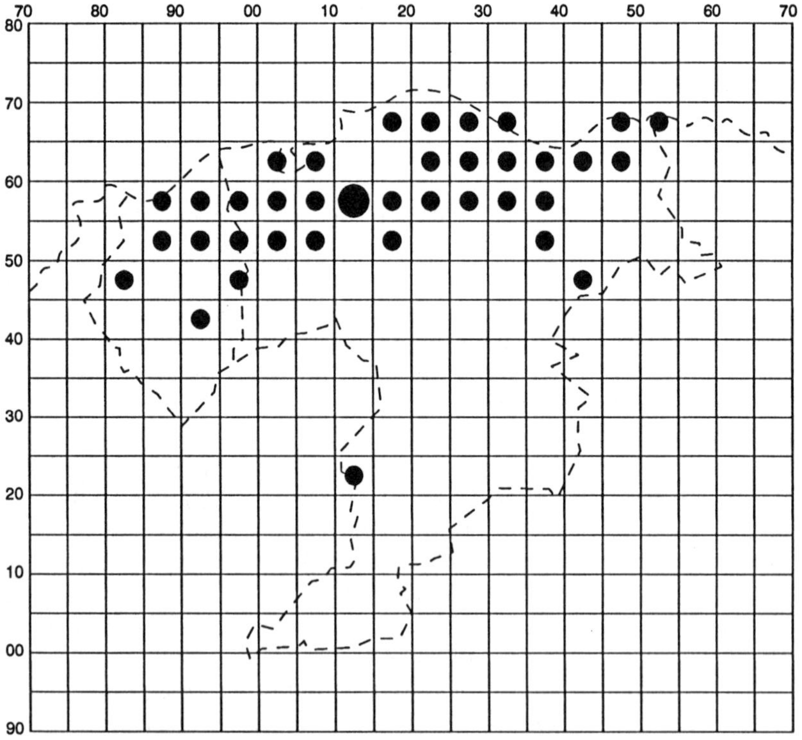

Figure 41 Chiffchaff distribution 1981–90 (April–July)

This rise is partly attributable to the greater number of observers and to fieldwork for the new Summer Atlas in 1988–9, but very few Chiffchaffs were found during the survey work for the first Atlas in 1968–72 and it seems certain that a genuine population increase has also taken place. Nearly all are within 10 km of the coast in shrubby woodland with at least a few mature deciduous trees. Many sing for several weeks and are probably unmated. At Loch Spynie in 1988 a male sang in the same clump of trees from 12 April until 25 September. Breeding has been proved at Pluscarden in 1971 and 1983 and near Elgin in 1973. Arrival is in late March and April with the earliest song heard at Loch Spynie on 29 March 1990. Possible late migrants have been seen in November on five occasions.

Chiffchaffs have been recorded during December–February in eight winters since 1971/5; there were two in 1976/7 and three in 1974/5. Two at Elgin sewage works between 16 January–30 March 1975 (one until 6 April) probably belonged to one of the Continental races *P.c.tristis* or *P.c.abietinus*.**[77]**

Willow Warbler

Phylloscopus trochilus

Summer visitor and common breeder.

An abundant species whose song is characteristic of woodlands throughout the Districts in early summer. They breed from the coast to the highest birch scrub in the glens and, in the Glenlivet and Tomintoul areas, they nest in juniper scrub up to 1.5 km from the nearest trees. Breeding densities are highest in younger woods, including plantations, where a thick understorey exists. They also occupy overgrown hedges, areas of scrub in farmland and country gardens. In 1984 19 pairs bred on a 58 hectare farm at Clochan.

Spring arrival is variable, depending on weather conditions, but the first song is usually heard by 20 April (the earliest being one at Pitgaveny on 8 April 1990), although sometimes later e.g. 26 April in 1977 and 1986. In July and August large numbers of Willow Warblers disperse around the Districts, feeding in almost any patch of shrubby vegetation. In 1985 79 were ringed in a small Clochan garden in 25 days. Most have left by early September but there are two October records, one near Keith on 17 October in 1986 and one ringed at Kinloss on 24 October in 1982.

Birds ringed locally in summer have been found on southward migration in the same year in Fife, Tayside, Lincolnshire (two – one within 12 days), Sussex and Kent. Five recoveries involving the Districts show spring passage through Kent (two), Merseyside, the Isle of May (two) and the Isle of Man.

PLATE 24 Willow Warbler attending young in the nest *(John Edelsten)*

Firecrest

Regulus ignicapillus

Accidental.

On 4 October 1970 three were well seen in the ravine of the Dorback Burn near Relugas (SB **6**:447). A single male was in a garden at Clochan on 2 November 1980 (SBR 1981).

Goldcrest

Regulus regulus

Common resident breeder.

Goldcrests are common breeders in coniferous and mixed woodland whose range has benefited from the expansion of forestry in the Districts. Outside the nesting season they associate with tit flocks when 20 or more may be seen together. They roam widely in autumn through all types of woodland, scrub and country gardens but appear to leave the conifer woods less frequently in winter, once leaf fall and colder weather have reduced insect populations on broadleaved trees. Unusual reports include one on the Nairn Bar on 28 November 1971 and singles dead on the Cairngorm plateau on 17 July 1976 [**49**], 13 June 1991 and 3 July 1991.

Spotted Flycatcher

Muscicapa striata

Summer visitor and common breeder.

A widespread breeder, it occurs sparingly in all types of mature open woodlands, though less commonly in conifers. Upland birchwoods along rivers and streams often hold a few pairs, as high as 470m altitude in Glen Builg. Others nest in large gardens and around farms, where their presence is advertised by their aerobatic pursuits after flying insects.

They are among the latest of spring migrants, usually not arriving before mid May; the earliest was one at Keith on 5 May 1987. Most leave by mid September; one at Braes of Glenlivet on 3 October 1990 was exceptionally late for an inland site.

Pied Flycatcher

Ficedula hypoleuca

Rare migrant. Has bred.

One pair bred near Aberlour in 1968 (SB **5**:349) and 1969 (SB **6**:119) and a single bird was seen at nearby Carron on 24 June 1973. There are only three other summer occurrences. In 1988 a male sang in a small oakwood at Raitcastle near Nairn from 10 May–1 June but remained unmated, while on 10 June 1989 a male was watched feeding among birches at Inchrory. On 10 June 1990 at Banchor a male was singing and seen entering a hole in a birch. It was not present on 22 June.

Birds are occasionally recorded on spring passage in early May, most notably on 13 May 1989 when five were at Mayne near Elgin and another at

Longmorn. Other reports (all singles) have come from Pitgaveny (9 May 1924), Gordonstoun (1–3 May 1953), Kinloss (7 May 1969), Loch Spynie and Lossiemouth (both 11 May 1975), Burghead (4 May 1977) and Knockando (6 May 1978). There is only one autumn record, a bird in the Findhorn valley on 17 September 1915.

Long-tailed Tit

Aegithalos caudatus

Common resident breeder.

A widespread breeder, frequently encountered in mixed and deciduous woodlands from the coast to the birchwoods in the glens. Nests are built in scrub or in forks of branches in taller trees of more open woods.

After the breeding season, groups comprising one or more family parties roam the countryside together, often in company with other tit species. The largest reported flocks were 45 at Loch Spynie on 29 December 1987 and 42 at Mundole on 27 August 1990. These flocks may be met with in all but the most open habitats, sometimes visiting gardens and even feeding at bird tables.

Willow Tit

Parus montanus

Former resident breeder, now extinct.

The Willow Tit was not recognised as a separate species in Britain until 1897 and earlier records of this species in Moray and Nairn were attributed to Marsh Tit *P.palustris*. There is no evidence that the latter species has ever occurred in the Districts.

St.John wrote in 1863 that Willow Tits were 'numerous in fir woods in winter' and he also described the nest and eggs although no locality was given. He asserted that they were more common than Coal Tits but gave no evidence for this.[**3**] Later in the century one was seen near Forres in winter 1878/9 and pairs nested at Darnaway and Drumduan (near Nairn) *c.*1894.[**4**] There are no reliable records since then, although they remained in upper Speyside until *c.*1950 [**49**] so it seems likely that a few were also in Moray and Nairn in the first half of this century.

Crested Tit

Parus cristatus

Numerous resident breeder.

Crested Tits gradually colonised Moray and Nairn from their upper Speyside strongholds between *c.*1860–*c.*1940. The direction of spread appears to have been down Speyside to Fochabers and then along the new coastal plantations to Forres and Nairn.

St.John stated in 1863 that they were probably in the woods near Dulsie but he gave no details.[**3**] The first record from Fochabers woods was of one seen in winter 1868 or 1869 and they were in Gordon Castle woods in 1886.[**7**] In 1899 two nests were found in this area and they were also seen closer to Elgin *c.*1901 (ASNH **12**:48–9). Other lower Speyside records last century included a pair in Glen of Rothes in July 1893 and breeding near Ballindalloch *c.*1895.[**4**] In autumn 1901 they were fairly numerous around Fochabers and by 1910 they had spread to the Forres–Nairn area, where they were found near Loch Loy on 16 May 1910 and in May 1915. Two other localities in the lower Findhorn valley held Crested Tits on 24 May 1910 and in September 1915 (BB **9**:302–3). In early July 1918 newly fledged juveniles were seen near Forres (BB **12**:165). By the 1940s they were on the Bin of Cullen [**78**] and four to six were regular in winters 1945–7 near Lossiemouth (SB **1**:40). They were clearly well established right along the coast by this time. Breeding surveys in 1968–72 [**65**] and 1979–80 [**78**] located Crested Tits in 18 out of 33 10 km-squares in the Districts with breeding proved in 11 and likely in the others. Strongholds were the coastal belt plantations with a more scattered population in the Speyside woods between Ballindalloch and Fochabers, a situation which remains true today. Outside the known usual range, breeding has recently taken place near Keith (1976), Dufftown (1988) and Tomintoul (1988), and in May–July 1988 pairs were located around the upper Findhorn at Ardclach, Dava and Rochuln with a single bird at Braemoray Lodge. They were seen on the Bin of Cullen on 16 October 1988 and 15 September 1991.

Crested Tits inhabit older Scots pine woods and mixed conifer plantations provided that substantial stands of Scots pine are present. The absence of adequate-sized stumps for nest holes is a limiting factor in young plantations, and areas of forest composed of mature, tall, smooth-boled trees appear much less attractive than when the trees are more scrubby with plenty of side branches.[**78**] Breeding density in suitable habitat in Culbin Forest was one pair/10 hectares *c.*1970 [**79**] and the density in the whole of Lossie Forest was one pair/100 hectares in 1979.[**78**] Nest boxes are regularly used, especially in Culbin Forest where 13 were occupied in 1987. Clutches are usually started in late April with fledging in early June; occasionally a pair is double brooded (SB **11**:227). In winter they sometimes visit bird tables, usually in gardens close to the forests, but one trapped in Clochan on 13 July 1985 was 2 km from the nearest pinewood.

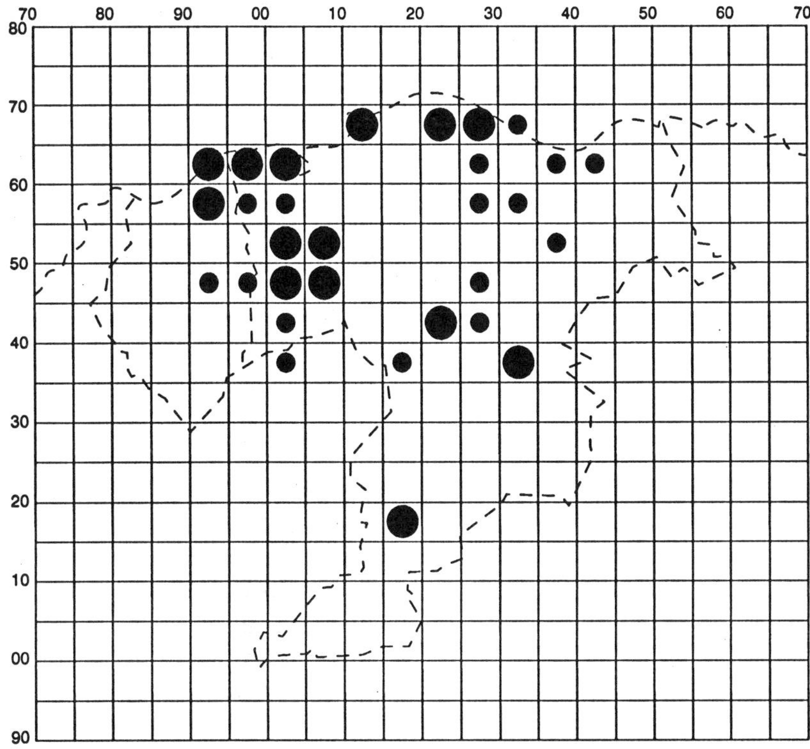

Figure 42 Crested Tit summer distribution 1981–90 (April–July)

Coal Tit

Parus ater

Common resident breeder.

A widespread and very common species in coniferous woodland, Coal Tits also breed in mixed and deciduous woods, large gardens and scattered trees in farmland and far up the glens, to at least 470 m in Glen Builg. Breeding density in Culbin Forest *c.*1970 was one pair per 3.4 hectares.[79] Nests are often at ground level among roots or in holes and they readily take to nest boxes. In the predominantly deciduous woodlands around Innes House in the 1980s, Coal

Tits only used the two boxes (out of 60) which were sited on conifers. Eggs are laid from late April.

In autumn and winter forest flocks can exceed 100; the most counted together were 270 at Cawdor on 7 January 1984 and 144 in Lossie Forest on 29 September 1985. They often associate with other tits, Goldcrests and Treecreepers. They regularly visit gardens where fat and peanuts are favourite foods.

Blue Tit

Parus caeruleus

Common resident breeder.

This is one of our most familiar garden birds, although it breeds mainly in woodland of almost any type which contains trees big enough to provide nest holes. There are fewer in conifer plantations but up to one pair per 23 hectares in Scots and Corsican Pine in Lossie Forest in the 1980s, where nest boxes are plentiful. Numbers fluctuate widely in response to breeding success and winter severity; the number of pairs occupying 210 nest boxes in Lossie Forest between 1978–88 ranged from three (in 1982) to 22 (in 1983).

In autumn and winter they join with other small woodland species in roving parties; the highest count was 27 at Elgin on 21 November 1981. They are common visitors to garden bird tables and nut bags where ringing reveals a large turnover of birds during a single day. The most distant ringing recovery is from Clochan to Huntly (25 km).

Great Tit

Parus major

Common resident breeder.

Great Tits breed in towns, gardens, farmland and woods of all types up to 350 m altitude near Tomintoul. Densities in coniferous plantations tend to be low due to lack of nest sites, a situation demonstrated in Lossie Forest where provision of 210 nest boxes in 500 hectares of pine increased the breeding population from two pairs (in 1978) to 49 pairs (in 1985), a density of one pair per 10 hectares. Song may be heard as early as January but eggs are not laid until early May, later in a cold spring. In autumn and winter they join feeding flocks with other small passerine species and are regular visitors to suburban and country gardens.

The most interesting ringing recovery is that of a bird ringed at Darnaway on 9 March 1983 and found 152 km south west at Oban three and a half weeks later.

Treecreeper

Certhia familiaris

Common resident breeder.

Treecreepers are widespread in the Districts, breeding from the coastal conifer plantations to the upland birchwoods. They are absent in summer only from younger woodlands where the trees are too small to provide nest sites. They will readily take to nest boxes, even of the conventional front-hole type, e.g. four to seven pairs annually in 210 boxes in Lossie Forest. Eggs are laid from late April, with first young on the wing in early June and second clutches following soon afterwards.

Outside the breeding season they also forage through more open country, where trees are only scattered, visiting willow and birch scrub and mature gardens. One or two often accompany tit flocks.

Red-backed Shrike

Lanius collurio

Rare migrant.

Gordon reported one killed at Gordon Castle woods, Fochabers in the second half of last century but there is no date or other details. Eight birds have been seen more recently:

1 ♀ Buckie	26 May 1973 (SB 8:274)
1 ♂ Orton	22 June 1975 (SB 9:230)
1 ♂ Burghead	23 May–late July 1984
1 ♀ Burghead	22 May 1984
1 ♀ Lossie Forest	19 May 1985

1 ♂ Mundole (Forres)	June 1988
1 ♀/immature Loch Spynie	17 Aug 1988
1 ♂ Loch Loy	2 June 1990

The two Burghead birds in 1984 were *c.*500m apart and, despite the male's long stay, there was no evidence of a breeding attempt.

Great Grey Shrike

Lanius excubitor

Scarce migrant and winter visitor.

The first recorded Great Grey Shrike was shot at Gordon Castle, Fochabers on 30 December 1793.[4] The total for the Districts, until the end of 1989, now stands at 45, 24 of them since 1950. The best years were 1889 (five), 1903 (four), 1967 (three) and 1982 (three). The monthly distribution of dated records is shown below:

Jan	Feb	Mar	Apr	May	Jun	Jul	Aug	Sep	Oct	Nov	Dec
7	7	4	6	0	1	0	0	1	2	9	7

All sightings have been of single birds except for two at Forres on 2 January 1860, two at Fochabers on 7 November 1903 and two at Auldearn on 1 January 1971. The midsummer record was inland in Nairn District on 30 June 1976 (SB **10**:113). Occurrences are widely scattered, mostly in the lowlands but as far inland as Ballindalloch (1982 and 1988) and Aitnoch (1989). A bird which wintered near Fochabers from 25 December 1967–late March 1968 occupied a defined home range of *c*.45 hectares consisting of young conifer plantation and birch/willow scrub beside the River Spey.[**80**]

Woodchat Shrike

Lanius senator

Accidental.

A male was watched on the dunes at Findhorn for 20 minutes on 2 June 1967 (BB **61**:355; SB **5**:110).

Jay

Garrulus glandarius

Scarce visitor, perhaps rare breeder.

The Old Statistical Account, relating to Rathven in the 1790s, describes Jays entering pigeon-houses and destroying the young.[**14**] There is no evidence that they were numerous elsewhere in Moray at the time and the culprits were perhaps more likely to have been Jackdaws. The next report was not until 8 February 1873 when one was shot at Dunphail. In January 1874 two were seen, and one of them shot, at Gordon Castle, Fochabers and another was shot a few days later at Innes House.[**7**] There were three records this century before the 1980s, three between Rothes and Craigellachie *c*.25 November 1921, one at Fochabers on 19 May 1968 and one in Lossie Forest on 28 August 1978.

Since 1984 Jays have been positively identified on 14 occasions and there are a number of other, anecdotal, reports. Only four occurrences relate to the breeding season: single birds at Caigellachie in mid April 1986, Lochs of Bogmussach on 15 April 1990, Boat o' Brig on 24 April 1990 and at Darnaway on several dates during summer 1990. These birds, together with reports of three to five together at Burgie, Dallas and Fochabers in recent winters suggest that breeding may occasionally be taking place, a logical extension of the progressive expansion of the species' Scottish range since the 1960s.

Magpie

Pica pica

Numerous resident breeder.

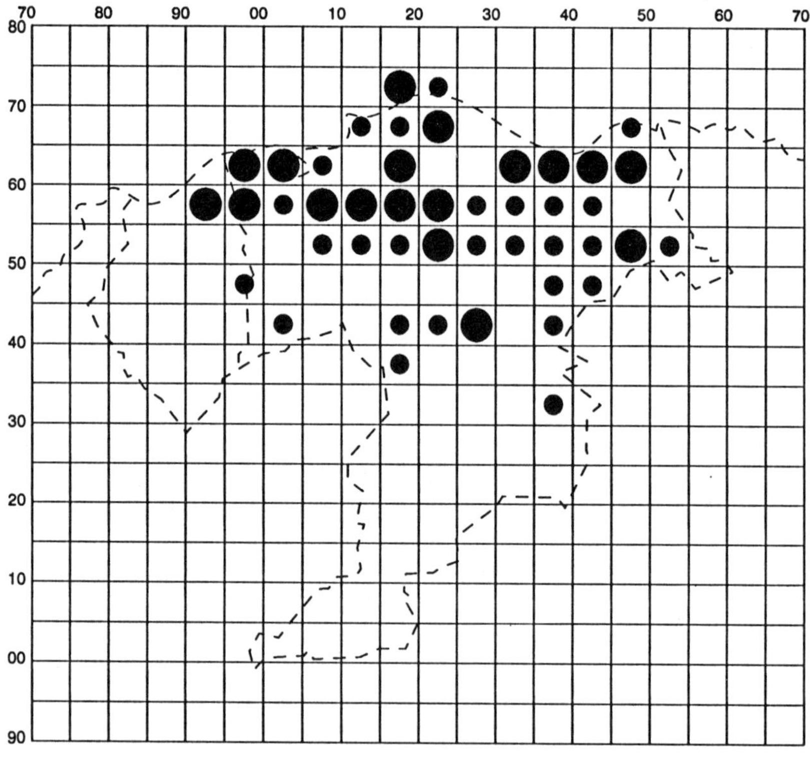

Figure 43 Magpie summer distribution 1981–90 (April–July)

Magpies were numerous in Moray in 1775 and abundant in 1863. Widespread persecution caused a progressive decline thereafter. They were last seen in Darnaway in 1865 and at Ardclach in 1890, both areas where they were formerly plentiful. Around Elgin they were still common around 1900 but had ceased to breed by 1910. There were no further records in the Districts until the 1930s when a slow recovery began; one pair bred at Spynie in 1935, 1936 and 1938 and another pair was at Gordonstoun in 1938–9 and 1946–7. They also nested at Pluscarden in 1947 and individuals were seen elsewhere in Moray almost every year between 1935–9 and 1945–8 (SN **60**:128). By the early 1960s there were 6–12 pairs in Moray and in 1968–72 Magpies were seen in the breeding season in 17 out of 33 10 km-squares in the two Districts.

Today Magpies are widely but thinly spread throughout the coastal lowlands with smaller numbers up county to the moorland edge. They remain very scarce in Nairn District where extensive fieldwork in 10 km-square NH 85 in 1988 failed to locate any and only one pair was found in 1989, near Cran Loch. The total breeding population of the two Districts is probably 100–150 pairs, most of them nesting on the edges of conifer plantations or in clumps of scrubby trees and feeding on short grassland nearby. Neighbouring pairs and their offspring may congregate into large groups in winter, the biggest group seen was 25 near Keith on 13 October 1987.

Jackdaw

Corvus monedula

Common resident breeder.

A widespread and common species, the Jackdaw breeds throughout the Districts in holes in trees, inland and coastal cliffs, quarries, ruins and chimneys, even in towns. From late summer onwards into winter they gather in flocks, often among Rooks, and feed on grassland and stubbles. Night time roosts, also often shared with Rooks, are usually in dense conifer plantations and may hold up to 2,000 birds (a minimum count at the Mosstodloch roost in December 1988). Future nest sites may be visited throughout the winter in open weather but most eggs are not laid until late April.

A Jackdaw ringed at Buckie in 1972 was found dead there 13 years later.

Rook

Corvus frugilegus

Common resident breeder.

Rooks are abundant over the farmland of the Districts but scarce or absent in the moors and uplands. The most recent survey of rookeries took place in 1975, using the old county boundaries.[**82**] The results are shown below:

County	*No. of rookeries*	*No. of nests*	*Av. nests/ rookery*	*Av. nests/ km²*
Banffshire	103	14,117	137.1	8.66
Morayshire	77	7,389	96.0	5.99
Nairnshire	21	1,993	94.9	4.72

The size distribution of the 201 rookeries was as follows:

1–25	*26–50*	*51–100*	*101–200*	*201–300*	*301–400*	*401–500*	*500+*
38	34	52	45	17	8	1	6

The largest were at Tarryblake (1,196 nests) and Ballindalloch (882 nests).[**83**] The biggest ever recorded was at Brodie where there were 1,714 nests *c.*1890.[**4**]

Rookeries are either in mature conifer plantations or tall deciduous trees in woods and farm shelter belts. Most are below 150m altitude and a small rookery at 410m in Glenlivet (NJ 217217) is possibly the highest in Scotland. They are reoccupied in February in fine weather and nesting is early with young on the wing by late May. After the breeding season flocks gather on short pasture and mown hayfields, feeding largely on soil invertebrates.

In winter large flocks, mixed with Jackdaws and gulls, feed on arable fields and their evening flights to roost are a familiar sight. Roosts, usually with Jackdaws, are mostly in dense conifer woods and may contain thousands of birds. A survey in 1970–5 [**84**] revealed four roosts over 5,000 in Moray and Nairn:

Carron House	25,000–30,000
Balnacoul, Mosstodloch	*c.*20,000
Dalmore Manse	5,000–10,000
Tarryblake	5,000+

Three of these roosts were still huge in 1989 but the one at Dalmore is no longer in use in winter.

The two longest movements shown by ringing are both of 17 km, one from Avoch (Black Isle) moved to Nairn, presumably across the Firth.

Carrion Crow/Hooded Crow

Corvus corone

Numerous resident breeder.

During the last 100 years the interbreeding zone between the two races of crow has crossed the Districts. In 1853 Hooded were most common and there were many hybrids but few, if any, pure black Carrion.[**3**] By the end of last century the two forms were equally common, at least in some areas,[**4,27**] and since then Carrion have become increasingly dominant. Today the great majority are Carrion or dark hybrids and it is unlikely that any pure Hooded Crows currently breed.

Crows are solitary breeders in most habitats from the coast to the moors. Nests are usually in tall trees on the woodland edge or in copses in open farmland. On moorlands low, isolated trees may be used as well as ruined buildings and cliff ledges. Nesting has also taken place on coastal cliffs at Covesea and Portknockie.

In autumn and winter crows assemble in loose flocks, the largest near the coast where maximum counts have been 220 at Findhorn Bay on 4 January 1988, 204 there on 22 November 1991, 172 at Culbin Bar on 20 October 1988 (over 20% hybrids) and 154 at Lossiemouth on 15 November 1981. In 1988 there were 63 at Culbin Bar as early as 18 June. Very small numbers of apparently 'pure' Hooded Crows are not uncommon in these flocks in winter; some of these may be Scandinavian immigrants. The proportion of hybrids is generally lowest in flocks in the east of the Districts.

Raven

Corvus corax

Scarce visitor, formerly widespread breeder.

In 1775 Ravens were 'numerous' in Moray.[**28**] By 1844 persecution was widespread and they were found commonly only in the less accessible uplands,[**6**] although in 1845 a few persisted as far down as the parishes of Knockando, Dallas, Rafford and Ardclach.[**13**] Nesting on the Ess of Glenlatterach continued until 1840.[**4**] By 1863 they were considered rare.[**3**] Further destruction of Ravens has taken place this century and in the early 1960s only occasional pairs remained, near Loch Avon and in the Ailnack gorge (where one pair nested until 1974) and just outside the District boundaries near Lochindorb,[85] where 13 were seen on 2 September 1972. There has been no further breeding attempt since 1974. On 12 August 1967 two were seen at Ben Rinnes and a pair was at Dulsie Bridge on 14 June 1978. Since then there have been occasional reports from the Lochindorb area, most recently two (one immature) near Carn a'Gharbh-ghlaic on 4 June 1988, two at Drynachan on 17 July 1989, five there on 18 May 1991 and two on 4 September 1991, six at Carn nan Clach Garbha on 30 September 1989, and one at Dava on 3 February 1991. In the Cairngorms in 1991 were two on Cairn Lochan on 20 August and two on Beinn Mheadhoin on 7 December.

Starling

Sturnus vulgaris

Common resident breeder and winter visitor.

At the start of the last century there were probably no Starlings in Moray and Nairn.[2] By the 1840s small flocks were being seen in spring and autumn, and breeding took place around that time at Lossiemouth, Gordonstoun and Elgin Cathedral.[4,6] In winter many roosted in the reeds at Loch Spynie,[4] where there were 'clouds' of birds in 1863.[3] By 1895 they were widespread and increasing breeders as far upcountry as Inchrory.[4]

Today Starlings breed commonly throughout the Districts, being absent only from open moorland and the highest uplands. In 1989 a pair reared a brood in a small, isolated birchwood near Lochindorb. Densities are highest close to human habitation where they nest in the roofs of houses, in walls and ruined buildings and in holes in trees. First broods are on the wing in late May when noisy flocks of juveniles assemble, sometimes moving onto upland grasslands and moors to feed; one was even on the Cairngorm plateau on 17 June 1964.[49] A flock of 1,100 at Findhorn Bay on 16 July 1989 were mostly juveniles.

In autumn many Continental immigrants arrive, mostly from Scandinavia. Birds ringed here during January–March have been found in May-June in Denmark, Finland and Norway (two). Flocks of up to 500 Starlings are not uncommon through the winter, feeding on farmland. They are also familiar birds of town and village, roaming through gardens emptying bird tables. Communal roosts are established in thickets, dense plantations and reedbeds. The largest is probably the long-established roost in the reeds at Loch Spynie, in use for over 140 years, which often holds *c.*10,000 birds in late autumn. A cave roost in the cliffs at Portknockie holds a few hundred birds, while others use the tower of the old Moss Street Church in Elgin, a conveyor-belt framework at Buckie maltings, old buildings around Burghead harbour and Monkey Puzzle trees in east Elgin.

Rose-coloured Starling

Sturnus roseus

Accidental.

One was shot at Loch Spynie on 21 June 1851.[3] The next occurrence was not until 1987 when an adult stayed at Allt A'Bhainne Distillery, Glen Rinnes from 13 June–5 July (BB **81**:587).

House Sparrow

Passer domesticus

Common resident breeder.

One of our most common and familiar species close to human habitation although scarce elsewhere,they nest under roofs, in walls and nest boxes and utilise a wide variety of sites around farm buildings.

In autumn and winter they remain in gardens feeding at bird tables or collect in flocks, often with finches and buntings, to forage around fields and farmyards. The largest reported flock was 140 at Clochan on 5 December 1981. On winter evenings they gather, chirruping noisily, in small roosts in thick hedges or scrub.

There are two interesting ringing recoveries: one marked at Avoch (Black Isle) in October 1959 was found at Roseisle the following March, 45 km away, assuming it crossed the Firth. Outstanding longevity was shown by the nestling ringed at Clochan on 28 May 1978 and retrapped there on 24 December 1988.

Tree Sparrow

Passer montanus

Numerous resident breeder.

Tree Sparrows were uncommon breeders last century. Today they have a curiously patchy distribution, regular and quite numerous in one area but absent from apparently similar habitat elsewhere. Most reports are of winter flocks and records of proved breeding, always in the coastal lowlands, are few, due in part no doubt to their secretive nature in the breeding season. They occupy farmland close to mature deciduous trees which provide nest holes and will readily use nest boxes, e.g. six pairs at Invererne House in 1990. In summers 1968–72 birds were located in nine 10 km-squares with breeding proved in only three. Since 1980 nesting has been proved or suspected in 14 localities; eight to ten pairs were located at Pitgaveny in 1989. A male was seen mating with a female House Sparrow in Elgin on 13 June 1975.

In winter they are easier to locate as they mix with finches to feed around farms and stubbles. Assemblies of 20–40 are regular in a few places e.g. Miltonhill, Clochan and the Lossiemouth area and are doubtless overlooked elsewhere. Occasional bigger flocks have included the highest counts of 120 at Lossiemouth airfield on 3 December 1983 and 100 at Miltonhill on 14 February 1986 and 19 February 1988.

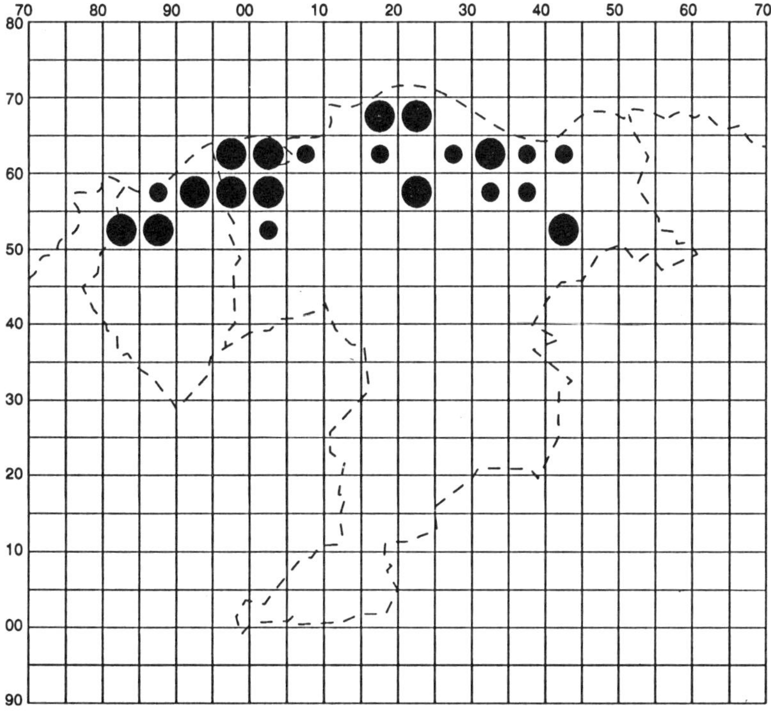

Figure 44 Tree Sparrow summer distribution 1981–90 (April–July)

Chaffinch

Fringilla coelebs

Common resident breeder, migrant and winter visitor.

The Chaffinch is one of our most widespread and abundant species, breeding in gardens and all forms of woodland including the highest upland birchwoods. Scattered pairs inhabit the birch and juniper scrub on the moorland edge, up to 470m in Glen Builg. It is one of the few species to have benefitted from afforestation which has allowed enormous expansion of the population. Exceptionally, one was feeding on picnic scraps on Ben Macdui summit on 24 September 1982.

In winter most birds move out of the forests and forage on adjoining farmland. Weedy turnip fields are particularly favoured and flocks of several hundred may build up. Peak counts were 2,000+ at Clochan on 7 December 1980 and 1,200 at Blairnamarrow near Tomintoul on 19 November 1983. Doubtless Continental Chaffinches form part of these large winter flocks but the extent of such immigration is unknown. The only ringing recovery to suggest it was the bird ringed on North Ronaldsay in October 1975 and found near Nairn in February 1978. Movements of the inland population towards the coast in winter may account for recoveries of birds ringed in Clochan in October and February and subsequently found at Aviemore and Archiestown in May–June. The same may apply to the Glenurquhart bird ringed in March 1983 and found in Lossiemouth the following January.

Brambling

Fringilla montifringilla

Common winter visitor and migrant.

Bramblings are irregular visitors with very few in some winters and large numbers in others, especially 1976/7, 1982/3 and 1983/4. Few are seen before October; the earliest was one at Clochan on 28 September 1985. They are usually found on arable land, often with Chaffinches, or feeding beneath beech trees. In 1976 up to 2,000 fed on beechmast in the Oak Wood, Elgin during December and *c.*2,500 were at Bow Bridge, Elgin on 12 February 1983. Other large flocks were 1,300 at Cawdor on 17 April 1983, 1,000 at Forres on 12 December 1976 and, up-country, 1,000 at Knockandhu (Glenlivet) on 26 December 1988. In spring good numbers may remain into May; the latest report was 400 at the Cabrach on 3 May 1970.

Greenfinch

Carduelis chloris

Common resident breeder.

A common and familiar species due to its attendance at garden peanut holders, the Greenfinch breeds chiefly in scrub, hedgerows and young conifer plantations but is absent from upland birchwoods. From the end of the nesting season until late winter they gather into flocks, often with other finches and buntings, in stubble fields and around farmyards; 500 birds were at Hopeman on 3 January 1988 and at Westerfolds on 17 February 1988. Flocks form early (e.g. 350+ at Mundole on 11 July 1989) and sometimes persist well into spring (e.g. 400 at Califer on 1 May 1976). Others feed in small groups in gardens in towns and villages. An exceptional record concerns one flying north-east over Garbh Uisge Beag (Cairngorm plateau) at *c.*1,150m on 1 April 1990.

Dispersal within Scotland has resulted in locally ringed birds moving to Aberdeen and Aberfeldy (Perthshire); one went as far as Northumberland. Others have moved into Moray and Nairn from Aberdeen and, notably, from Campbeltown (Strathclyde), a distance of 291 km.

Goldfinch

Carduelis carduelis

Numerous resident breeder.

Goldfinches were quite numerous in the Districts early last century [2] but were a favourite target of bird catchers and between 1840–80 they were almost wiped out. Single birds were subsequently at Ardclach in 1882, Forres in 1887 and a pair at Ferness in 1892.[4] There were no records in the first half of this century and they still 'seem(ed) to be quite extinct' in 1965.[**45**] First signs of recovery came in 1968 when there were three records: one at Elgin on 19 January, four at Kinloss on 3 February and four at Aberlour on 5 April (SB **5**:352). During summers 1968–72 Goldfinches were seen in eight 10 km-squares [**65**] but there was no confirmation of breeding until 1977 when a nest was found near Clochan. In winters 1981/2–1983/4 they were found in 18 10 km-squares [**68**] and the increase has continued since.

Today Goldfinches are widely but thinly spread from the coast to Tomintoul. Scrub and large, mature gardens appear to be the commonest breeding sites, although they can be seen in spring and summer up to the moorland edge, e.g. three at Johnstripe (Dunphail) on 21 April 1988. From late summer until winter small groups are encountered feeding on thistle heads or weed seeds. Largest flocks were 44 at Pitgaveny on 19 November 1990, 40 at Spey Bay on 7 January 1987 and 40 at Garmouth on 2 September 1990. Some, at least, remain far up-country, e.g. five at the Cabrach on 4 February 1988.

A Goldfinch ringed near Ardersier in December 1982 was found at Loch Spynie the following July.

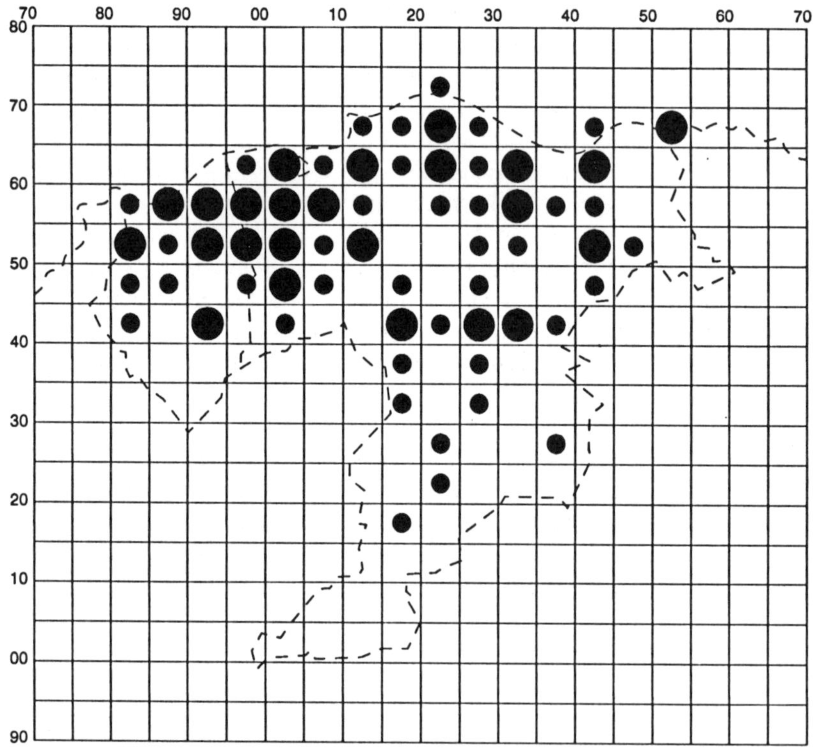

Figure 45 Goldfinch summer distribution 1981–90 (April–July)

Siskin

Carduelis spinus

Common resident breeder and migrant.

Although always quite numerous in the Districts, Siskins have only recently become familiar garden birds since the development of the habit of feeding on peanuts in red mesh bags since the mid 1970s.

In the mid nineteenth century they were said to nest frequently in Moray and small flocks were present in autumn and winter.[**3**] They were commonly taken as cage birds; a porter at Aberlour station caught over 20 in a decoy trap fixed to a telegraph pole in autumn 1893. In 1895 they were 'fairly abundant residents'.[**4**] This century their coniferous woodland breeding habitat has expanded greatly and as plantations have matured Siskins have also increased their range and numbers, notably since the 1960s.

In autumn and winter, flocks containing an unknown proportion of Scandinavian migrants feed on riverside alders and birches; 50–100 together are not unusual and the highest count was 350 at Culraggie (Glenlivet) on 11 January 1989. A large number of local birds move south to winter in southern England, returning north in March–April at which time numbers visiting local gardens for peanuts greatly increase.

Over 110 Siskins ringed elsewhere in Britain have been recovered in the Districts. Evidence of winter emigration to southern England is provided by 54 birds ringed there between December and April and recaptured in Moray and Nairn in spring and summer. The return north can be rapid, e.g. Hertfordshire to Elgin in 15 days. More unusual was the movement of a bird from Jersey in October 1981 to Elgin in December of the same year.

Linnet

Carduelis cannabina

Common resident breeder and partial migrant.

Linnets are common breeders in lowland arable country but scarce in the uplands. Small numbers nest in the larger river valleys as far as Tomintoul but they are certainly not abundant in Glen Fiddich and Strathavon as they were described in 1895.[**4**] Favourite habitat is gorse scrub but bushes and hedges in farmland and large gardens may also hold nests.

In autumn and winter the interior is largely deserted and few sizeable flocks are seen more than 30 km inland. Near the coast flocks feed on weed seeds on arable land and sometimes on dunes and saltings. Highest counts have been 500 at Nairn (19 January 1975), Clochan (28 November 1982) and Westerfolds (17 February 1988).

Twite

Carduelis flavirostris

Numerous resident breeder, a few on the coast in winter.

At the end of last century the Twite was a widespread breeder, 'universal' on high ground up to *c*.400m. Good numbers were reported in Glenlivet, Glen Avon, Cabrach and around Ardclach. Large autumn and winter flocks fed on stubbles and plough and even foraged for seeds on the thatched roofs

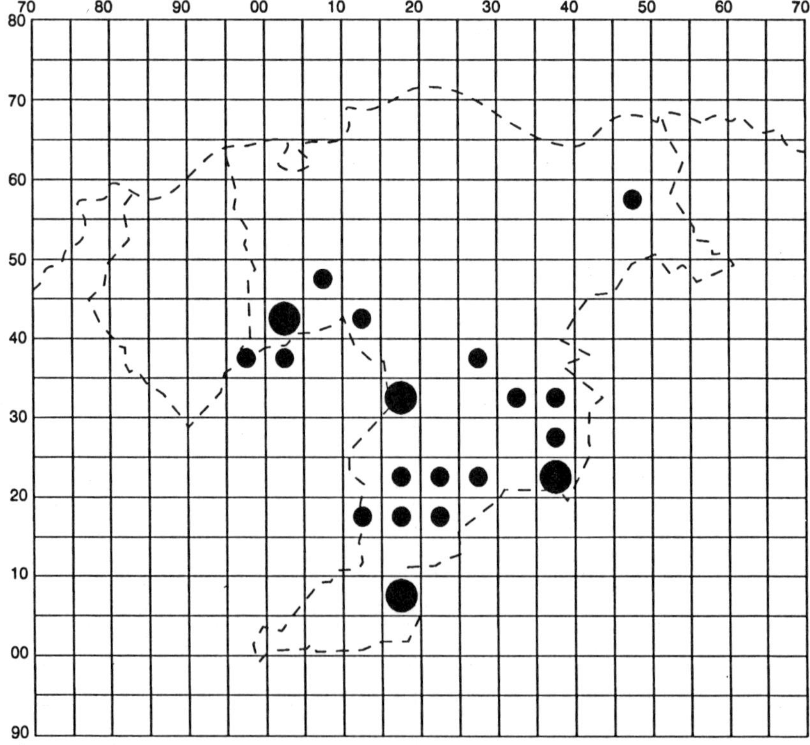

Figure 46 Twite summer distribution 1981–90 (April–July)

of farmhouses. Movement to lower ground and the coast was observed in winter.[**4,27**]

Since that time Twite have declined greatly, due in part, perhaps, to the demise of many upland crofts.[**86**] In summers 1968–72 they were found in 17 10 km-squares [**65**] but in most areas density was very low. Recently they have appeared even more local and only the Glenlivet/Cabrach/Tomintoul area holds a significant population. Here they breed thinly over upland farmland, the moorland edge and in young conifer plantations. A few pairs are also scattered over the western Moray moors especially in the Braemoray/Dava area, where a flock of 16 was counted on 8 April 1989. Good flocks sometimes buld up in Glenlivet in weedy turnip fields; best counts have been 225 at Tombae on 7 December 1987 and 215 at Achdregnie on 8 April 1986. Smaller flocks have been seen near Tomintoul (e.g. 80 at Conglass on 30 December 1988) and in the Cabrach (max. 50 on 21 January 1988). On 24 August 1990 a Twite was heard at *c.*1,150m over Garbh Uisge Beag in the Cairngorms.

In winter small numbers can sometimes be found on the coast mainly in the Findhorn/Culbin area (max. 25 at Culbin on 20 February 1983).

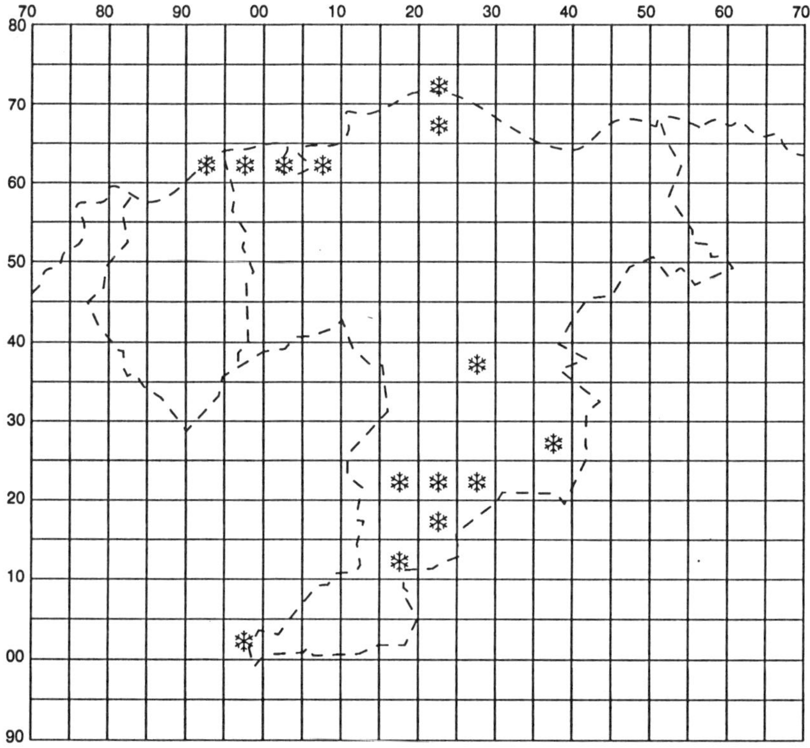

Figure 47 Twite winter distribution 1981–90 (November–February)

Redpoll

Carduelis flammea

Common resident breeder and migrant.

Redpolls are plentiful nesters in suitable habitat throughout Moray and Nairn. Formerly most pairs or small groups bred in damp willow scrub and birchwoods, but they have become much more widespread this century as young plantations have been colonised.

From late summer onwards, they form flocks, sometimes with Siskins, to feed on seeds of birch and alder. They also congregate in turnip fields and on waste ground with other finches. Highest counts have been 375 at Dunphail on 28 December 1983 and 300+ near Loch Flemington on 21 March 1989, although flocks of up to 50 are much more usual. Continental Mealy Redpolls *C.f.flammea* have been identified at Spey Bay (three on 30 November 1975), near Loch Flemington (two on 21 March 1989) and at Strathavon Lodge (one on 24 October 1991). Others have been suspected at times among winter flocks of local birds in western Moray. Most unusual were two Redpolls over Stac an Fharaidh, Cairngorm at 1,100m on 24 July 1989.

Common Crossbill

Loxia curvirostra

Irregular scarce visitor and probable breeder.

Scottish Crossbill

Loxia scotica

Resident breeder.

The status of the two crossbill species in the Districts is confused. They were not specifically separated until the mid 1970s and since that time the majority of local birds have not been conclusively identified either way. The issue is further complicated by the fact that on Deeside, although *scotica* is restricted to native pinewoods or mature pine plantations, *curvirostra* may be found breeding in the same woods and feeding on Scots pine cones.[**87,107**] Presumably the same situation may hold true for Moray and Nairn and so the commonly-held belief that a crossbill in Scots pine is *scotica* may result in misidentifications. *Loxia scotica*, however, is most unlikely to be seen, and will almost certainly not breed, in plantations of larch and spruce.

The first historical reference to *curvirostra* involved large numbers of crossbills feeding on larch cones at Cluny Hill, Forres in September 1868,[**4**] doubtless part of an irruption into Scotland from the Continent. In 1909–10, following another large invasion, the species was again reported in Moray woods and a probable male, which may have been breeding, was shot at Carron on 10 April 1910.[**87**] Small numbers were seen in October–December 1962 (e.g. 12 at Forres on 16 November, nine at Rothes on 27 October and six at Elgin on 24 October) and 120 crossbills at Tomintoul on 21 August 1981 were most likely to have been *curvirostra*. In 1990 Britain saw a large influx of Continental birds and crossbills were widely reported, although mainly unidentified, throughout the Districts. Of particular note were the undoubted *curvirostra* flocks among spruces and larches in the Daugh of Edinvillie plantation. On 12 November a group of 76 was plucking larch cones from a single tree. Breeding by Common Crossbills has yet to be proved but is likely to take place, especially following an invasion. On 18 February 1984 18 were watched in a mature spruce plantation at Tervieside, Glenlivet, where a number of males were excitedly calling and displaying around the treetops.

In 1895 the breeding range of 'crossbills' included the Nairn and Findhorn valleys, Forres, all through the Laich of Moray and as far east as Cullen and Rothiemay.[**4**] Although the specific identity of all these birds cannot now be proved, it is relevant that museum skins exist of certain *scotica* which were obtained at Fochabers in August and November 1902 and at Elgin in March 1910.[**108**] In the 1930s and 1940s Scottish Crossbills apparently nested in all the large pinewoods, but around 1960 they became scarcer and deserted Loch na Bo woods and Speymouth Forest. The populations also fell in Culbin and Darnaway.[**87**] By 1968–72 there had been some recovery and 'crossbills' were found in summer in 19 10 km-squares out of 33 surveyed, with breeding proved in nine.[**65**] In 1975 Nethersole-Thompson suggested that there was a breeding population of *c.*50 pairs of Scottish Crossbills in Moray, Nairn and Banff counties, moving from wood to wood in different years.[**87**]

The situation today is that crossbills are widely distributed in older Scots pine plantations in the Districts, although the population in any one wood continues to be very variable. On Deeside the only plantations where Knox found *scotica* were over 80 years old and stands of pine of around this age exist in Moray in places such as Culbin and Speymouth Forests. Although no specimens have been obtained and no calls analysed, it seems very likely that the heavy-billed birds breeding in these woods are indeed Scottish Crossbills. The best recent count was a flock of 35 in Speymouth Forest on 13 May 1978. The true identity of small groups of crossbills encountered flying noisily over the trees in 40–60-year-old plantations will, meantime, have to remain undetermined, although a pair closely watched while nest building in a 40-year-old compartment of Lossie Forest in February 1980 certainly had the appearance of *scotica*.

Bullfinch

Pyrrhula pyrrhula

Common resident breeder.

Bullfinches breed at low density throughout the Districts wherever there are thickets of vegetation such as dense deciduous woodlands, willow scrub or young plantations.

After the breeding season they feed on a variety of seeds, frequenting the margins of weedy fields, hedgerows and scrub. Heather seeds are taken on the moorland edge up to 600m altitude. They normally forage in small groups of less than 10 but occasionally much larger flocks are encountered; the largest was of 59 in rank heather beside the Lecht Road on 19 November 1983.

There have been four recoveries of birds ringed locally; the longest movement was 5 km.

Hawfinch

Coccothraustes coccothraustes

Accidental.

There are possibly three records of which only the most recent is beyond doubt. St.John gave an undated record of one described to him as having been seen near Forres prior to 1863.[**3**] Another is reputed to have been caught by an illegal bird-trapper in Forres *c.*1980 and sold for aviculture in Edinburgh. In 1988 one was seen in a garden at Clochan on 30 October (SBR 1988).

Lapland Bunting

Calcarius lapponicus

Rare visitor.

There have been six records involving a total of 12 birds:

1 Culbin	6 Oct 1974 (SB **8**:465)
2 Speymouth	18 Oct 1975 (SB **9**:234)
5 Spey Bay	19 Oct 1977 (SB **10**:152)
1 Burghead	23 Nov 1982 (SBR 1982)
2 Aldunie, Cabrach	21 March 1988 (SBR 1988)
1 ♂ Kinneddar, Lossiemouth	11 Feb 1991 (MNBR 1991)

All were near the coast except the Cabrach birds which were at 350m on the moorland edge. There was also one at Whiteness Head, just outside the Nairn boundary, on 24 December 1972 (SB **7**:383).

Snow Bunting

Plectrophenax nivalis

Common winter visitor and rare breeder.

The earliest summer record was of a male on Ben Macdui on 4 August 1830 and a pair was seen on the rocks above Loch Avon, below Ben Macdui, on 1 June 1870. The first nest in the Districts, in fact the first in the Cairngorms, was found on 5 June 1893 at 1,140m on Ben Avon. The nest and eggs were collected and deposited in the British Museum. Breeding also took place on

Ben Macdui between 1900–10 and in 1912.[88] Since that time a very few pairs of Snow Buntings have continued to nest in southern Moray among the corries and boulderfields of the high tops. Studies in this area between 1987–9 revealed average densities of less than one pair/km^2 in the small areas of suitable habitat, with nests seldom closer together than 500 m. Breeding success, however, was high with pairs regularly rearing two broods (R.Smith). A male on the summit of Ben Rinnes on 1 May 1989 was not seen subsequently.

The first autumn immigrants arrive in September; the earliest were two at Speymouth on 13 September 1969, but large numbers are unusual before late October. During winter, flocks feed among the coastal dunes where main areas are as follows:

	Usual numbers	*Peak count*
Speymouth	20–40	200 on 18 Nov 1972
Lossiemouth	50–100	250 on 16 Jan 1989
Findhorn–Nairn	100–200	500 on 24 Jan 1989

The origin of these birds is indicated by recoveries in Iceland, in March–April 1990, of two Snow Buntings ringed at Lossiemouth during winter 1988/9.

Ringing has also shown that Snow Buntings are very mobile around the Moray Firth and the size and composition of coastal flocks is highly variable, even from day to day. Birds caught at Lossiemouth in winter 1987/8 were retrapped at Dornoch (after six weeks) and Wick (next winter). Incomers to Lossiemouth had been ringed at Ardersier (nine days earlier) and Newburgh, Grampian, (five and a half weeks before). Evidence of exchange between coastal and inland flocks comes from the bird ringed at Ardersier on 22 December 1987 and caught at the Lecht, Tomintoul on 25 March 1988. Regular baiting with grain (as has recently been done at Lossiemouth to catch birds for ringing) can establish larger and more permanent flocks, a habit turned to their advantage by the crofters of Glenlivet last century. The birds were shot in great numbers (e.g. 118 'at one discharge'), plucked and then boiled or roasted.[4]

They were apparently far more numerous inland last century than is now the case. In Glenlivet in 1895 there were large flocks on all hills, sometimes in 'astonishing numbers'[4] and there were big flocks in stackyards and fields around Ardclach in 1900.[27] Today groups are usually smaller, although a Cabrach flock peaked at 500 on 31 January 1988 and 300 were at Knockando on 31 January 1975. During the three winters 1981/2–1983/4 their distribution was as follows:[68]

	10km-squares surveyed	*Birds seen in one day* 1–8	9–50	51+	*% squares containing Snow Buntings*
Coastal	10	0	3	5	80
Inland	23	4	5	4	57

They sometimes visit high hills and mountain tops, even in mid winter, e.g. 30 on Ben Rinnes summit on 20 December 1987 and 100 between Cairn Gorm and Ben Macdui in December 1961.[**49**] There is a regular flock around the ski carpark at the Lecht during the skiing season. Most winter visitors have left the Districts by the end of March; the latest records at the coast were singles at Lossiemouth on 22 April 1979 and at Spey Bay on 5 May 1972.

Yellowhammer

Emberiza citrinella

Common resident breeder.

Yellowhammers are widespread in Moray and Nairn from the coast to the moorland edge but never far from agricultural land. They breed in hedgerows, open scrub and particularly favour thickets of gorse. Last century they were much persecuted because of superstitions alleging connections with the Devil but this seems to have had little effect on their abundance and by 1900 the habit was dying out.[**6,27,52**]

In winter flocks are attracted to farmyards and stubbles, where they mix with finches and sparrows; 300 at Miltonhill on 14 February 1986 was exceptional, otherwise 160 near Buckie on 14 January 1984 is the highest count.

Reed Bunting

Emberiza schoeniclus

Numerous resident breeder.

A widespread although only locally common breeder throughout the lowlands and inland to 350m at Tomintoul, Reed Buntings occupy a variety of habitats, chiefly reedbeds, marshes and damp scrub but occasionally also drier gorse commons, young plantations and even well-vegetated dunes. Three pairs bred on Nairn Bar in 1990.

Results of the ornithological Atlas surveys [**65,68**] are shown below:

	10 km-squares surveyed	*10 km-squares occupied by Reed Buntings*		
		summer 1968–72	*winter 1981/2–1983/4*	*summer 1988–90*
Within 20 km of the coast	17	16	15	14
Over 20 km inland	16	13	3	8

These surveys indicate a decline in the inland breeding population and also suggest movement away from inland haunts in winter.

During the winter Reed Buntings feed around marshes, reedbeds and dunes but also among scrub and stubbles on farmland. Numbers seen together are usually small, but there were 40 at Drainie on 2 January 1988. Communal roosts often form in reedbeds such as at Kingston and Loch Spynie.

Corn Bunting

Miliaria calandra

Numerous resident breeder.

Breeding Corn Buntings are closely associated with growing cereal crops and are conspicuous as they utter their jangling song from prominent perches such as telephone poles and wires. In 1844 they were 'resident in great abundance';[6] and at the turn of the century they were still very common

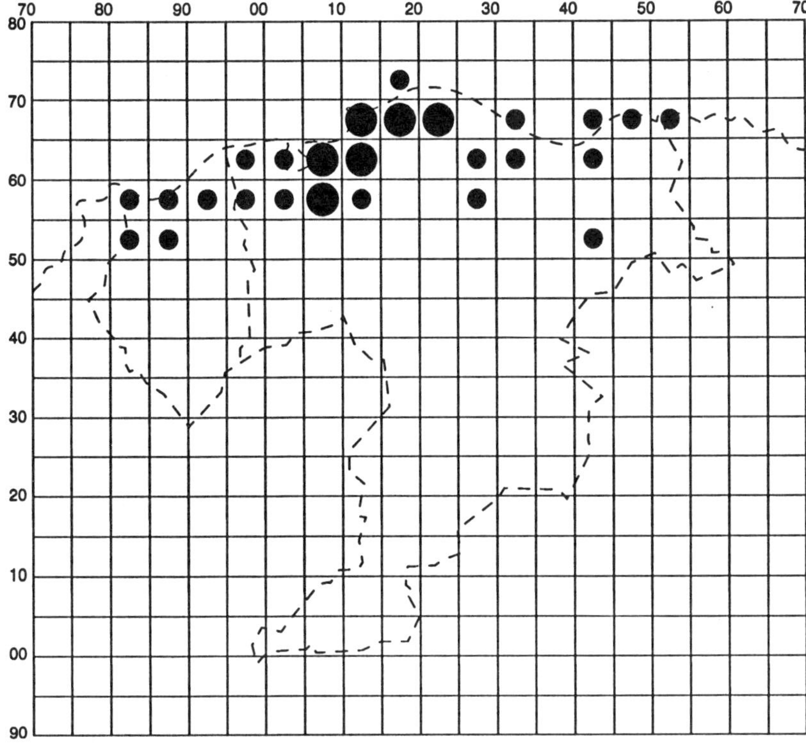

Figure 48 Corn Bunting summer distribution 1981–90 (April–July)

on farmland throughout the Laich of Moray, but more local further inland.[4] In December 1948 about 150 were roosting in marshy ground near Loch Spynie (BB **43**:370) and in the early 1960s they were still numerous in the coastal plain,[**45**] nesting in crops and among gorse. In summers 1968–72 they were present in 21 10 km-squares out of 33 surveyed, with breeding proved in 11 including NJ 12 in Strathavon.[**65**] Since then a very marked decline has taken place; in summers 1985–90 birds were seen in only ten 10 km-squares. Breeding density is mostly low, although 'pockets' of higher population still exist in the Alves and Hopeman areas, around Lossiemouth airfield and between Portgordon and Cullen. The current breeding population is probably in the region of 50–100 pairs and the decline may now have halted. In 1989 several new sites were occupied within the 'stronghold' areas and 11 singing males were found around Drainie.

In winter Corn Buntings assemble in small gatherings in open country to feed on stubbles and waste ground. Few flocks are seen today; they were recorded in only four out of 33 10 km-squares during winters 1981/2–1983/4. A flock of 90 at Findochty on 28 February 1990 was by far the largest group reported in recent years, the best in the 1980s being 23 near Lossiemouth on 21 January 1987.

Appendix 1: Grid references of localities mentioned in the text

Aberlour	NJ 265428	Birnie	NJ 206592
Achavraat	NH 911482	Blackhills	NJ 272586
Achdregnie	NJ 245246	Black Loch	NH 986555
Achnatone	NH 923490	Blacksboat	NJ 184388
Aikenway	NJ 291500	Blackwater	NJ 335287
Ailnack	NJ 150154	Blairnamarrow	NJ 210154
Airdrie	NH 980469	Boar's Head Rock	NJ 289680
Aitnoch	NH 981397	Boat o' Brig	NJ 319517
Aldroughty	NJ 185625	Bochel, The	NJ 232232
Aldunie	NJ 369269	Bogmoor	NJ 357627
Altyre	NJ 025535	Bow Fiddle Rock	NJ 495688
Alves	NJ 135623	Bowmans	NJ 358266
Archiestown	NJ 230442	Braemoray	NH 998428
Ardclach	NH 955453	Braes of Glenlivet	NJ 244214
Arndilly	NJ 290475	Bridge of Brown	NJ 124206
Auchindoun	NJ 355400	Bridge of Marnoch	NJ 605495
Auchlochan	NJ 023416	Broadley (Moray)	NJ 395618
Auchness	NJ 115491	Brodie	NH 978572
Auldearn	NH 918555	Brokentore	NJ 183549
Auldich	NJ 196348	Buck, The	NJ 412235
Aultahuish	NJ 140494	Buckie	NJ 425657
Aulthash	NJ 374558	Buckie Loch	NJ 002647
Aultmore	NJ 470580	Buckpool	NJ 412653
		Buinach	NJ 181561
Ballindalloch	NJ 178365	Burghead	NJ 114689
Balnacoul	NJ 323595	Burghead Bay	NJ 080670
Banchor	NH 912407	Burgie	NJ 093593
Beinn Mheadhoin	NJ 023017		
Ben Aigan	NJ 310482	Cabrach	NJ 385270
Ben Avon	NJ 133018	Cairn Dregnie	NJ 260270
Ben Macdui	NN 989989	Cairn Eney	NJ 020443
Ben Main	NJ 351359	Cairnfield	NJ 415623
Ben Rinnes	NJ 255355	Cairn Gorm	NJ 005040
Berryburn	NJ 059454	Cairn Lochan	NH 985026
Bin of Cullen	NJ 480643	Califer	NJ 082571
Binn Hill	NJ 305656	Carnach	NJ 009490
Birkenhill	NJ 224600	Carn a'Gharbh-ghlaic	NH 895351

Carn an t-Suidhe	NJ 261269	Delnies	NH 845563
Carn Ghuibhais	NJ 082453	Deskford	NJ 508617
Carn Kitty	NJ 090428	Drainie	NJ 215687
Carn Meilich	NJ 162232	Drumdivan	NH 844547
Carn Mor	NJ 266184	Drumduan	NH 917567
Carn na Cailliche	NJ 188475	Drumin	NJ 185303
Carn nan Clach Garbha	NH 945345	Drumlochan	NH 943410
Carn Shalag	NJ 118428	Drybridge	NJ 435625
Carron	NJ 222414	Drynachan	NH 865397
Carse of Delnies	NH 830565	Dufftown	NJ 324397
Caskieben	NH 853550	Duffus	NJ 170688
Cawdor	NH 845500	Dulsie Bridge	NH 933415
Caysbriggs	NJ 248670	Dunphail	NJ 010480
Chapeltown, Glenlivet	NJ 242210	Dyke	NH 990585
Clochan	NJ 402608		
Cloddach quarry	NJ 200591	Edinkillie	NJ 040470
Clunas	NH 882465	Elfhill	NJ 212557
Clunas reservoir	NH 860460	Elgin	NJ 215625
Cluny Hill	NJ 081533	Ess of Glenlatterach	NJ 195534
Coire Grealach	NJ 145076		
Coire Raibeirt	NJ 003030	Feith Buidhe	NH 990015
Coltfield	NJ 117637	Ferness	NH 963448
Conglass	NJ 174223	Findhorn	NJ 040645
Cook's Cairn	NJ 302278	Findhorn Bay	NJ 045625
Corsemaul	NJ 388402	Findochty	NJ 465680
Cothall	NJ 019549	Findrassie	NJ 195652
Coulmony House	NH 975477	Fleenas	NH 913500
Covesea	NJ 186705	Fochabers	NJ 345585
Covesea Skerries	NJ 197719	Forres	NJ 035585
Coxton	NJ 253360		
Craigellachie	NJ 290450	Garbh Uisge Beag	NH 995010
Craigenroan Reef	NJ 445675	Garbh Uisge Mor	NH 998000
Craig Watch	NJ 386355	Garmouth	NJ 338644
Cran Loch	NH 945590	Garrowood	NJ 502507
Creag Mhor	NJ 057048	Geddes	NH 883527
Culbin Bar	NH 965627	Gilston	NJ 205662
Culbin Forest	NH 990620	Glen Avon	NJ 100060
Culbin Sands	NJ 020640	Glenferness	NH 937428
Cullen	NJ 513671	Glen Fiddich	NJ 320336
Culraggie	NJ 209225	Glen Latterach	NJ 192516
		Glenlatterach reservoir	NJ 192530
Dallas	NJ 124525	Glenlivet	NJ 260233
Dalmore Manse	NH 920540	Glenmullie	NJ 196168
Dalvey	NJ 006577	Glen of Rothes	NJ 260520
Darnaway	NH 990520	Glen Rinnes	NJ 285345
Daugh of Edinvillie	NJ 282404	Gordon Castle	NJ 350596
Dava	NJ 005387	Gordonstoun	NJ 183690
Delnabo	NJ 160170	Gow Moss	NJ 382534

Grange	NJ 490510
Hatton, Kinloss	NJ 093641
Hillockhead	NJ 402500
Hill of Dalnapot	NJ 160375
Hill of Towie	NJ 382473
Hilton of Delnies	NH 845563
Hopeman	NJ 145695
Inchbroom	NJ 254669
Inchrory	NJ 179081
Innes House	NJ 279650
Invererne House	NJ 031606
Inverharroch	NJ 382312
Johnstripe	NJ 050479
Keith	NJ 430505
Kellas	NJ 172543
Kildrummie	NH 866535
Kilravock	NH 813494
Kincorth House	NJ 012617
Kinermony	NJ 254420
Kingston	NJ 337655
Kinloss	NJ 065618
Kinneddar	NJ 223694
Kintessack	NJ 002603
Kirkhill	NJ 247628
Kirkmichael	NJ 180130
Knockandhu	NJ 213237
Knockando	NJ 182429
Knock Hill	NJ 537552
Knock of Braemoray	NJ 011418
Ladder Hills	NJ 266184
Lecht	NJ 245133
Lein	NJ 334657
Leuchars	NJ 258648
Lhanbryde	NJ 275615
Lochan Buidhe	NH 983011
Loch Avon	NJ 015025
Loch Builg	NJ 188031
Loch Belivat	NH 953470
Loch Dallas	NJ 093477
Loch Dubh	NJ 024417
Loch Etchachan	NJ 006005
Loch Flemington	NH 810520

Lochindorb	NH 975365
Lochinver	NJ 182618
Loch Loy	NH 933587
Loch na Bo	NJ 283600
Loch Noir	NJ 093454
Loch of Blairs	NJ 023557
Loch of Boath	NH 886453
Lochs of Bogmussach	NJ 136473
Loch of Cotts	NJ 268669
Lochs of Little Benshalag	NJ 111437
Loch of the Clans	NH 834532
Loch of the Cowlatt	NJ 123443
Loch Oire	NJ 288608
Loch Park	NJ 354430
Loch Spynie	NJ 235665
Logie	NJ 012505
Longmorn	NJ 235584
Lossie estuary	NJ 243700
Lossie Forest	NJ 270680
Lossiemouth	NJ 235710
Maverston	NJ 300635
Mayen	NJ 581477
Mayne	NJ 208608
Meikle Balloch Hill	NJ 472496
Meikle Hill	NJ 144505
Millbuies	NJ 243569
Mill Our	NJ 199528
Millton	NJ 105321
Milton Brodie	NJ 093628
Miltonduff	NJ 183602
Miltonhill	NJ 099630
Monaughty	NJ 125608
Monaughty Forest	NJ 132595
Morinsh Forest	NJ 225300
Mortlach Hills	NJ 370370
Moss of Dunphail	NJ 026482
Mosstodloch	NJ 333600
Moy	NJ 015602
Muir of the Clans	NH 835525
Mulben	NJ 355505
Mundole	NJ 013569
Nairn	NH 883567
Nairn Bar	NH 922603
Netherton	NJ 038612
Newmill	NJ 435525
Newton of Budgate	NH 826499

Newtyle	NJ 055525
Oakenhead	NJ 242686
Ordiga	NJ 373605
Ordiquish	NJ 338572
Orton	NJ 317543
Parkmore	NJ 339415
Pikey Hill	NJ 214513
Pitchroy	NJ 176380
Pitgaveny	NJ 240652
Pittendreich	NJ 194613
Pluscarden	NJ 147568
Pooltown	NH 814536
Portessie	NJ 440666
Portgordon	NJ 395642
Portknockie	NJ 490685
Rafford	NJ 061562
Raitcastle	NH 890528
Rathven	NJ 444657
Relugas	NH 992487
Riff Bank	NH 785605
Rochuln	NJ 072472
Rosehaugh	NJ 166644
Roseisle	NJ 138666
Rothes	NJ 277495
Rothiemay	NJ 547483
Sanquhar Loch	NJ 041581
Sluie	NJ 007525
Spey Bay	NJ 354653
Speymouth	NJ 345656
Speymouth Forest	NJ 375585
Speyslaw	NJ 284668
Spynie canal	NJ 235666
Stac an Fharaidh	NJ 008030
Strathavon	NJ 145252
Strathlene	NJ 449674
Strypes	NJ 278585
Tarras	NJ 062597
Tarryblake	NJ 520495
Tearie	NH 988569
Teindland	NJ 280562
Ternemny quarry	NJ 557528
Tervieside	NJ 232308
Thornton	NJ 487515
Tips of Corsemaul	NJ 394396
Tombae	NJ 219254
Tomcork	NJ 043465
Tomdow	NJ 005447
Tomhommie	NH 823542
Tomintoul	NJ 170185
Tomlachlan Burn	NH 933377
Tomnavoulin	NJ 213260
Towiemore	NJ 395457
Tulchan	NJ 128356
Upper Manbeen	NJ 188577
Urquhart	NJ 286627
Wellhill	NJ 001612
Wester Elchies	NJ 254430
Westerfolds	NJ 195679
Westfield	NJ 163653
Whiteash Hill	NJ 375585
Whiteness Head	NH 805587
Williamston	NJ 160691

Appendix 2: Moray and Nairn Checklist

Use this list to record the species you have seen in Moray and Nairn.

_______ Red-throated Diver
_______ Black-throated Diver
_______ Great Northern Diver
_______ White-billed Diver
_______ Little Grebe
_______ Great Crested Grebe
_______ Red-necked Grebe
_______ Slavonian Grebe
_______ Black-necked Grebe
_______ Black-browed Albatross
_______ Fulmar
_______ Sooty Shearwater
_______ Manx Shearwater
_______ Storm Petrel
_______ Leach's Petrel
_______ Gannet
_______ Cormorant
_______ Shag
_______ Bittern
_______ American Bittern
_______ Little Egret
_______ Grey Heron
_______ Black Stork
_______ White Stork
_______ Glossy Ibis
_______ Spoonbill
_______ Mute Swan
_______ Bewick's Swan
_______ Whooper Swan
_______ Bean Goose
_______ Pink-footed Goose
_______ White-fronted Goose
_______ Greylag Goose
_______ Snow Goose
_______ Canada Goose
_______ Barnacle Goose
_______ Brent Goose
_______ Ruddy Shelduck
_______ Shelduck
_______ Wigeon
_______ American Wigeon
_______ Gadwall
_______ Baikal Teal
_______ Teal
_______ Mallard
_______ Pintail
_______ Garganey
_______ Shoveler
_______ Pochard
_______ Ring-necked Duck
_______ Tufted Duck
_______ Scaup
_______ Eider
_______ King Eider
_______ Long-tailed Duck
_______ Common Scoter
_______ Surf Scoter
_______ Velvet Scoter
_______ Goldeneye
_______ Smew
_______ Red-breasted Merganser
_______ Goosander
_______ Ruddy Duck
_______ Honey Buzzard
_______ Black Kite
_______ Red Kite
_______ White-tailed Eagle
_______ Marsh Harrier
_______ Hen Harrier
_______ Goshawk
_______ Sparrowhawk
_______ Buzzard
_______ Rough-legged Buzzard
_______ Golden Eagle

_______ Osprey
_______ Kestrel
_______ Merlin
_______ Hobby
_______ Gyrfalcon
_______ Peregrine
_______ Red Grouse
_______ Ptarmigan
_______ Black Grouse
_______ Capercaillie
_______ Red-legged Partridge
_______ Grey Partridge
_______ Quail
_______ Pheasant
_______ Water Rail
_______ Spotted Crake
_______ Little Crake
_______ Corncrake
_______ Moorhen
_______ Coot
_______ Crane
_______ Little Bustard
_______ Great Bustard
_______ Oystercatcher
_______ Avocet
_______ Stone Curlew
_______ Ringed Plover
_______ Kentish Plover
_______ Dotterel
_______ Golden Plover
_______ Grey Plover
_______ Lapwing
_______ Knot
_______ Sanderling
_______ Little Stint
_______ Temminck's Stint
_______ Baird's Sandpiper
_______ Pectoral Sandpiper
_______ Curlew Sandpiper
_______ Purple Sandpiper
_______ Dunlin
_______ Broad-billed Sandpiper
_______ Ruff
_______ Jack Snipe
_______ Snipe
_______ Great Snipe
_______ Woodcock
_______ Black-tailed Godwit
_______ Bar-tailed Godwit
_______ Whimbrel
_______ Curlew
_______ Spotted Redshank
_______ Redshank
_______ Marsh Sandpiper
_______ Greenshank
_______ Lesser Yellowlegs
_______ Green Sandpiper
_______ Wood Sandpiper
_______ Common Sandpiper
_______ Turnstone
_______ Wilson's Phalarope
_______ Red-necked Phalarope
_______ Grey Phalarope
_______ Pomarine Skua
_______ Arctic Skua
_______ Long-tailed Skua
_______ Great Skua
_______ Mediterranean Gull
_______ Little Gull
_______ Black-headed Gull
_______ Ring-billed Gull
_______ Common Gull
_______ Lesser Black-backed Gull
_______ Herring Gull
_______ Iceland Gull
_______ Glaucous Gull
_______ Great Black-backed Gull
_______ Kittiwake
_______ Ivory Gull
_______ Sandwich Tern
_______ Roseate Tern
_______ Common Tern
_______ Arctic Tern
_______ Little Tern
_______ Black Tern
_______ White-winged Black Tern
_______ Guillemot
_______ Razorbill
_______ Black Guillemot
_______ Little Auk
_______ Puffin
_______ Pallas's Sandgrouse
_______ Rock Dove/Feral Pigeon
_______ Stock Dove
_______ Woodpigeon
_______ Collared Dove

________ Turtle Dove
________ Cuckoo
________ Yellow-billed Cuckoo
________ Barn Owl
________ Snowy Owl
________ Tawny Owl
________ Long-eared Owl
________ Short-eared Owl
________ Nightjar
________ Swift
________ Alpine Swift
________ Kingfisher
________ Roller
________ Hoopoe
________ Green Woodpecker
________ Great Spotted Woodpecker
________ Skylark
________ Shore Lark
________ Sand Martin
________ Swallow
________ House Martin
________ Richard's Pipit
________ Tawny Pipit
________ Tree Pipit
________ Meadow Pipit
________ Rock Pipit
________ Yellow Wagtail
________ Grey Wagtail
________ Pied Wagtail
________ Waxwing
________ Dipper
________ Wren
________ Dunnock
________ Robin
________ Nightingale
________ Bluethroat
________ Black Redstart
________ Redstart
________ Whinchat
________ Stonechat
________ Wheatear
________ Grey-cheeked Thrush
________ Ring Ouzel
________ Blackbird
________ Fieldfare
________ Song Thrush
________ Redwing
________ Mistle Thrush
________ Grasshopper Warbler
________ Sedge Warbler
________ Marsh Warbler
________ Lesser Whitethroat
________ Whitethroat
________ Garden Warbler
________ Blackcap
________ Wood Warbler
________ Chiffchaff
________ Willow Warbler
________ Firecrest
________ Goldcrest
________ Spotted Flycatcher
________ Pied Flycatcher
________ Long-tailed Tit
________ Willow Tit
________ Crested Tit
________ Coal Tit
________ Blue Tit
________ Great Tit
________ Treecreeper
________ Red-backed Shrike
________ Great Grey Shrike
________ Woodchat Shrike
________ Jay
________ Magpie
________ Jackdaw
________ Rook
________ Carrion Crow/Hooded Crow
________ Raven
________ Starling
________ Rose-coloured Starling
________ House Sparrow
________ Tree Sparrow
________ Chaffinch
________ Brambling
________ Greenfinch
________ Goldfinch
________ Siskin
________ Linnet
________ Twite
________ Redpoll
________ Common Crossbill
________ Scottish Crossbill
________ Bullfinch
________ Hawfinch
________ Lapland Bunting
________ Snow Bunting

________ Yellowhammer
________ Reed Bunting
________ Corn Bunting

Additional Species

________ ____________________
________ ____________________
________ ____________________
________ ____________________
________ ____________________
________ ____________________
________ ____________________
________ ____________________
________ ____________________
________ ____________________
________ ____________________
________ ____________________
________ ____________________
________ ____________________
________ ____________________
________ ____________________
________ ____________________
________ ____________________
________ ____________________
________ ____________________
________ ____________________
________ ____________________
________ ____________________
________ ____________________

Reference List

1. BarretJ. & Barret,C.F. (1985) Divers in the Moray Firth, Scotland. *Scot.Birds* **13**:149–54.
2. Baxter,E.V. & Rintoul,L.J. (1953) *The Birds of Scotland*. Edinburgh: Oliver & Boyd.
3. St.John,C. (1863) *Natural History and Sport in Moray*. Edinburgh: Edmonstone & Douglas.
4. Harvie-BrownJ.A. & Buckley,T.E. (1895) *A Vertebrate Fauna of the Moray Basin*, 2 vols. Edinburgh: David Douglas.
5. Aspinall,S.J. & Mudge,G.P. (1986) *Seaducks and Divers in the Moray Firth 1985–1986*. Unpubl. RSPB report.
6. Gordon,G. (1844) A Fauna of Moray. II Birds. *Zoologist* **2**:502–15.
7. Gordon,G. (1889) *The Fauna of Moray*. Elgin: J & J.A.Watson.
8. MacDonald,M. (1934) *Bird Watching at Lossiemouth*. Elgin: Courant and Courier.
9. Allen,D.S. (1979) *Seaducks in the Moray and Dornoch Firths, Scotland, winter of 1978/79*. Unpubl. RSPB report.
10. FisherJ. (1952) *The Fulmar*. Glasgow: Collins.
11. FisherJ. (1966) The Fulmar population of Britain and Ireland, 1959. *Bird Study* **13**:5–76.
12. Wynne-Edwards,V.C. (1953) Leach's Petrels stranded in Scotland in October–November 1952. *Scot.Nat.* **65**:167–89.
13. *New Statistical Account of Scotland*, 1845 Vol XIII: *Banff, Elgin, Nairn*. Edinburgh: Blackwood.
14. *The Statistical Account of Scotland* 1791–99, ed Sir John Sinclair, Vol XVI: *Banffshire, Moray and Nairnshire*.
15. Watt,H.B. (1908) A List of Scottish Heronries, past and present. *Ann.Scot.Nat. Hist.* **17**:218–23.
16. Boece,H. (1526) *Scotorum Historiae a prima gentis origina*, Bellendens translation.
17. Rawcliffe,C.P. (1958) The Scottish Mute Swan Census 1955–56. *Bird Study* **5**:45–55.
18. Ogilvie,M.A. (1981) The Mute Swan in Britain 1978. *Bird Study* **28**:87–106.
19. Brown,A.W. & Brown,L.M. (1985) The Scottish Mute Swan Census 1983. *Scot.Birds* **13**:140–8.
20. Spray,C.J. (1983) East of Scotland Mute Swan Study. *Scot.Birds* **12**:197–8.
21. Hewson,R. (1963) Whooper Swans at Loch Park, Banffshire 1955–61. *Bird Study* **10**:203–10.
22. Hewson,R. (1973) Changes in a Winter Herd of Whooper Swans at a Banff Loch. *Bird Study* **20**:41–9.
23. MacGillivray,W. (1837–1852) *History of British Birds*.

24. Ruttledge,R.F. & Ogilvie,M.A. (1979) The past and current status of the Greenland White-fronted Goose in Ireland and Britain. *Irish Birds* **1**:293–363.
25. Berry,J. (1939) *The Status and Distribution of Wild Geese and Wild Duck in Scotland*. Cambridge: Cambridge University Press.
26. Atkinson-Willes,G.L. & Matthews,G.V.T. (1960) The past status of the Brent Goose. *Brit.Birds* **53**:352–7.
27. Thomson,R. (1900) *The Natural History of a Highland Parish (Ardclach, Nairnshire)*. Nairn: George Bain.
28. Shaw,L. (1775) *The History of the Province of Moray*. Edinburgh: William Auld.
29. Moore,N.W. (1957) The past and present status of the Buzzard in the British Isles. *Brit.Birds* **50**:173–97.
30. Ratcliffe,D.A. (1980) *The Peregrine Falcon*. Berkhamsted: Poyser.
31. Barrett,J. (1983) *Moray Firth Seaducks: winters 1981–82 and 1982–83*, Report to Britoil of surveys carried out by RSPB.
32. St.John,H.C.(ed) (1901) *Charles St.John's Notebooks* 1846–1853. David Douglas.
33. Milne,H. (1961) Eiders breeding in Morayshire. *Scot.Birds* **1**:491.
34. Mudge,G.P. (1978) *Seaducks in the Moray and Dornoch Firths, Scotland. Winter of 1977/78*. Unpubl. NCC and RSPB report.
35. Milne,H. (1965) Seasonal movements and distribution of Eiders in Northeast Scotland. *Bird Study* **12**:170–80.
36. Barrett,J. (1984) *Moray Firth Seaducks: Winter 1983–84*. RSPB report to Britoil.
37. Mudge,G.P. & Aspinall,S.J. (1985) *Spring, autumn and winter concentrations of seaducks and divers in the Moray Firth 1984–1985*. Unpubl. RSPB report.
38. Aspinall,S.J. & Mudge,G.P, (1986) Seaducks and divers in the Moray Firth 1985–1986.
39. Harvie-Brown,J.A. & Buckley,T.E. (1887) *A Vertebrate Fauna of Sutherland, Caithness and West Cromarty*. David Douglas.
40. Meek,E.R. & Little,B. (1977) The spread of the Goosander in Britain and Ireland. *Brit.Birds* **70**:229–37.
41. Watson,A. (1986) In *The Atlas of Wintering Birds in Britain and Ireland,* compiled by Peter Lack. Berkhamsted: T. & A.D.Poyser.
42. Rintoul,L.J. & Baxter,E.V. (1927) On the decrease of Blackgame in Scotland. *Scot.Nat.* **1927**:5–13.
43. Pennie,I.D. (1950) The history and distribution of the Capercaillie in Scotland. *Scot.Nat.* **62**:65–87; 157–78.
44. Norris,C.A. (1945) Summary of a report on the distribution and status of the Corncrake (*Crex crex*) *Brit.Birds* **38**:162–8.
45. *The Third Statistical Account of Scotland 1965*, ed. Henry Hamilton, *The Counties of Moray and Nairn.*
46. Cadbury,C.J. (1980) The status and habits of the Corncrake in Britain 1978–1979. *Bird Study* **27**:203–18.
47. Swann,R.L. (1985) Highland Oystercatchers. *Ringing & Migration* **6**:55–9.
48. Prater,A.J. (1976) Breeding Population of the Ringed Plover in Britain. *Bird Study* **23**:155–61.
49. Dennis,R.H. (1984) *The Birds of Badenoch and Strathspey*. Roy Dennis Enterprises.
50. Alexander,W.B. (1945) The Woodcock in the British Isles (Part I). *Ibis*

87:512–50.

51. Alexander,W.B. (1947) The Woodcock in the British Isles (Part VI). *Ibis* **89**:1–28.
52. Watson,J. (1889) *Some Local Wild Birds (to be found in the vicinity of Elgin).* J. & J.A. Watson.
53. *Catalogue of British Birds in the Elgin Museum.*
54. *Catalogue of Birds in the Dr.Muirhead Collection in Elgin Museum.*
55. Bainbridge,I.P. & Minton,C.D.T. (1978) The Migration and Mortality of the Curlew in Britain and Ireland. *Bird Study* **25**:39–50.
56. Bourne,W.R.P., Smith,A.J.M. & Dowse,A. (1978) Gulls and terns nesting inland in northeast Scotland. *Scot.Birds* **10**:50–3.
57. Cramp,S., Bourne,W.R.P. & Saunders,D. (1974) *The Seabirds of Britain and Ireland.* Glasgow: Collins.
58. Cramp,S. (1971) Gulls nesting on buildings in Britain and Ireland. *Brit.Birds* **64**:476–87.
59. Monaghan,P. & Coulson,J.C. (1977) Status of Large Gulls Nesting on Buildings. *Bird Study* **24**:89–104.
60. Thom,V.M. (1986) *Birds in Scotland.* Berkhamsted: T. & A.D.Poyser.
61. Norman,R.K. & Saunders,D.R. (1969) Status of Little Terns in Great Britain and Ireland in 1967. *Brit.Birds* **62**:4–13.
62. Clarke,W.E. (1895) On the recent visitation of the Little Auk (*Mergulus alle*) to Scotland. *Ann.Scot.Nat.Hist.* **4**:97–108.
63. Sergeant,D.E. (1952) Little Auks in Britain 1948 to 1951. *Brit.Birds* **45**:122–33.
64. Harvie-Brown,J.A. (1894) On the extension of the distribution of the Stock Dove (*Columba oenas*) in Scotland. *Ann.Scot.Nat.Hist.* **3**:3–8.
65. Sharrock,J.T.R. (comp.) (1976) *The Atlas of Breeding Birds in Britain and Ireland.* BTO/IWC.
66. Hudson,R. (1965) The spread of the Collared Dove in Britain and Ireland. *Brit.Birds* **58**:105–39.
67. MacMillan,A.T. (1961) The Collared Dove in Scotland. *Scot.Birds* **1**:480–9.
68. Lack,P. (comp.) (1986) *The Atlas of Wintering Birds in Britain and Ireland.* Berkhamsted: T. & A.D.Poyser.
69. Stafford,J. (1962) Nightjar Enquiry 1957–58. *Bird Study* **9**:104–15.
70. Harvie-Brown,J.A. (1892) The Great Spotted Woodpecker (*Picus major*,L.) in Scotland. *Ann.Scot.Nat.Hist.* **1**:4–17.
71. Harvie-Brown,J.A. (1908) The Great Spotted Woodpecker's resuscitation in Scotland since 1841 or 1851. *Ann.Scot.Nat.Hist.* **17**:210–6.
72. Mead,C. & Mead,V. (1966) Sand Martin safari. *Ringers' Bulletin* **2**:No.9 pp 14–5.
73. McGinn,D.B. (1979) Status and breeding biology of Swallows in Banffshire. *Scot.Birds* **10**:221–9.
74. Hewson,R. (1967) Territory, behaviour and breeding of the Dipper in Banffshire. *Brit.Birds* **60**:244–52.
75. Harrison,J.G. (1967) Grey-cheeked Thrush in Morayshire. *Brit.Birds* **60**:55–6.
76. Nethersole-Thompson,D. & Watson,A. (1974) *The Cairngorms.* Glasgow: Collins.
77. Elkins,N. (1976) Probable Siberian Chiffchaffs wintering in Morayshire. *Scot.Birds* **9**:164–6.

78. Cook,M.J.H. (1982) Breeding status of the Crested Tit, *Scot.Birds* **12**:97–106.
79. Deadman,A.J. (1973) *A population study of the Coal Tit* Parus ater *and the Crested Tit* Parus cristatus *in a Scottish Pine plantation*. Unpubl. Ph.D. thesis, Aberdeen University.
80. Hewson,R. (1970) Winter home range and feeding habits of a Great Grey Shrike in Morayshire. *Scot.Birds* **6**:18–22.
81. Duncan,A.B. (1938) The Magpie in Scotland. *Scot.Nat.* **1938**:65–79.
82. Castle,M.E. (1977) Rookeries in Scotland – 1975. *Scot.Birds* **9**:327–34.
83. Sage,B.L. & Vernon,J.D.R. (1978) The 1975 National Survey of Rookeries. *Bird Study* **25**:64–86.
84. Munro,J.H.B. (1975) Scottish winter Rook roost survey – central and northern Scotland. *Scot.Birds* **8**:309–14.
85. Holyoak,D.T. & Ratcliffe,D.A. (1968) The distribution of the Raven in Britain and Ireland. *Bird Study* **15**:191–7.
86. Hewson,R. (1967) The status of the Twite. *Scot.Birds* **4**:508–9.
87. Nethersole-Thompson,D. (1975) *Pine Crossbills.* Berkhamsted: T. & A.D.Poyser.
88. Nethersole-Thompson,D. (1966) *The Snow Bunting*. Edinburgh: Oliver & Boyd.
89. Williamson,K. (1954) American birds in Scotland in Autumn and Winter 1953–1954. *Scot.Nat.* **66**:13–29.
90. Swann,R.L. & Mudge,G.P. (1989) Moray Basin wader populations. *Scot.Birds* **15**:97–105.
91. RSPB (1980) *RSPB Moorland surveys 1980; Morayshire*. RSPB internal document.
92. Shepherd,K.B., Brown,A.F., Calladine,J.R. & Smedley,M. (1989) *A survey of breeding birds of some moorland areas in Morayshire in 1989*. Chief Scientist Directorate Commissioned Research Report No.951.
93. Nethersole-Thompson,D. & Nethersole-Thompson,M. (1979) *Greenshanks*. Berkhamsted: T. & A.D.Poyser.
94. Baxter,E.V. & Rintoul,L.J. (1921) The Pintail as a Scottish Breeding Species. *Scot.Nat.* **1921**:37–42.
95. Nethersole-Thompson,D. (1951) *The Greenshank*. Glasgow: Collins.
96. Watson,D. (1977) *The Hen Harrier*. Berkhamsted: T. & A.D.Poyser.
97. Edward,T. (1860) A List of the Birds of Banffshire, accompanied with Anecdotes. *Zoologist* **18**:6968–70.
98. Everett,M.J. (1967) Waxwings in Scotland, 1965/66 and 1966/67. *Scot.Birds* **4**:534–48.
99. Burn,D.N. & Mather,J.R. (1974) The While-billed Diver in Britain. *Brit.Birds* **67**:257–96.
100. Knox,A.E. (1872) *Autumns on the Spey*. London: John van Voorst.
101. Prater,A.J. (1989) Ringed Plover *Charadrius hiaticula* breeding population of the United Kingdom in 1984. *Bird Study* **36**:154–9.
102. Millais,J.G. (1913) *British Diving Ducks*.
103. Marquiss,M., Smith,R. & Galbraith,H. (1989) Diet of Snowy Owls on Cairn Gorm plateau in 1980 and 1987. *Scot.Birds* **15**:180–1.
104. Gladstone,H.S. (1910) The American Bittern in Scotland. *Ann.Scot.Nat.Hist.* **19**:70–4.
105. Watson,A. (1965) Research on Scottish Ptarmigan. *Scot.Birds* **3**:331–49.

106. Hewson,R. (1969) Roosts and roosting habits of the Dipper. *Bird Study* **16**:89–100.
107. Know,A.G. (1990) Probable long-term sympatry of Common and Scottish Crossbills in northeast Scotland. *Scot.Birds* **16**:11–8.
108. Knox,A.G. (1990) Identification of Crossbill and Scottish Crossbill. *Brit.Birds* **83**:89–94.
109. Davis,B. (1988) *Recent recorded incidents of lead poisoning among wildfowl in Scotland.* Unpublished NCC Report.
110. Lloyd,C. Tasker,M.L. & Partridge,K. (1991) *The Status of Seabirds in Britain and Ireland*, London: T. & A.D. Poyser.

Index of Birds' Names

Index of Place Names